2nd Edition

Aussie Rules

FOR

DUMMIES®

by Jim Main

WILEY

Wiley Publishing Australia Pty Ltd

Aussie Rules For Dummies®

2nd edition published by
Wiley Publishing Australia Pty Ltd
42 McDougall Street
Milton, Qld 4064
www.dummies.com

Copyright © 2003, 2008 Wiley Publishing Australia Pty Ltd

The moral rights of the author have been asserted.

National Library of Australia
Cataloguing-in-Publication data

Main, Jim, 1943– .

Aussie rules for dummies.
2nd ed.

Includes index.
ISBN 978 0 7314 0595 4 (pbk.).

1. Australian Football League. 2. Australian football. I. Title.

796.336

Cover image: GSP Images/AFL Photos

10 9 8 7 6 5 4 3 2 1

About the Author

Jim Main is one of Australia's best-known sports writers and is a noted football historian. He abandoned a law degree course at the University of Melbourne for his preferred career of journalism, but later graduated with a Bachelor of Arts (majoring in history) from La Trobe University.

Although Jim spent his formative years in journalism as a general reporter and subeditor, he eventually gravitated to sports writing. After working on the Melbourne *Herald*, he moved to England and worked on London's *Daily Express* from 1970 to 1971. During this time he was granted leave of absence to cover the 1970 Commonwealth Games in Edinburgh for the News Limited group. Soon after his return to Australia, Jim won a Walkley Award (Australian journalism's most prestigious award) and moved to sports writing in general, and the Aussie Rules scene in particular.

Jim went on to serve as Melbourne sports editor of the *Australian* for more than a decade, while simultaneously pursuing a freelance career, producing more than 60 books and regularly contributing articles to the *Australian* and *Inside Football*.

His sports-writing career includes covering three Commonwealth Games (Edinburgh in 1970 and 1986, and Brisbane in 1982), the 1984 Los Angeles Olympics and various assignments in England, Ireland, the United States and Japan.

Jim's published books include two Australian murder anthologies, a travel guide to Europe, and numerous Aussie Rules, tennis and cricket titles. His football books include *The Encyclopedia of AFL Footballers* and *This Football Century* (both with Russell Holmesby), *Whatever It Takes* (with Jim Stynes), *Fallen: The Ultimate Heroes* (with David Allen) and *Pants: The Darren Millane Story* (with Eddie McGuire). In 2003, he was inducted into the Melbourne Cricket Ground Media Hall of Fame for his contribution to the coverage of sports at the MCG.

Dedication

To all those who have been part of my life in Aussie Rules, and especially to my wife, Libby, for her unswerving loyalty and patience.

Author's Acknowledgments

To Richard Smart for introducing me to this wonderful project, to Kristen Hammond for her incredible enthusiasm in guiding me through the *For Dummies* style, to acquisitions editors Jane Ogilvie and Charlotte Duff for their thoughtful and invaluable advice, to editors Nicole McKenzie and Carolyn Beaumont for their patience, persistence and skill and, in this second edition, Kerry Davies for her marvellous editing skills and unlimited patience. Thanks also to the rest of the editorial team, and to those who helped with information and suggestions. These include fellow football historian Russell Holmesby and the AFL's walking, talking football encyclopedia, Col Hutchinson. Special thanks also to the AFL's Lawrie Woodman for his invaluable contribution in checking material.

Publisher's Acknowledgments

We're proud of this book; please send us your comments through our Dummies online registration form located at www.dummies.com/register/.

Some of the people who helped bring this book to market include the following:

Acquisitions, Editorial and Media Development

Project Editor: Kerry Davies

Acquisitions Editor: Charlotte Duff

Technical Reviewer: Lawrie Woodman

Editorial Manager: Gabrielle Packman

Production

Layout and Graphics: Wiley Composition Services, Paul Lennon and the Wiley Art Studio

Cartoons: Glenn Lumsden

Proofreader: Joy Montgomery

Indexer: Karen Gillen

The author and publisher would like to thank the following copyright holders, organisations and individuals for their permission to reproduce copyright material in this book.

© AFL Auskick: pages 103–4 (code of conduct)

© John Wiley & Sons Australia: page 155, photos by Sandra Jane

© Inside Football online: page 264.

Every effort has been made to trace the ownership of copyright material. Information that will enable the publisher to rectify any error or omission in subsequent editions will be welcome. In such cases, please contact the Permissions Section of John Wiley & Sons Australia, Ltd, who will arrange for the payment of the usual fee.

Contents at a Glance

Table of Contents

Introduction

*W*elcome to the second edition of *Aussie Rules For Dummies*, your handy guide to a uniquely Australian form of football, officially known as Australian Rules Football and affectionately called Aussie Rules.

Aussie Rules may be the most popular sport in Australia today, but that's not because it's an easy game to play or follow. You have to understand quite a lot about the rules, the plays and even the history of the game just to carry on a polite social conversation, let alone start kicking goals. No worries!

Aussie Rules For Dummies guides you through the ins and outs and behind posts of the entire sport from the viewing stands to the grounds and even behind the scenes. Whether you're fully acquainted with this exciting game or a beginner keen to understand what on earth its devoted fans are shouting about, this book introduces you to all the details and nuances of Aussie Rules.

About This Book

This book helps you find out just what you want to know about Aussie Rules in general, and the AFL (Australian Football League) in particular. However, it's not a book to read from start to finish, from page to page, although you can do this if you want. Rather, the book has been written and designed so that you can pick it up to find out about any aspect of Aussie Rules at any given time. Say, for example, you're watching an AFL game on television and something happens to make you think, 'Why is that?' This book can help you discover the answer.

If you prefer, you can skip around first and learn the rules, and then go to where I explain how to develop the skills of the great Australian football code. Feel free to flip from page to page and absorb the information in your own time.

Whether you're an established AFL star or a newcomer to the game doesn't matter — there's something for you in this book.

Why You Need This Book

This friendly yet comprehensive guide to Australia's most loved code of football provides a detailed explanation in plain English of the rules of Aussie Rules and how they came into being, techniques and strategies for actually playing the game, and key facts and figures to back you up in any game debate.

If you attend a lot of Aussie Rules games or watch them on television and ask everyone around you a lot of questions, you may eventually get a fair understanding of the rules and history of the game. But when one fan tells you one thing and another gives you a slightly different answer, sooner or later you want to know the right answer from a reliable authority. *Aussie Rules For Dummies* can help you discover information about Aussie Rules that many diehard fans are yet to learn.

If you're eager to start playing, or already play but want to improve your form, this book is full of tips and tricks of the game to help you become a well-rounded player. I also provide lists of great players, past and present, who can serve as inspiring role models for players at every skill level.

Archaeologists centuries from now may come across weird and wonderful figures such as 15.10 (100) d. 15.8 (98) and scratch their heads. Unless, of course, they happen to unearth a copy of this book; then they'll be able to decipher what a score in Aussie Rules actually means. Even if you already know how Aussie Rules scoring works, you may find some other aspects of the game as puzzling as 40th-century archaeologists may find them.

How This Book is Organised

This book is divided into sections called, cleverly enough, parts. These parts are divided into chapters. Each part covers a different aspect of the game. I start with the basics in Part I and build from there, making this your easy-to-follow guide to Aussie Rules. The following list explains what's in each part.

Part I: Before the First Bounce

If you're a newcomer to Aussie Rules, this part is the place to start — right at the beginning of the book. In this part, I explain the many benefits of following or playing Aussie Rules, as well as the basics of the game — the rules, the scoring system. You find information on what equipment you'll need to play the game and how to read, rather than climb, a ladder.

Part II: Playing the Game

Now, I really get down and dirty by explaining the nitty-gritty of the game. The part starts off with a chapter on the various playing positions. The terms 'centre half-back' and 'ruckman' will soon make sense and you'll be able to identify those players when watching a game. Thinking of becoming an Aussie Rules champion? In this part, you'll also find chapters covering the skills involved — kicking, and marking, handballing, bouncing and running, baulking and defending, and tackling — and routines for you to practise each.

Part III: Taking Your Game to the Next Level

This part takes you through the different levels of playing Aussie Rules, from Little League and AFL Auskick, right through to the senior ranks, as well as the great big football world of suburban and country competitions around the country and the game as it's played around the world. I also cover how the 'draft' works, training, how to avoid and treat injury, and information you need if you want to coach.

Part IV: The Australian Football League

The indigenous Australian code of football is known officially around the world as Australian Rules Football, but the game's governing body is the Australian Football League (AFL). In this part, I define the AFL and its development, including the historical influences on its formation in the late 19th century.

I also cover the people who run the game at AFL level and how they make their decisions. Aspects of each of the 16 AFL clubs — including their history and champions — are discussed at length, too, as well as the various medals they can win and the grounds they play on.

Part V: The Spectator Sport

So, you don't want to play Aussie Rules. You just want to go to a game or even watch it on television. No worries! You can be involved in a lot of different ways. In this part, you'll find information on how to join a club and follow the AFL competition via the various media available — newspapers, radio, television and the Internet. I show you how to get involved in tipping competitions and assess a football form — basically all the important and fun aspects of being a spectator.

Part VI: The Part of Tens

This part is my favourite, as I get to name who I believe to be the ten best players and goal kickers, and which teams and games I think are the best — ever! Writing this part was a labour of love, but it was far from being an easy task. This part is sure to stir discussion and even controversy.

See what you think.

Part VII: Appendixes

Here, you'll find some helpful reference material. You'll find lengthy lists of the premiership and medal winners, as well as books that I highly recommend for further reading. And, to get you in the know, I've included a list of the lingo used in the stands and the umpires' signals. Enjoy!

Icons Used in This Book

You'll find the following icons throughout the book, which signify particular information:

This icon indicates terms used in the vocabulary of the game. Master this lingo and you'll sound like an Aussie Rules veteran in no time.

A book on Aussie Rules just wouldn't be the same without reference to the great incidents and characters of the past. This icon flags stories about the game's incidents and heroes, right from the birth of Aussie Rules.

Because I've followed the AFL competition almost from the time I could walk, and I've been a football writer for more than 30 years, I've seen and experienced many amazing incidents. When I have my own tale to tell or want to throw in my five cents worth, I mark it with this icon.

The Tech Stuff icon provides technical information that you don't need to know but you may find interesting.

The Remember icon indicates things you shouldn't forget, because you may find the information useful in the future. (Now, where are those car keys?)

You can find lots of helpful information and advice in paragraphs marked with the Tip icon.

This icon points you to Web sites that can help you find out more about this wonderful game.

Part I
Before the First Bounce

Glenn Lumsden

'Sorry to break the news to you, but we actually play Aussie Rules up here...'

In this part . . .

To get you started, this part provides an introduction to Aussie Rules and what the game is all about. If you're new to the sport, you can find out what you need to know to follow a game in this part.

In Chapter 1, you discover why fans the world over believe the game is so great; you'll also find a quick rundown on the object of the game. In Chapter 2, I introduce you to the basic rules of play, the role of each of the umpires in upholding those rules and the glory of final fever. In Chapter 3, you can find out all about the scoring system and how teams are rated, and then, in Chapter 4, I detail the gear needed to play.

Chapter 1

Australia's Greatest Game

*A*t first sight, Aussie Rules may look like a wild-card combination of soccer, rugby, American football, basketball and a little beach volleyball thrown in, but it's actually a wonderful, organically home-grown game that wasn't invented by anyone and isn't closely related to any of those other sports. From being a hotchpotch kick with a leather ball in the mid-19th century, Aussie Rules has developed into a hugely popular game in Australia, with interest developing all around the world.

From Australian football's humblest beginnings, just a century and a half ago, the game now attracts an aggregate attendance of more than 7 million a season (attendances for 2007, including finals matches, totalled 7,049,945). That averages out at about 38,000 fans to each AFL game! Yet, way back when the competition was founded as the Victorian Football League (VFL) in 1897, the total attendance that season was just 38,000 at an average of 5,133 per game. (For more history of the game, see Chapter 14.)

These figures relate only to the AFL competition, but hundreds of other competitions, small and large, are also growing in popularity. That means you can participate in or support local clubs at all kinds of levels, from junior to professional, wherever you live. Aussie Rules games are played all over Australia every weekend in winter, with the game now spreading its wings to places such as Britain, the United States, Europe and Japan, just to name a few. (See Chapter 8 for a detailed listing of leagues and competitions around Australia and the world.)

The growing popularity of Aussie Rules can be attributed to a number of factors, but the main reasons are: It's fun and fast-paced for both the players and spectators; it has a simple goal but room for complex strategies and tactics; and, on the home front at least, it inspires national pride in a sport that is uniquely Australian.

Why some play and some watch

I watched the 1989 Hawthorn–Geelong grand final with Scotland soccer international Ray Stewart, who had competed in an international super-kick competition (with representatives from all the football codes from around the world), and he was easily able to follow the game. However, he was in shock at some of the extremely heavy physical contact, which left Hawthorn's Robert DiPierdomenico coughing blood from a punctured lung and teammate Dermott Brereton with cracked ribs. Stewart turned to me late in the game and said: 'I would not play this game for a million dollars.' Oh, by the way, Hawthorn won by 6 points. This was regarded as one of the toughest, tightest grand finals for decades, but this grand final was surpassed for excitement by those of 2005 and 2006. The Sydney Swans and the West Coast Eagles clashed in both games, with the Swans defeating the Eagles by just 4 points in 2005. Then, in 2006, the Eagles pipped the Swans by just 1 point. Both these grand finals already have been labelled classic encounters.

The Object of the Game — Simplified

Aussie Rules might look like a complicated game, but in reality it's fairly simple. The basic object is to score more points than the opposition by kicking, handpassing and running the ball between the goalposts for goals or into the scoring zone for fewer points.

One of the field umpires starts the game (and each quarter of 20 minutes) by standing in the centre square, holding the ball high and blowing a whistle. This action signals for the timekeepers to start the clock. (For details of the playing field and the location of the umpires, see Chapter 2.)

The field umpire then bounces the ball in the centre circle. Two players, one from each team (the *ruckmen*), then jump for the ball with the intent of hitting it to their teammates. The players then try to move the ball towards their goals by either *handpassing* (holding the ball in one hand and punching it with the other hand) or kicking it. When in possession of the ball, a player must bounce it on the ground at least every 15 metres. For information on positions, see Chapter 5 and, for the skills of the game, see Chapters 6 and 7.

If a player kicks the ball and another player, either his teammate or the opposition, catches it (called a *mark*) then that player can stop play without fear of being tackled by the opposition. When a team has the ball within reach of a goal, usually 50 metres or closer, they then try to kick a goal.

One of the two timekeepers signals the end of each quarter and the game by a whistle.

The game is stopped only in one of the following circumstances:

- ✔ A goal is scored, in which case the ball is bounced in the centre circle again, as at the start of the match.
- ✔ A *behind* is scored (when the ball goes between a goalpost and a behind post or is touched as it goes between the goalposts), in which case the opposition kicks the ball from the goal square back into play.
- ✔ The ball goes out of the boundary lines, in which case a boundary umpire throws the ball back into play.
- ✔ One, or more, of the players is injured.
- ✔ An umpire sends a player from the field because of the *blood rule*.

Players can obstruct opposing players off the ball — called *shepherding* — if they're within 5 metres of the ball, but they can't push or tackle a player who doesn't have possession of the ball. If they do so, a free kick is awarded to the opponent. Free kicks are also awarded for: Throwing the ball; being tackled fairly by your opponent and then dropping the ball; and kicking the ball out of bounds on the full.

Why Aussie Rules Is the Best

Every fan of every code of football argues that his or her code is the world's best. But, in my humble opinion, only Aussie Rules fans are right: It undoubtedly is the best game of all. And, although it's not an international code, progress is being made in that direction (see Chapter 8 for more information on the global movement of the game).

How do I know Aussie Rules is the best? Simple! Because it's the only football code in the world that has fans roaring with excitement from start to finish.

In comparison, soccer involves magnificent skills but you could go to sleep waiting for a score. And I can't stay interested in a game that could tie at 0–0. Likewise, the stop-and-start nature of American football means a stop-and-start reaction with my emotions. Either of the rugby codes, union or league, just makes me question why it's called a code of football, as it looks more like mobile wrestling to me! Give me Aussie Rules any day. (But then, I *am* biased: Come on, Swans!)

The Main attraction

As a boy, I never, ever missed a South Melbourne match. I went wherever the Swans were playing until I left junior football ranks to play in a suburban competition on Saturday afternoons. Even then I had someone listen to the radio to follow the Swans' progress. The Swans relocated to Sydney in 1982, making it much more difficult for me to see them play every week. However, I now go to all their matches in Melbourne and fly to Sydney for 'home' games once or twice a season. Yes, I'm a tragic Swans fan. But I'm not alone: Thousands of loyal fans travel great distances to keep up with their favourite teams — when you're hooked on Aussie Rules, it's a lifetime commitment.

The 2005 and 2006 Sydney–West Coast grand finals created enormous excitement (refer to the sidebar 'Why some play and some watch' earlier in this chapter). Australia came to a standstill while these games were played at the Melbourne Cricket Ground in front of 92,000 fans. These grand finals truly reflected the enormity of the interest in football on a national scale. The matches were played between one team from Sydney and the other from Perth, on opposite sides of Australia, and played in Melbourne. You can't get much more national than that. You could have fired a rocket down the main streets of these three cities without hitting anyone. Everyone was watching the grand finals in both years.

Whether you want to play the game, watch it from the stands or from the comfort of your lounge chair, following, in no particular order, are the reasons why you need to be involved in the greatest game of all.

Having heaps of fun

Watching or playing Aussie Rules is heaps of fun. Just imagine the sun is shining, the grass is mown and you're going to play the world's great game. Or it's Sunday, you're sitting on the couch with a beverage and a snack and a match is about to play. In fact, the word 'fun' is entirely inadequate. Perhaps I should use the term 'unbridled joy'. Yeah, that's better!

Aussie Rules builds camaraderie among members of a team, members of a club and even between fans who don't know each other but find themselves cheering for the same team in a bar halfway around the world. Footballers at all levels revel in the mateship of playing together. Lifelong friendships are made and countless team reunions are held across Australia every week of every season. Additionally, sitting with people who feel the same way as you do about the game and a particular team can help build friendships.

Football may be a winter game, but it can be played all year round. For example, Aussie Rules is played in Darwin in summer because, believe it or not, the winters there are too dry and the weather too hot. The rain during the wet season in summer softens the grounds and therefore reduces the risk of injury. Elsewhere in Australia, Aussie Rules is generally a winter sport, but played almost any day of the week. You can find many, many weekend competitions, with games played on Saturdays and/or Sundays, but you may also seek out a few weekday competitions.

And you don't have to play the game to enjoy it; watching Aussie Rules or coaching it are just as enjoyable. Most women have never played Aussie Rules, but some of them are the game's greatest fans. For example, former Victorian premier Joan Kirner is a devoted Essendon fan. (See Chapter 8 for more information on women's teams and Chapter 13 for the full list of AFL teams.)

Additionally, you can have lots of fun as part of a club. Current estimates indicate that more than five million Australians are keen, if not avid, AFL fans. For more information on the advantages of being a member of a club, see Chapter 17.

Finding fitness and health

What better way to get fit than by training for and playing Aussie Rules? The benefits are enormous. Playing this code of football requires the highest possible level of fitness at the elite level, but even the average 'hack' suburban footballer needs some aerobic capacity to play the game. So, do your body a favour and get involved.

No cheers, just tears

The camaraderie involved in football can be best exemplified by the reaction of Essendon captain James Hird when he learned before the start of the 2002 season that teammate Damien Hardwick was being traded to rival club Port Adelaide. Hird shed a tear at Essendon's annual general meeting when he was told his 2000 premiership teammate was moving on. When Hird retired at the end of the 2007 season, he was given a hero's farewell, and teammates likewise shed quiet tears.

Even if you're the worst player in Aussie Rules history, the exercise will do you good. Even if you don't get a kick or a handpass, or even if you fail to touch the ball, just running around can give you a cardio workout, improve your coordination and tone your leg muscles. Playing the game is a whole lot healthier than eating pies and hot-dogs in the grandstand.

Plus, the sport has a range of benefits for your mental wellbeing. What better way to relax and forget the worries of life than sitting through a match for more than two and a half hours? Believe me, when the game is in progress and you're supporting your team, nothing else matters. You'll forget your work and your worries. The time becomes yours, and you'll have nothing else in mind but the big game.

On top of that, physical restrictions are no barrier to the game. For some sports you have to be a certain height or a specific size, but not so with Aussie Rules. You can be just 168 centimetres (or even smaller) to get a game, or be as big as Fremantle's Aaron Sandilands, who, at 212 centimetres, is the tallest man to have played at VFL/AFL level. Lean, heavily built, tall, small. It doesn't matter. Aussie Rules is a game for everyone.

Enjoying the passion and challenge

The passion that's generated when you take the playing field with 17 like-minded players is amazing. You change into your playing gear as individuals and, hey presto, as soon as you take the field you're part of the team. And, believe me, when the scores are close, near the end of play, you'd be amazed at how much passion the difference between victory and defeat can generate.

Always on a Sunday

I couldn't get enough football as a junior. I played three matches a week — with my house team at school, with the school team and, on Sundays, with my club team, West Preston YCW (Young Christian Workers). My school had banned football with a club, but how was it going to learn of my rule breaking? Several boys from that team went on to play in the VFL (now AFL) and they included Brendan Hackwill, Gary Lazarus and John Bahen (all Fitzroy), and Kevin Hall (Carlton). Yet today's footballers complain that playing even once a week is a tough call. Mind you, I played lowly amateur football; in professional AFL the hits are much harder.

Ask and you shall receive

During pre-season training in 1992, a tall young man walked into the rooms at Essendon's Windy Hill ground and asked if he could have a trial with the Bombers. Sight unseen, Steve Alessio was given a trial and proved to be a revelation. He made his Essendon debut that year and went on to become a premiership ruckman. See, it can happen to anyone.

To the casual observer, Aussie Rules appears to be a dangerous sport — and it can be. The players wear little or no padding and the tackling can be ferocious. (For details on the gear you need to play, see Chapter 4.) But the best way to play the game is without fear, and playing it is a good way to fight your fears.

Aussie Rules may be a relatively dangerous game because of the lack of padding and other protection, but I believe this aspect can build character. Besides, it doesn't have anywhere near the in-your-face aggression of rugby union or rugby league. Overcoming your own fears is a great lesson for life.

Playing Aussie Rules can also lead to a professional career. Yes, this scenario may be stretching the imagination, but it *can* happen. Who knows how good you may become? Everyone has to start somewhere, and AFL history is riddled with cases of 'unknowns' becoming stars of the game.

Don't Just Be a Television Fan

Aussie Rules is great to watch, 'live' or on television. If you live in a remote area of Australia or overseas, you may be unable to see a live match. But, if possible, make the effort to get to a game.

You never forget the experience of a live Aussie Rules game. Apart from observing the skills and excitement of the game itself, you can relish mixing with fans from all walks of life and chuckle at their banter, good-humoured or otherwise. Like thousands of other fans, you can fall in love with the colour, spectacle and non-stop flow of the game.

Good things come in small packages

Jim 'Nipper' Bradford, who played seven games with Collingwood in 1943 and nine with North Melbourne in 1949, is believed to be the smallest man to play at VFL/AFL level. Bradford stood just 152 centimetres, or 5 feet in the old imperial measure.

Players also get a buzz, with Sydney's 1996 preliminary final win over Essendon the perfect example. The Swans won by a point on the last kick of the game to enter their first grand final for 51 years. The players were so excited they formed a human pyramid by jumping on each other in sheer joy. Then, when the Swans won the 2005 grand final, the tears of long-suffering fans of the red and white ran down thousands of cheeks. It was arguably the most emotional triumph in football history. The Swans hadn't won a flag since 1933, had been banished from South Melbourne to Sydney in 1982, had overcome near extinction and finally had triumphed. It's also a two-way street, and the more the fans support the team, the more the team supports each other and the fans. Geelong, in 2007, also experienced the joy of winning a premiership after a long drought, with a resounding win of 119 points. The score was Geelong 24.19 (163) to Port Adelaide's 6.8 (44). The Cats' previous premiership was in 1963, so little wonder Geelong fans celebrated long and hard.

If you happen to miss an important game for your favourite team or can't quite get to all the live games you want to see, you can enjoy Aussie Rules anyway, through radio, television, the Internet, and newspapers and magazines (see Chapter 19 for more on football media). Thousands of fans who can't get to games still follow every kick, every handpass, every score through the media.

Ownership of the pink swan kind

Fancy owning a football team? Well, once upon a time, you could have done just that. No AFL club currently has private ownership, but the Sydney Swans and the Brisbane Bears (now Lions) once were in private hands. The Swans at one stage during the mid-1980s were owned by the flamboyant doctor Geoffrey Edelsten, whose other claim to fame was flying around Sydney in a pink helicopter. The Bears at one stage in the late 1980s were owned by businessman Christopher Skase, who later fled Australia to escape his creditors.

Chapter 2

Getting a Grip on the Basics

. . . .

In This Chapter

▷ Timing the game

▷ Defining the umpires — they're not referees

▷ Signalling the game

▷ Ruling on the play

▷ Gauging the grounds

▷ Following the season

▷ Fronting for the finals and the grandest day of all

. . . .

*A*ustralian football has evolved from a rough-and-tumble affair into today's highly sophisticated sport with specific rules and a unique playing structure. The result is a true Aussie game with a charm that appeals to ever-growing numbers of people around the country.

The code of Aussie Rules is constantly evolving, watched over by the Australian Football League and its Rules Review Committee, which fine-tunes the game from season to season. Although no single change over the past four or five decades can be said to have revolutionised the game, almost every year sees a subtle change to one rule or another, each designed to keep the game moving forward.

For example, in the past, a player kicking off after a behind had to wait for the goal umpire to finish waving a flag before he could take his kick. The AFL recently changed this rule so that the goal umpire only has to signal with one finger that a behind has been scored and the player can take his kick.

Another recent change is to the past practice of using only one ball for an entire game, unless it had been kicked out of the ground and someone had stolen it (it has happened), or using a new ball for each quarter in wet and heavy conditions. Now bags of balls sit behind each set of goalposts. This change makes the game much faster and it's now common to see teams score what are known as *coast-to-coast* goals. That is, the player kicking out after a behind quickly moves the ball to a running teammate, who, in turn, passes to other teammates for a goal, without the opposition touching the ball. Easier said than done, but highly entertaining when it comes off.

The key to the game's appeal and success is its momentum. You won't find stop–start play in Australian football. Aussie Rules is go, go, go! That's why marching bands and drum majorettes are rarely seen at an Aussie Rules ground. In Australian football, the football is the entertainment, and Aussie Rules fans constantly make it clear that this is how they want it.

Australian football can be a complicated sport to the uninitiated, so an understanding of the basic rules and scoring makes the game a lot easier to follow. If you're a newcomer to Aussie Rules, this chapter helps you watch a match without asking the fan sitting next to you: 'What on earth is happening?' If you're an old hand, sit back and enjoy the ride, because I guarantee to deliver plenty of fascinating Aussie Rules trivia to get you through your next quiz night.

In this chapter, I unravel the reasons why Aussie Rules is such a popular football code, and I cover the basics of the game. You can discover the reason the game is divided into quarters, the size of the field, the length of the season and, most important, what makes your emotions soar at finals time.

Swan dive

With much fanfare in the 1980s, the Sydney Swans introduced a group of marching girls called the Swanettes. This glamorous team amused the crowds for a while, but went the way of the dodo after a couple of years, when the promoters realised that the squad of long-legged beauties was having no effect on ticket sales.

Cheerleaders are no longer part of the game. It was a short-lived experiment and no-one seems to miss them. Besides, they never appeared during the quarter- and three-quarter-time breaks because these breaks between play last just 6 minutes, and because the players remain on the ground in team huddles.

Half-time breaks last 20 minutes, and almost all matches at AFL level have Little League (school-age) or *AFL Auskick* (a program designed to introduce youngsters to playing the game) matches during the main break.

Instead of dancing girls to open the day's entertainment, many competitions pit their reserves sides against each other in what is called a *curtain-raiser*. These pre-match reserves games have been included for more than 60 years, except for a short period just before and after World War II, when baseball matches were played to entertain the fans in the lead-up to senior matches. Baseball was scrapped in favour of reserves matches as curtain-raisers when officials saw the opportunity to promote the Australian sport. Reserves matches as curtain-raisers may still be common in suburban and country football, but are rarely played before AFL matches. There's no specific AFL reserves competition and the only real chance of seeing a reserves team in action is to go to a Geelong match at its Skilled Stadium home, where, a couple of times a season, the Geelong reserves are in action. The Geelong Football Club fields a side in the Victorian Football League (once the Victorian Football Association) competition against teams like Port Melbourne, Sandringham or North Ballarat.

Four Quarters Make a Whole

Before the game's basic rules (known as *codification*) were drawn up in 1859, games of Australian football often lasted an entire day. Because no rules existed, teams had any number of players and massive scrimmages were common.

The basic idea was to push the ball over a goal line — yes, just once — and the first team to do this was declared the winner. A victory usually took time — plenty of time. In fact, games often lasted four or five hours, and teams often resumed the battle the next day, or the next week.

These games were played with no breaks and, although some players had a rest on the sidelines if necessary, any number of other players joined the fray. In other words, games usually were free-for-alls. (Check out Chapter 14 for more details on the establishment of the Victorian Football League.)

One famous football match between Scotch College and Melbourne Grammar School lasted two days, with the scores level at the end of the first day's play. Eager to have a result, the combatants decided to return the following week, with Scotch College finally successful — and MGS probably surrendering exhausted!

Even in the latter part of the 19th century, when lengthy games were the norm, the game was divided into four quarters, and this structure has continued since the establishment of the AFL. What has changed, however, is the length of the quarters. Until 1997, each quarter lasted 25 minutes, plus what is known as time on. Today, each quarter lasts 20 minutes, plus time on.

Counting Time On

Time on is extra time added to each quarter to make up for dead time during the play. For example, play may be suspended while an injury receives attention, while the ball goes out of play, while the ball is taken back to the centre after a goal is scored and so on. Each of these gaps in play is called *dead time*.

Two independent timekeepers, appointed by the AFL for each match, keep track of time on by following whistles and signals from the field umpires. The amount of time on due in a quarter is a closely guarded secret.

Only the timekeepers — and maybe sports writers who sit next to the timekeepers — know precisely how much time on is to be added to the game. So only the timekeepers know when the last second of the game has been reached, and this secret is what can make the conclusion of a game so exciting.

FOOTY FLASHBACK

Saints and sirens

One of the timekeepers in the famous 1966 St Kilda versus Collingwood grand final, Fred Farrell (an avid St Kilda supporter), was so excited by the Saints' 1-point win that he blew the siren for more than ten seconds. Rumour has it that a colleague had to prise Farrell's finger from the button.

The day is remembered too as the day that St Kilda fans jigged with delight in the aisles to celebrate their team's first — and so far only — premiership.

Excited fans have been known to invade grounds and cause numerous incidents in the mistaken belief that the final siren has blared. South Melbourne fans were so excited by their team narrowly leading Collingwood in the final minutes of a match at the Lake Oval in 1970 that they jumped the fence, following several fans who thought the siren had sounded. Police had to clear the ground before the match could re-start. South eventually won by just 1 point.

St Kilda was involved in another siren sensation in the 2006 season, against Fremantle at the Aurora Stadium, Launceston. St Kilda was trailing by 1 point when the timekeepers signalled the end of the match. However, the umpires failed to hear the siren and St Kilda's Steven Baker scored a behind. The match therefore was a draw, or was it? The AFL investigated and, two days later, declared the game should have ended when the timekeeper pressed the siren button and the match was awarded to Fremantle.

Imagine a scene where a team is leading by just 1 point, and the other team can win with just seconds to go. The cheering crowds are on their feet, their suspense enhanced by the fact that they don't know how long time on is going to last. Finally, the last second is counted off, agreed by the two timekeepers. One of the timekeepers presses the button and the loud siren — never referred to as a hooter — sounds across the ground, and the crowd and the players suddenly realise the game is over.

The Men Who Call the Shots

Umpires control the game of Australian football. They use a range of signals to call infringements or decisions on the play, and your understanding of these signals is the key to how much you enjoy watching the game.

For example, when an umpire stops play and makes the signal to award (or pay) a free kick, you're going to enjoy the whole procedure more if you know exactly why the game has been stopped and the exact nature of the infringement. See 'Umpiring Signals' later in this chapter.

But the umpiring of Aussie Rules, with its vigorous signals and colourful characters, wasn't always the sophisticated game you see played today. In the early years of the code, the competing captains called rule infringements. Naturally this system was far from ideal, with captains creating strange and wonderful interpretations of the rules.

Umpiring is a highly specialised skill mostly taken up by people who prefer the official side of the sport to playing the game. A famous exemption to this rule was Lawrence 'Lardie' Tulloch, who captained Collingwood to two premierships in 1902 and 1903. He then turned his hand to umpiring and became the main man for the 1907 grand final, in which Carlton defeated South Melbourne.

Field and boundary umpires for decades wore all-white shirts and shorts, and black socks. This tradition changed in the 1990s when the AFL introduced red and blue to the shirts, and blue socks. Then, for the new millennium, the AFL introduced coloured uniforms for umpires. They now wear red, yellow, green or even orange shirts, shorts and socks, depending on the colours worn by the competing teams because their uniforms can't show any favouritism. For example, if Sydney (red and white) plays Hawthorn (gold and brown) the umpires would probably wear a neutral green uniform.

Field umpires

The first use of a field umpire was in a Melbourne versus Carlton game in 1866. However, umpires weren't used in major matches until 1872. Popular belief has it that the first umpire to wear a white uniform was George Coulthard in South Australia in 1880. Figure 2-1 shows the dress code of a modern-day field umpire. Regardless of the colours they wear, umpires still cop abuse from fans, who once called them 'white rabbits' — now they call them yellow or green rabbits — and worse.

Until 1975, only one field umpire controlled the game in the senior Victorian Football League (now AFL) competition. The use of two umpires was introduced in 1976 and expanded to three umpires for senior games in 1994. Most junior and amateur matches still use two field umpires.

Figure 2-1:
The current
uniforms
of the goal
umpire
(left), and
boundary
and field
umpires
(right). Field
umpire
uniforms are
distinguished
by a number
on the back.

Boundary and goal umpires

In addition to field umpires, Aussie Rules today has two boundary umpires and two goal umpires. Their roles are as follows:

- ✔ **Boundary umpires** wear similar uniforms to those of field umpires (see Figure 2-1) — the only difference is that field umpires have a number on the back of their shirts — and patrol either side of the ground to decide when the ball has gone out of play (over the boundary line).

  The first recorded use of boundary umpires was in a match at Ballarat in 1891; however, the league didn't officially introduce boundary umpires until 1903.

✔ **Goal umpires**, up until recently, wore long trousers, white coats and hats (see Figure 2-2). These uniforms were, to say the least, quaint. When the AFL played a series of exhibition matches in the United States and Canada in 1988, fans regarded the goal umpires as part of the attraction. They now wear long trousers, a coloured shirt and baseball-type cap (see Figure 2-1). Goal umpires decide whether to record a goal (6 points) or a behind (1 point) and keep the official tally of these scores. (For more information on, er, behinds, check out Chapter 3.)

The official score tally of the goal umpires decides the match result, even though the scoreboard may indicate a different score. All AFL scoreboards are operated by attendants, with some of these scoreboards electronic and some operated manually. These attendants rarely make mistakes, although every now and then an extra behind can be added or missed.

At the end of each quarter, goal umpires signal the scoreboard attendants to confirm whether the scores are correct. If the goal umpires cross their flags, the signal represents an incorrect score. Waving the flags indicates a correct score.

Footballers can no longer 'hide' from umpires and rarely get away with infringements of the rules, especially at AFL level, where video cameras follow every angle of the game. Players can be cited on video offences and are frequently warned: If you do the crime, you do the time. In other words, if a player is found guilty of punching, gouging and so on, he is suspended.

Figure 2-2:
The old uniform of the goal umpire.

Umpiring Signals

Umpires have developed a number of common signals over the years to indicate long distance by hand gestures when a violation or score is made or when the ball goes out of bounds. This section explains some of the most common signs you may see umpires using on the field today.

Study these signals carefully and you'll be able to follow the game much more easily. Memorising the umpires' gestures helps you know which rules have been infringed and why umpires pay particular free kicks. (You can also join in the arguments about penalties or whether the ball was in or out more quickly if you recognise the umpires' signs.)

General signals during play

Field umpires use a number of signals to indicate exactly which decision they've made in certain circumstances. This part of the game was developed over several seasons about 20 years ago. Officials realised that fans needed to know why certain decisions were made, so umpires responded to this need with informal signals. These signals have slowly been incorporated into the game and are well recognised by the game's devotees.

Following are the signals you're most likely to see field umpires use during play:

- **A 50-metre penalty:** These penalties are awarded against players who try to slow down an opponent by holding on to him for an unnecessarily long time after a free kick or mark, or running between the player with the ball for a set kick and the man on his mark. These penalties are also paid if a player on the mark or one of his teammates abuses the umpire. The field umpire then puts up a hand and waves the offending player towards him while he runs backwards to mark out the 50-metre penalty.

- **All clear:** After a team has scored and the goal umpire has made his signal, the field umpire puts both hands to his mouth and calls 'all clear'.

- **Around the neck:** Grabbing or touching a player around the head, neck or shoulders is illegal. These are no-go zones for safety reasons, and an umpire paying a free kick in such cases puts his right hand across his left shoulder, or vice versa if he is left-handed.

✔ **Ball-up:** The field umpire crosses his arms in front of his chest to signify that he will take the ball and bounce it to clear congestion in play. This often follows a legitimate tackle that cannot result in a free kick to the tackler because the player being tackled did not have prior opportunity to get rid of the ball by hand or foot. The term *prior opportunity* is therefore critical in these decisions.

✔ **Blood rule:** When a player is ordered from the ground because he has blood on his body or playing uniform, the field umpire informs the player and then raises his forearms and crosses them in front of his face. The game is stopped until the player sent from the field is replaced by a teammate in exactly the same position.

✔ **Clean mark:** If a player, for example, takes a disputed mark in a pack and the field umpire rules it legal, he puts his hands in front of his face sideways (as shown in Figure 2-3) as a signal that the player has, indeed, taken the mark.

✔ **Holding the ball:** If the player being tackled *has* had prior opportunity to get rid of the ball and is deemed by the field umpire to have held the ball too long or to have incorrectly disposed of the ball, a free kick is paid to the tackler. The umpire will bend at 45 degrees to the ground and then cross his arms with a sweeping motion. Fans, after almost every tackle, sweat on the umpire's movements and know exactly which sign they wish to see, or not see, depending on which team they support.

✔ **In the back:** Pushing an opponent in the back is illegal in Aussie Rules and the umpire paying a free kick because of this infringement merely imitates a push by pressing his hands forwards as if into an imaginary back.

Figure 2-3: The field umpire's signal for a clean mark.

✔ **Kicking in danger:** Trying to hack the ball out of the pack by foot is illegal, because it may put other players in danger of injury. This free kick is not paid very often because footballers are aware of dangerous play. However, when a 'kicking in danger' free kick is paid, the field umpire signifies this decision by taking an imaginary kick.

✔ **Running too far:** If a player runs more than 15 metres with the ball without bouncing it, the field umpire will pay a free kick to the opposition. He will signal this by twirling his wrists over each other in a whirling motion. This gesture is similar to the 'travelling' signal in basketball.

✔ **Touched, play on:** Many times a player feels he has taken a mark, yet the ball has been touched by another player — teammate or opposition — downfield or even in the pack. In such instances, the field umpire calls out 'play on' and waves his hands in the air.

✔ **Trip:** A trip can be made by hand or foot and any tackle below the knee is regarded as a trip. In either case, the field umpire lifts a leg and wraps a hand around the ankle to signal the trip, as shown in Figure 2-4.

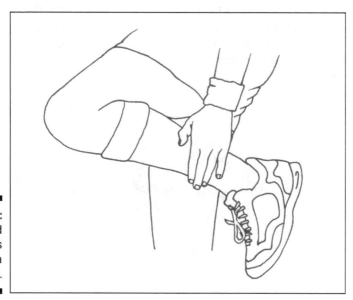

Figure 2-4:
The field
umpire's
signal for a
trip.

Goal signals

The goal umpire determines the results of any kick for goal by the following signals:

- ✔ **Behind:** The goal umpire raises just one finger, much to the dismay of some fans and the delight of the others. A behind is scored when the ball goes between a goalpost and a behind post, or if it goes through the goals but is touched by any player. A behind is worth 1 point.

- ✔ **Goal!!!:** The goal umpire raises a finger of each hand and points them forwards, much like an imaginary gunslinger. Of course, the crowd sweats on these decisions, especially if the shots for goal are very close.

- ✔ **Hit the post:** If the ball hits a goalpost, whether or not it bounces through, it's a behind, and the goal umpire pats that goalpost to indicate what is known to fans as a *poster*, and is worth a point.

- ✔ **Out of bounds on the full or on the bounce:** The ball is out of bounds if it goes over the boundary line or hits the behind post. If it hits the behind post *on the full* (without hitting the ground after being kicked and without being touched), a free kick is awarded against the player who kicked the ball. To indicate 'out of bounds on the full', the goal umpire runs to the nearest behind post and extends one arm parallel to the ground, as shown in Figure 2-5. This signal assists the boundary umpire, who may be 20 metres or more away, during a quick passage of play. If it's not out on the full, and therefore is *on the bounce*, the goal umpire runs to the nearest behind post and points to the ground to indicate that the ball didn't go out of bounds on the full and that it should be thrown in by the boundary umpire on that side of the ground.

- ✔ **Touched:** The goal umpire uses one hand to tap the top of his other hand, indicating the ball was touched before it went through the goals. He then raises one finger to signal a behind.

Figure 2-5: The goal umpire's signal for 'out of bounds on the full'.

Boundary signals

The boundary umpire generally decides whether the ball has crossed the boundary line. Here are their signals:

- ✔ **Touched over the line:** If the ball goes over the boundary line after being touched or hitting the ground, the boundary umpire raises his right arm and blows a whistle to signify there will be a throw-in. The boundary umpire then throws the ball over his head and back into play.

- ✔ **Out on the full:** Any time the ball goes over the boundary line, it is said to be 'out'. If the ball goes over the line on the full without being touched, the boundary umpire points to the boundary line where the ball crossed the line in the air. The opposition then takes a free kick.

Aussie Rules, Okay!

To the casual observer, Australian football looks like a freewheeling, spontaneous sport, devoid of rules. Not so! Whole books are filled with the rules of the game, but the hitch is that most of these rules and sub-rules are open to interpretation.

For example, holding on to an opponent who doesn't have the ball in possession is illegal. However this situation begs the question of what constitutes holding an opponent. Does holding an opponent mean using a full-nelson wrestling hold to restrict an opponent, or is it just grabbing a rival by the back of the shorts?

Strictly speaking, any holding of an opponent is illegal. However, umpires generally interpret the holding rule to mean the holding of a player who doesn't have the ball and who's trying to win possession of the ball.

FOOTY FLASHBACK

To's and throws

The game of Aussie Rules banned throwing the ball back in the game's early days. Then the Victorian Football Association (formed in 1897) introduced a throw rule in 1920.

The throw rule played a part in Australian football for more than 20 years. But controversy raged — controversy raging is a major art form in Aussie Rules — and the 1940s saw the end of the throwing rule.

The victors in this clash were the members of the Victorian Football League, who convinced the Association that the passing of the ball with a clenched fist (also known as *handball*) was an essential skill.

In other words, holding of the player must be obvious and restricting. This may sound confusing if you're not familiar with the game, but with practice you can tell when a player in your favourite team is being restricted. And it won't take you long to join the other fans trying to educate the umpire through that strange Aussie Rules language that consists of loud hooting and derision.

Australian football has about 20 main rules. Each has a large number of sub-rules, and most are open to interpretation. Sub-rules are helpful to know, but won't necessarily improve your enjoyment of the game. Try these for a bit of fun:

- **Metallica:** Players are banned from wearing jewellery, because rings, bracelets and neck chains can cause injury.

- **Weigh cool:** The dry weight of the ball must be between 450 grams and 500 grams.

- **Bad vibes:** A player is not allowed to shake a goalpost while a rival is trying to score.

- **Medico no-no:** A free kick can be awarded against a team whose club medical officer interferes with the ball.

To fully enjoy the game of Australian football, you don't need to overly concern yourself with learning these endless curios. In fact, only a handful of the most dedicated fans know and understand these intricacies in the rules. However, knowing the following rules is essential to understanding and enjoying Australian football:

- **Passing the ball:** A ball can only be kicked or handpassed with a clenched fist. Throwing the ball is illegal. Handpassing, or handballing, is the game's most distinguishing feature and has become a highly developed skill. (Check out Chapter 7 for more details on passing the ball.)

- **Catching the ball:** If the ball is kicked more than 15 metres and isn't touched in flight, a player can catch the ball and claim a mark, which I discuss further in Chapter 6. This means the player has the option of stepping back to take his kick or handpassing, or he can play on. Playing on, he immediately runs away from where the mark was taken. (I talk more about playing on in Chapter 7.)

- **Holding an opponent:** Holding on to an opponent who doesn't have the ball is illegal. However, if an opponent is in possession and plays on, he's open game. A player in this position can be tackled and thrown to the ground — the harder the better, to make sure he's just that little more hesitant the next time he tries to play on. The tackle must be below the shoulders, but not below the knee, which would allow the umpires to call an illegal tackle.

✔ **Being thoroughly mean and nasty:** Pushing an opponent in the back or throwing an opponent to the ground after he has kicked or handpassed the ball is illegal. Other illegal moves include:

- Deliberately kicking the ball out of bounds on the full (which means the ball flies over the boundary line without bouncing, or being touched by another player)

- Tripping an opponent

- Kicking an opponent

- Striking or maiming an opponent

- Striking an umpire (Heaven forbid!)

✔ **Being racist:** Racial vilification is no longer tolerated in Australian society; nor is racism accepted on the football field. Any AFL player who makes a racist or ethnic remark or gesture must go through a conciliation process or face the consequences — usually suspension.

If any breaches of these rules occur, one of the field umpires awards a free kick against the offending player. If an infringement occurs after a free kick, the field umpire can declare an additional penalty and the ball is moved 50 metres downfield against the offending team. This is known as a *50-metre penalty*.

Kicked out

David Rhys-Jones, who played with Sydney and Carlton from 1980 to 1992, has the dubious distinction of appearing before the League tribunal more times than any other player.

Rhys-Jones was reported 25 times, found guilty of 11 charges and suspended from 22 matches. A ferocious competitor and a brilliant footballer, Rhys-Jones was awarded the Norm Smith Medal (see Chapter 15 for more on this medal and Appendix A for a list of winners) as the best player on the ground in the 1987 Carlton–Hawthorn grand final (won by Carlton). The judges' decision was unanimous. I know, because I was one of the five judges.

A much earlier counterpart of Rhys-Jones was Richmond's Bill Burns, who was found guilty of kicking an opponent in 1909 and was suspended from playing in 46 matches. That was one tough tribunal!

Size Doesn't Necessarily Matter

Official Australian football grounds come in many sizes, but only one shape — oval. And why an oval for a football game? Australian football was invented as a way to keep cricketers fit during the winter months. For this reason, Australian football has always been played on an oval-shaped field similar to a cricket field. Indeed, many grounds are still used for cricket and football, with the Melbourne Cricket Ground (MCG) the classic example.

The AFL's *Laws of the Game* stipulates that 'the playing ground shall be oval in shape, between 135 and 185 metres in length and between 110 and 155 metres in width'. All grounds must be marked with a circle 3 metres in diameter in the centre (for the centre bounce), and have a centre square of 50 metres, where only designated players are allowed for the bounce of the ball at the start of each quarter or after a goal has been scored.

As well, two goalposts set 6.4 metres apart are placed at each end, with behind posts set another 6.4 metres from each goalpost. Lines are marked to 9 metres from each goalpost to form a kick-out area after behinds have been scored (see Chapter 3). Figure 2-6 illustrates how the ground appears (with these elements marked).

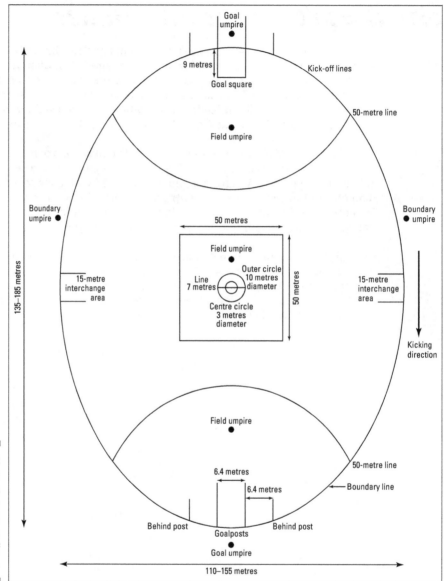

Figure 2-6:
The
dimensions
of the
playing field
plus the
location of
the umpires.

The long and the short of it

The Sydney Cricket Ground (SCG) — home of the Sydney Swans — has the shortest playing surface in AFL competition, 153 x 137 metres.

On the other hand, Geelong's Skilled Stadium has a playing surface of 171 x 117 metres, making this stadium traditionally the narrowest playing field in the competition. However, in 2001, the Sydney Swans signed an agreement to play several games a season at the Sydney Olympics venue, Telstra Stadium, at Homebush. The stadium has an adjustable playing ground, varying from 130 to 160 metres wide.

Whatever its width, Telstra Stadium's 75,000 capacity and ultra-modern structure make it a very desirable venue.

Seasons that Make Sense

Every competition has a season, a period of play that's usually based on the number of teams taking part in the competition. For example, a 10-team competition may play an 18-round season in which the teams play each other twice on a home-and-away basis. The AFL, with 16 teams, is unable to use this system because 32 rounds of matches plus the finals simply takes up too much time. How would we fit in the cricket season? Contrary to the view of most football fans, players do need a summer break from the sport. Today, 22 rounds of matches make up the AFL competition, the season lasting six months.

Home and away

The term *home and away* refers to where a team is playing — that is, whether the team is playing at the club's ground or the opponent's ground. Simple? Not quite, because at AFL level a club's 'home' can occasionally include more than one stadium. For example, the Sydney Swans' main home ground is the Sydney Cricket Ground. However, the team can also play a number of games at Telstra Stadium. Both locations are called home games because the Swans play at both on a regular basis. The moral of this story is to check where the game is to be played, because turning up at the wrong venue is a great way to spoil your day!

One way to help you work out the location of a game is to check your newspaper and see how the game you want to attend is listed. As a general rule, *fixtures* (sporting events held at prearranged locations on prearranged dates) are drawn up with the home team named first. For example, if the fixture reads Collingwood v Melbourne, the home team is Collingwood.

Today's AFL competition originated in 1897 with 8 clubs and 16 rounds, and fixtures were easy to organise. The competition has shrunk and expanded many times over the years, evolving into today's 16-club competition, which began in 1997, when Port Adelaide joined the AFL.

With 16 teams and 22 rounds, not every club can play each other twice in the one season. The AFL tries to correct this imbalance by ensuring teams not matched against each other twice in the one season do so within the next two seasons. The AFL season may not be as even as everyone would like, but the mix is the best that can be made of a 16-team competition. For a list of the 16 teams, see Chapter 13.

On the road again

The term 'home and away' has been used from the earliest days of football, when fans began travelling from one side of a city to another to watch their favourite team play.

For example, fans travelled from the suburb of Collingwood to St Kilda, 12 kilometres away. In those days, this was a considerable distance and fans referred to going 'away' or staying at 'home' to see their team play.

Even farther from the suburbs of Melbourne were the games in Geelong, which fielded a team against the seven Melbourne-based clubs in the early days of the Victorian Football League.

Geelong is approximately 80 kilometres from Melbourne, but that didn't stop fans catching the train to support their team playing an away game in Geelong. Train travel to Geelong was common until the 1950s and '60s, when most families finally were able to afford a motor vehicle.

In Melbourne, many thousands of fans continue to travel to Aussie Rules matches by tram, the most convenient means of public transport.

Trams are extremely popular in Melbourne and are packed on match days, going to the MCG or Telstra Dome. Trams are superb people-movers, and football fans in other cities, including the residents of Adelaide and Sydney, face much harder travel conditions without trams.

Kick-off time

The AFL season starts late in March, with the grand final played on the last Saturday in September. (The year 2000 was an exception to this rule because the AFL avoided a clash with the Sydney Olympics and the footy finals by moving the first games forward to early March.)

Table talk

Many football competitions around the world describe the list of wins and losses as *tables*. In Australian football, a table is known as a *ladder*. The team leading the competition sits at the top of the ladder, the team with the least points at the bottom. The AFL ladder is based on wins, losses and draws, with 4 points awarded for a win, 2 for a draw and none for a loss. Some competitions, notably the South Australian National Football League, use a system of 2 points for a win and 1 for a draw.

Adding up points is the easy bit. The tricky part comes when, for example, two teams have 13 wins and 9 defeats each at the end of the season. To work out which team is placed above the other on the ladder, the AFL uses what are known as *percentages*.

To calculate a team's percentage, take the total points the team has scored in the season, multiply the number by 100 and then divide the result by the total number of points scored against the team.

For example, in a season a team may score 2,000 points with 1,900 points scored against the team. Multiply the 2,000 points by 100 and you reach 200,000. Divide this by 1,900 and you come up with the figure 105.3, which is the team's percentage for the season.

I know this figure is accurate because I worked it out on a calculator. However, Aussie kids aged 6 and above, who are Rules fans, can work out a team's percentage to the last decimal point — in their heads. In fact knowing how to work out your team's percentage is one of the essentials of Australian (Rules) life.

Finals Fever

When all the matches have been played and the ladder has been formulated down to the last percentage point, the *final eight* can be declared. Now, the top eight clubs play off in a finals series, while the bottom eight teams go home to pack their guernseys in mothballs and eat cream buns and drink soft drink of the amber kind for the first time in eight months.

Again, that's the easy version of the story. Understanding exactly how the finals series works is a mystery beyond even the most dedicated fans and the popular belief is that only rocket scientists are able to work out which teams should play which in the first weeks of the finals.

I'm no rocket scientist, but I'm now going to describe to you how the AFL footy finals are devised — once and once only, mind you! It's more than my sanity's worth to try this too often. If you learn this by rote, you can impress your friends forever as someone who can really understand how the AFL finals system works.

The finals are played over four weeks, in this order:

- ✔ **Week one:** The 1st placegetter plays the 4th, the 2nd plays the 3rd, the 5th plays the 8th, and the 6th plays the 7th. (The losers in the 5th–8th and 6th–7th games are eliminated.)

- ✔ **Week two:** The winner of the 5th–8th match plays the loser of the 1st–4th game in one semi-final, while the winner of the 6th–7th match plays the loser of the 2nd–3rd match in the other semi-final. (The losers of these two semi-finals are eliminated.)

- ✔ **Week three:** The winners of the first week's round of games between the 1st and 4th placegetters, and the 2nd and 3rd placegetters, have now had a week's rest, and are ready to do battle against the winners of the two semi-finals of the previous week. These matches are known as *preliminary* finals.

- ✔ **Week four:** The winners of the two preliminary finals matches play off in the grand final.

Easy to understand, isn't it?

At the MCG — Grand Final Mania

The AFL grand final is The Big Day on the Australian football calendar and one of the biggest annual events in Australia. The big match, as the grand final is known, is televised live around the world and has an audience of hundreds of millions of football fans.

Filling the stands

The grand final is traditionally played at the Melbourne Cricket Ground (MCG) and always attracts a capacity crowd. The ground currently has a capacity of around 100,000 — the MCG used to stretch to over 100,000 in the days when standing room was acceptable. The record attendance for any sporting event at the MCG was set in 1970 when Carlton defeated Collingwood and 121,696 fans were screaming their teams on to a win.

I've been to most grand finals in the past 30 years and the excitement this match generates continues to amaze me. It's almost possible to grasp the spirit of excitement that invades the city of Melbourne as its population gears up for the big match.

FOOTY FLASHBACK

The final version?

Over the years since 1897, the finals round has included either four, five, six or eight teams.

In 1897, the top four clubs played a round-robin finals series. For the following three years, a much more complicated system involved all eight clubs in the finals.

In the period between 1900 and 1931, four other systems were used until Percy Page and Ken McIntyre devised the final-four system. The Page–McIntyre system was used until 1971, at which time the league introduced a final five for 1972. The final six was introduced in 1991 and the final eight was introduced in 1994. Phew!

Australian football fans initially greeted this relatively recent expansion of the finals series from six teams to eight with considerable scepticism. Today, however, the final eight is considered a welcome opportunity for more fans to be able to boast that their team has made the finals.

As proof of this, under the final-four system, the average attendance at finals was around 380,000, whereas under the final-eight system, the attendances for finals matches are around 600,000 per year — a considerable jump. This rise means more people are enjoying the sport and the clubs and promoters are happy at the flow-on increase in earnings from television and other media rights.

Chumps to champs

Fitzroy finished the 1916 home-and-away season on the bottom of the ladder with just two wins and a draw from 12 matches. And yet the club went on to win the 1916 premiership!

The reason the team was able to achieve this amazing feat was that the competition that year included just four teams, due to the impact of World War I.

Fitzroy found form in the final-four system finals, made the grand final and then defeated Carlton by 29 points. From chumps to champs in four weeks!

In 1990, as a radio commentator for the Collingwood versus Essendon grand final, I was on the hallowed turf of the MCG to describe the atmosphere as the teams ran onto the ground. At that moment, the roar of the massive crowd virtually knocked me off my feet. It was truly deafening and, since that day, I have envied the players who experience the emotion of running onto the MCG for a grand final.

Flying the flag

The premiership is decided in a contest between the two teams that survive the first three weeks of the finals. Until 1958, the winning club of the Australian football grand final was presented with a premiership flag. Traditionally, this was unfurled at the premiership club's opening home game the following year and then proudly flown throughout the season at all home games. Other clubs flew their pennants at home games as well.

In 1959, the League introduced a premiership cup (see Figure 2-7) and the first of these now-familiar trophies was presented to Melbourne captain John Beckwith after his team defeated Collingwood in the grand final.

Figure 2-7:
The Australian football premiership cup is presented at the end of every grand final with much fanfare and cheering.

LEAGUE LINGO

The presentation of the trophy is now a huge part of the premiership celebrations. Players on the premiership team are each presented with medallions and the player voted the *best on the ground* in the grand final is presented with the Norm Smith Medal (see Chapter 15 and Appendix A for more details). The winning club's theme song is blared time and time again on the PA system and, as the winners slowly jog a lap of honour to show their fans the premiership cup, the PA thumps out Queen's pop hit 'We Are the Champions'.

Grand grounds

In the modern era of Australian football, every grand final has been played at the MCG, except for the 1991 game. In that year — when Hawthorn defeated West Coast at Waverley Park — the MCG was unavailable because of the construction of the Great Southern Stand.

The only other grand finals played away from the MCG since the earliest years were those in 1943, 1944 and 1945, due to the fact that the famous ground was occupied by the armed forces during World War II.

Grand finals not played at the MCG were played at the following locations:

- **1943:** Richmond defeated Essendon at Princes Park.

- **1944:** Fitzroy defeated Richmond at the Junction Oval. After the win, jubilant Fitzroy supporters had to walk back to their Brunswick Street Oval ground to celebrate, because Melbourne was hit by a public transport strike.

- **1945:** Carlton defeated South Melbourne at Princes Park.

- **1991:** Hawthorn defeated West Coast at VFL Park.

Chapter 3

Settling the Score

In This Chapter

▶ Scoring and goals of the game

▶ Climbing the ladder

*A*ustralian football is as unique to this country as the kangaroo — and so is the way the game is scored. For example, in soccer the ball goes into the net and a goal is scored. Simple! At the end of a game, if one soccer team has three goals to the other team's two goals, the final score is 3 to 2. How easy is that?

In the case of rugby union and rugby league, different amounts of points are awarded for tries, penalties and goals. To work out the score, you simply multiply the number of tries, goals and penalties by their relevant values and then total the results. At the end of the game, the score may read 24 to 21. Easy!

Oh, if only scoring were so simple in Australian football! Instead, scoring is a relatively complicated system in which 6 points are awarded for a *goal* (when the ball is kicked between the goalposts) and 1 point for a *behind* (when the ball is kicked between the goalposts and the behind posts), so a game is scored as follows:

✔ Team A scores 15 goals and 10 behinds, producing a score of 100. That is, 15 goals multiplied by 6 equals 90 points, while 10 behinds multiplied by 1 equals 10 points: $(15 \times 6) + 10 = 100$.

✔ Team B scores 15 goals and 9 behinds, producing a score of 99.

✔ Team A wins by 1 point. The final score is written:
Team A 15.10 (100), Team B 15.9 (99).

Aiming high

Geelong holds the record score for any AFL match with 37.17 (239). The team achieved this feat in a 1992 game against Brisbane at the Carrara Oval on Queensland's Gold Coast.

Carlton was the first team to break the 200-point barrier with a score of 30.30 (210) against Hawthorn at Princes Park in 1969. Only 29 matches have seen scores of 200 points or more. The Sydney Swans is the only team that has scored 200 points or more in consecutive matches. In a 1987 match against West Coast at the Sydney Cricket Ground (SCG), the winning Swans scored 201 points and the following week the Swans scored 236 points against Essendon, also at the SCG.

With these incredible victories on record, the Swans went out the following week onto the same field and scored 198 against Richmond, failing by just 2 points to make three *double tons* (as scores of 200-plus are known) in a row.

Scores of Ways to Make a Point

The aim of the game is to score more points than the opposition and, because both goals and behinds are part of the scoring, the best way to achieve victory is to score as many 6-pointers (goals) as possible. That said, a team can be defeated when the opposition scores less goals but at least seven more behinds, as the following shows:

- ✔ Team A scores 15 goals and 10 behinds, which is written 15.10 (100).

- ✔ Team B scores 14 goals and 17 behinds, which is written 14.17 (101).

Despite this situation, scoring goals is still preferable to scoring behinds, because the opposition has to work that much harder to match goal points.

Scoring a goal for 6

A goal is scored when a footballer kicks the ball through the two goalposts at his team's end of the ground. The distance the ball travels — 50 centimetres or 50 metres — is irrelevant as long as the ball travels through the goalposts untouched by any other player. As well, the ball must be propelled by any part of the footballer's leg below the knee — his boot, shin or even ankle bone! This achievement is worth 6 points (as indicated by the goal umpire's signal as shown in Figure 3-1)! Hear the crowd shout in delight . . . or anguish!

The laws of the game stipulate that the two goalposts be 6.4 metres apart and not less than 6 metres in height. The two behind posts at either end should be placed 6.4 metres to the side of each goalpost and have a minimum height of 3 metres.

Figure 3-1:
The goal umpire points with his index fingers to signal a goal.

Kicking a behind is not a bummer

Although scoring goals is the aim of the game, scoring behinds is not to be scoffed at, because even one behind (worth 1 point) can make the difference between victory and defeat.

A behind is scored when

- ✔ **The ball travels between the goal and behind posts.**

    Figure 3-2 shows why sending the ball through the goalposts untouched is so much more difficult than sending the ball through any other part of the scoring area.

- ✔ **The ball goes between the goalposts but has been touched by a player after leaving the first player's boot, foot or shin.**

    Aussie Rules footballers try to prevent the opposition scoring a goal, even if a behind is conceded as a result. Players achieve this by deliberately touching the ball before it goes over the goal line. Behinds (worth single points) scored in this manner are described as *rushed*, as in 'rushed through the goals'.

- ✔ **The ball hits a goalpost before going through the goalposts.**

    Known as a *poster*, a ball hitting the goalpost brings groans of dismay from fans whose team came so close to scoring a 6-point goal.

- ✔ **The ball is carried or punched over a team's goal line by an opposition player.**

    These behinds occur when a team is under defensive pressure and prefers to concede a behind rather than take the risk of the other team scoring a goal. In other words, losing 1 point is far better than losing 6 points.

Figure 3-2:
The goalposts take up only a fraction of the ground's area.

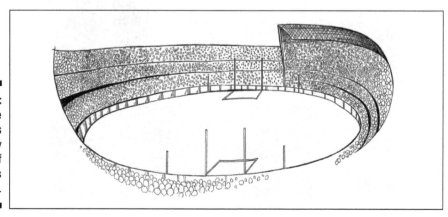

Falling way behind

Over the years, a number of AFL games have resulted in no goals being scored, but this only happened in the earliest years of competition when scoring was more difficult and the game flowed less freely than the rules allow today. The last time a team finished with zero goals was in 1961 when Richmond scored 0.8 (8), losing to St Kilda 12.19 (91) at the Junction Oval.

In the history of the game, no team has played an entire AFL match without scoring at least 1 point. St Kilda, however, holds the questionable record of scoring just one behind (1 point) in a match against Geelong (162 points) in 1899.

Fitzroy came close to going the same way in 1953. With just one minute to play in a match against Footscray at the Western Oval, Fitzroy's score was nil. Club captain Allan Ruthven saved the day in that final minute by kicking a goal, and the match, played on a waterlogged ground, ended in Footscray defeating Fitzroy 66 points to 6.

Australian football is mainly about the positive skills of kicking, handpassing and *marking* (catching a kicked ball in flight). (See Chapters 6 and 7 for more information on the skills of football.) However, playing a tactical game also requires defensive skills, including knowing when to reach for the ball in flight to take a mark in defence, and when to knock the ball clear.

Coaches don't take kindly to defenders who consistently try to out-mark the opposition because the ploy can easily fail and cost the team a goal. The less risky approach is to try to knock the ball clear of an opponent trying to mark, even if a player has to hit the ball through the posts and give a behind point to the opposition.

Discovering draw-backs

If the scores at the final siren are drawn, then this result stands because no extra time is allowed in Aussie Rules. When two teams draw, the 4 match points, which would have been awarded to the winning team, are shared — 2 points to each team. Draws are rare in Australian football and generally average out to one each season.

I say extra time isn't allowed in Australian football. But, like all rules, this has exceptions too. Extra time of ten minutes is added to finals matches that result in a draw. If a draw still exists at the end of this extra time, another ten minutes is played. However, no extra time is allowed to resolve a grand final draw. Instead, the teams meet again for a nail-biting replay.

Level-pegging

The first recorded drawn match was between Fitzroy and South Melbourne on June 22, 1897, with both teams scoring 43 points. The pair clashed again later in the season and South Melbourne defeated Fitzroy by just 1 point.

In the 1921 Victorian Football League (now AFL) season, a record five draws were scored, whereas only two grand finals have ended in a draw — the 1948 match between Essendon and Melbourne and the 1977 match between North Melbourne and Collingwood. In the resulting match replays, Melbourne won the 1948 contest and North Melbourne won the 1977 replay.

The other possible anomaly that may affect the result of a match is a *protest*. In the modern era of the game, no result has been changed due to a protest; however, in 1909 Geelong protested against St Kilda for playing an unregistered player, resulting in a victory for Geelong, despite the fact that St Kilda had won the match by just 1 point.

The Ladder to Success

To compile a season's *ladder* (the table showing where the teams stand in relation to each other), points are awarded for match results. In most competitions, including the AFL, 4 *match points* are awarded for a win, 2 for a draw, and a loss means that zero, zilch, zip points are awarded! Match points are the difference between playing in the final eight and spending the last weeks at home watching the other teams play off in the finals on telly.

Compiling the ladder

After the first round of matches in the 16-team AFL competition, each team is given its position on the ladder, according to the number of match points the team wins. The team with the most points goes on top, the team with the second best tally is next and so on. And the pecking order changes because a new ladder is compiled at the end of each round throughout the season.

At the end of the season's competition — after the AFL's 22 rounds, for example — the order of teams is known as the *final ladder*. The first eight teams then play the finals.

Mid-season and final ladders look much the same — the only difference is that teams change position and numbers increase as the season progresses.

Understanding the headings on the various columns in a ladder is important. Check out the final ladder in Table 3-1, which is based on the 2007 AFL season results. Here, I explain the codes and what they mean:

✓ **'P' is for played.** The number 22 represents the total number of games played. If every team records the number 22, then all teams have played 22 matches and this is the final ladder at the end of the season. (In other leagues, the total may be just 18 or 20.)

Listing the number of games played is essential because some teams may have played more games than others by a particular time in the season.

✓ **'W' is for won.** All the team's victories are recorded round by round.

✓ **'L' is for lost.** This column is for the number of games a team has lost.

✓ **'D' is for drawn.** Although draws don't happen often, they still need to be recorded.

✓ **'For' is for all the points scored by the team.** This column adds up how many points the team has scored by the end of each round.

✓ **'Against' is for all the points scored against the team.** Unfortunately teams give up points too, and this column adds up how many points the team has had scored against them by the end of each round.

✓ **'%' is for a team's percentages at the end of each round.** I talk about the importance of percentages in Chapter 2.

Percentages are those statistics that result from the points *For* being multiplied by 100 and then divided by the points *Against*.

✓ **'Points' is for total match points.** This column represents the number of points a team has collected in terms of victories and draws.

In most competitions, including the AFL, a team is awarded 4 match points for each win, 2 match points for each draw, and no match points for a defeat.

Understanding the ladder

In Table 3-1, the team with the most match points is at the top of the ladder, and the team collecting the lowest number of match points is at the bottom. Places in between are decided on match points and, in some circumstances, by percentages (refer to Chapter 2).

A ladder contains many subtleties, such as the placing of teams that win and lose the same number of games. For example, in Table 3-1, Hawthorn is above Collingwood because Hawthorn has the greater percentage. (Refer to the preceding section, 'Compiling the ladder', for an explanation of the table headings.)

Table 3-1				Final Ladder for the 2007 AFL Season				
Team	*P*	*W*	*L*	*D*	*For*	*Against*	*%*	*Points*
Geelong	22	18	4	0	2542	1664	152.8	72
Port Adelaide	22	15	7	0	2314	2038	113.5	60
West Coast	22	15	7	0	2162	1935	111.7	60
Kangaroos	22	14	8	0	2183	1998	109.3	56
Hawthorn	22	13	9	0	2097	1855	113.0	52
Collingwood	22	13	9	0	2011	1992	101.0	52
Sydney	22	12	9	1	2031	1698	119.6	50
Adelaide	22	12	10	0	1881	1712	109.9	48
St Kilda	22	11	10	1	1874	1941	96.5	46
Brisbane	22	9	11	2	1986	1885	105.4	40
Fremantle	22	10	12	0	2254	2198	102.5	40
Essendon	22	10	12	0	2184	2394	91.2	40
Western Bulldogs	22	9	12	1	2111	2469	85.5	38
Melbourne	22	5	17	0	1890	2418	78.2	20
Carlton	22	4	18	0	2167	2911	74.4	16
Richmond	22	3	18	1	1958	2537	77.2	14

Carlton spoons it up

The term 'wooden spoon' was originally used at Cambridge University in the United Kingdom and described the spoon that was presented to the student achieving the lowest score in the mathematical honours degree.

While no-one knows precisely why the term was adopted so wholeheartedly by fans of Australian football, the very mention of the wooden spoon sends a shiver up the back for fans whose team is a candidate to win this dubious honour.

Of the 8 clubs that formed the Victorian Football League in 1897, through to the 16 clubs that form the AFL today, only 1 club, Carlton, had avoided the dreaded wooden spoon, until the 2002 season. Carlton had never finished at the bottom of the ladder and the club's fans (and officials, players and promoters) were devastated at the club's first wooden spoon. To make matters worse, Carlton also collected the 2005 and 2006 wooden spoons.

Studying the ladder

AFL ladders are published in the major newspapers and on various Web sites on the Internet. Ladders are studied assiduously by fans after every round, so you want to make sure you take your ladder with you if you're heading for a barbecue with fans from opposing teams. The AFL site (www.afl.com.au) keeps the ladder updated after every round.

The ladder allows you to answer the questions Aussie Rules fans ask. How many match points does your team need to close the gap on the top eight? How can your team get above the fifth-placed side? How can your team avoid finishing last? Each of these questions is relevant, but particularly the last.

Even if a team doesn't make the top eight, fans don't want their team to finish on the bottom of the ladder. In Aussie Rules, a team that finishes on the bottom of the ladder must carry the stigma of *collecting the wooden spoon* — a mythical trophy to be avoided at all cost!

Chapter 4

Gearing Up for the Game

Australian football is basically a game of kick and catch, so, although Australian footballers wear a distinct uniform, few add-ons such as shoulder pads or helmets are required to play the game. The basic uniform consists of a footy jumper, shorts, socks and boots. Add a football to this combination and you're ready to play.

Having made that broad statement, I need to add that an enormous range of accessories, designed for practical and safety purposes, is available for players to fine-tune their success on the field. This chapter explains the clothing and equipment choices you make when you — or someone in your family — need to be kitted out for Aussie Rules.

Wearing the Whole Kit and Caboodle

Australian football players may deny having a passion for fashion, but few players are likely to wear a kit designed a decade ago. Tight shorts and baggy shorts, woolly jumpers and cotton jerseys . . . the game's seen the gamut over the years. In recent times, many of the design changes have come about for safety reasons, which is why choosing the right equipment is so important.

These boots are made for kicking . . .

Boots are the most important part of a player's uniform, because a player's feet and toes are put through a vigorous and violent workout during a game of Aussie Rules. A high-quality pair of boots also gives a player the necessary grip on both dry and wet grounds.

Up to 1970, footballers wore distinctive ankle-high boots with a special protective pad over the anklebone. Since those days, football footwear has come a long way and professionals now take two styles of boots along to every game — a pair of *rubbers* and a pair of *studs*, as shown in Figure 4-1.

 ✔ **Rubbers:** As the name implies, these boots have moulded rubber soles with well-defined tread, and give the player excellent grip on a firm, dry field.

 ✔ **Studs:** These boots have rows of hard plastic studs generally screwed to the sole of the boot. The studs are about 10 millimetres in length, though some are longer, and dig into soft or muddy soil, providing the player with the necessary grip in wet ground conditions. Studs are also known as *stops*.

Most players prefer to play in the more comfortable rubbers and often wear these more simple shoes (optimistically) in the first quarter. As a result, you often see an entire team discovering the delights of slipping and sliding on the field and then promptly switching to studs during the first break.

The key to comfort and safety is choosing boots that fit perfectly. Stroll into a sports shop and you may well be amazed to discover how many different brands of football boots are available. The most popular brands include Adidas, Puma, Lotto, Fila and Nike, but this doesn't mean you should ignore other brands.

In an ideal world, you buy a pair of rubbers and a pair of studs when you're shopping for football boots. However, if the hip pocket is a little lean, go for boots capable of taking studs because, after all, football is a winter sport and rain is more often than not the name of the game. (Make sure you remember to screw in the studs before games or training.)

In the early days of football, studs didn't exist, so footballers nailed strips of leather to a pair of working boots. Known as cleats, these leather strips were removed after the match and the player wore the boots to work during the week.

Figure 4-1:
The moulded soles (left) have dimples that can grip a hard surface, whereas longer studs (right) dig into the turf in heavy or rain-soaked conditions.

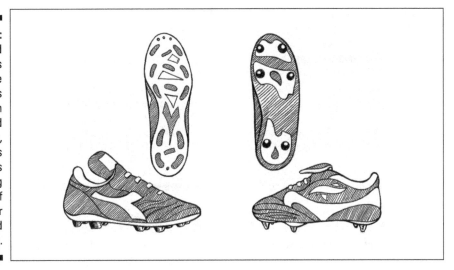

In my very modest playing days, I wore ankle-high boots with leather studs, or stops, which were very difficult to wear in at the start of the season. I remember having blistered feet at the start of every season due to stud-nails pushing through the soles. Now, however, football boots are more like slippers and usually made of the lightest possible leather. In my time, there was no choice of colour. Just black! Now, white boots are more common than black ones, and some players wear red, blue, yellow and even gold boots.

Field fashions and top dressing

What do the Channel Isles have to do with Australian football? Nothing whatsoever. However, because certain styles of pullovers originated on the Channel Isles of Guernsey and Jersey, Australians have long used the terms *guernsey* and *jersey* to describe a pullover. And, for generations, Australian football jumpers — pullovers, guernseys, jerseys or whatever you choose to call them — were made exclusively from wool.

Not any longer! These days, footy jumpers are made from a clever range of materials that usually include a type of synthetic. This fabric provides warmth in cold conditions, and allows the air to circulate in hot and humid conditions. As a result, the Australian football jumper now looks more like a soccer shirt with one major difference — somebody forgot to sew on the sleeves. (At least, that's how it's worn in the upper echelons of the game.)

FOOTY FLASHBACK

When the Essendon Football Club was founded in 1872, officials decided on black and red as the official colours. The only problem was that the guernseys had to be made in England and, while waiting for these to arrive, Essendon temporarily wore navy blue guernseys. Also, the Fitzroy Football Club decided on its founding, in 1883, to adopt the colours of maroon and blue. Fitzroy also had its guernseys made in England and, when their consignment arrived, the guernseys had yellow chamois-leather patches across the shoulders. Fitzroy therefore wore maroon and gold for many years before wearing maroon and blue and, in the 20 years before the club's demise in the merge with Brisbane in 1996, maroon, gold and blue.

A ripping yarn!

In days gone by, jumpers with long sleeves were the norm in Aussie Rules. Then, in the 1920s, a few players decided the sleeves were too restrictive, so the lads literally ripped the bloody arms off!

Club officials weren't impressed by this treatment of the uniforms, so a number of clubs began ordering sleeveless jumpers for their players.

Jumpers with long sleeves do exist and are used by players in particularly wet or cold conditions. The League doesn't have a rule about sleeves and usually the matter is a personal choice.

For example, recently retired (2007) Essendon champion James Hird usually (but not always) wore a jumper with sleeves, as did former Hawthorn champion Michael Tuck.

When I played amateur football and lacked a certain amount of muscle definition, I preferred a sleeved jumper to hide my inadequacies. In the same vein, junior teams generally wear sleeved jumpers — after all, how many juniors have bulging muscles to scare off the opposition?

South Melbourne full-back John Heriot decided in the 1960s that both long-sleeved and sleeveless jumpers were uncomfortable, so he designed his own! Heriot's famous number 21 footy jumper had tailor-made short sleeves that ended just above the elbow, and several AFL players today still wear Heriot's design, although the AFL frowned upon them late in 2002.

The AFL at the start of the new millennium decided that clubs needed alternative uniforms. All clubs were told to come up with new designs so there would be no colour clashes in matches. All clubs complied, some with minor changes, others adopting more radical designs. Collingwood, for example, refused to wear anything but its famous black and white stripes, but compromised by changing the back of its guernsey from black to white as an alternative uniform. The Brisbane Lions, Carlton and the Western Bulldogs in 2007 introduced basically white away outfits.

The AFL each season plays a *Heritage Round* in which it recalls past eras. Clubs are asked to wear old designs. For example, the Sydney Swans for these rounds over the past few seasons switched from white with a red 'opera house' yoke on the front and a red back to white with a red vee. Adelaide in one Heritage Round match wore the old South Australian state colours of red with blue and yellow vees. But Adelaide has not been brave enough — yet — to wear the colours South Australia wore in interstate matches before World War II — turquoise and chocolate brown!

Short tales!

In the 1950s, Carlton became the first team to wear shorts in a colour other than black or white. However, the club had to get a special dispensation from the AFL before kitting the team out in navy blue shorts to match their footy jumpers.

Colourful shorts then began to replace the blacks and whites, through the football clubs of the 1970s, mainly due to the introduction of colour television. In days gone by, shorts were knee-length and by the 1990s they were extremely short (as worn by Sydney and Brisbane full-forward Warwick Capper in the 1980s).

The style now is for slightly looser and longer shorts for comfort.

The low-down on shorts

Football's earliest heroes wore *knickerbockers* — knee-length shorts that fitted snugly over the top of knee-high socks — because even a glimpse of leg flesh was in those days deemed immodest. Oh, how times change! In the 1970s and '80s footballers appeared to have their shirts spray-painted onto their bodies and, if the players' shorts had been any tighter, they'd have had trouble running.

While baggier shorts are being seen on the field these days, many coaches object to the bigger look, believing these shorts are an easy target for opposition players to grab during a tackle.

Professional footballers are required to have at least two pairs of shorts — one for home games and one for away games. Until about 20 years ago, the home team wore black shorts and the away team wore white shorts to help umpires and fans differentiate between teams with similar club colours on their jumpers.

With the introduction of brightly coloured shorts, most teams began to wear their home shorts to every game, except when playing an away game against a team wearing the same colour shorts. At AFL level, for example, Richmond players wear black shorts with a yellow stripe, but switch these for white shorts when playing an away game against Essendon, which has black shorts with a red stripe. (Check out Chapter 13 for the rundown on the AFL clubs and their colours.)

FOOTY FLASHBACK

Supermen and knickerbockers

Former Fitzroy and North Melbourne defender-ruckman Michael Reeves, who played in the AFL competition from 1980 to 1987, had a problem with corked thighs as a result of internal bleeding.

To protect his legs, he wore padded protection in his shorts — the first player to do so. The result was that Reeves looked as though he were wearing knickerbockers. Then, as happens with fashion on and off the football fields, the idea caught on and, today, many Aussie Rules players wear a similar type of padding.

Melbourne ruckman Jeff White, who throws himself into heavy packs, uses padding under his shorts and undershorts. These undershorts, which are skin-tight and knee-length, protect the groin and hamstring areas from cold. Some footballers, including White, put padding under the undershorts. White also wears a protective pad over his shins, as he once suffered a terrible gash that took years to heal.

South Melbourne ruckman Jack Graham literally died of a football injury, even if many years after his career (227 games from 1935 to 1949). Graham gashed a shin and the wound never healed. Many years later the wound was still so bad he was advised to have surgery. However, he died of infection following this surgery.

Undershorts came in all colours of the rainbow when they first became popular in the mid-1990s. However, the AFL now insists undershorts be in skin tones.

Put a sock in it . . .

Professional players are required to wear team socks, and members of junior teams can be fined small amounts of money for wearing odd socks or socks in the wrong colour when playing for their teams.

Jocks and other jazz

An enormous assortment of football accessories is available, ranging from shin guards to thigh pads. Most exist for practical and safety reasons, whereas others are designed to satisfy the whim of individual players. This equipment includes:

- **Athletic supports:** The old jockstrap appears to be going out of fashion, but players who don't wear athletic supports should wear tight underpants, preferably made of lycra or another strong, elastic fabric. In fact, to put it delicately, body-hugging daks are essential for personal protection.

✔ **Gloves:** At AFL level, gloves are required to be in club colours. Until the late 1990s, no self-respecting footballer wore gloves, regarded as strictly anti-macho. However, Australian footballers discovered gloves while playing unofficial *Test matches* (international matches played as a 'test' of skill) against the Irish in Ireland in 1984 and 1987. The Irish, mainly because of the bitter cold in the Emerald Isle, wear gloves to keep their hands warm and these gloves have evolved to include rubber dimples on the palm-side, for better grip. Australian footballers suddenly realised gloves were a good idea after all and many now wear gloves, especially in wet conditions. The gloves must be in a team's basic colour. For example, Richmond players must wear black gloves, whereas Sydney players must wear red ones.

✔ **Injury aids:** A range of items is available that either help to prevent injury or protect a previous injury. (See Chapter 11 for more on protective gear.) These include:

- **Mouthguards:** Every footballer should wear a mouthguard to protect teeth and gums. Who wants to wear dentures? Who wants to go gap-toothed? Mouthguards are the answer, so see your dentist. They are essential!

- **Padding:** A piece of padding is particularly relevant when you're trying to protect an old injury or wound. For example, Carlton's Glenn Manton chose to wear a black rubber protective cover over his left elbow; his elbow was badly scarred after he fell through a plate-glass window as a teenager.

- **Shin guards:** These leg guards are highly recommended because Australian football can be a rough-and-tumble game.

- **Tape:** Taping is an exact art and is best done by a trainer or medical officer. The enormous value of taping is shown in the fact that most football clubs go through literally kilometres of tape every season.

- **Thigh pads:** At AFL level, thigh pads can be worn as part of the undershorts and must be in skin tone.

- **Wrist straps:** Many footballers use wrist straps, mainly to protect old injuries. For example, a bruised thumb is bound by tape, which is then wrapped around the wrist. Some footballers also use tape to stiffen wrist joints. A common football injury is a broken scaphoid, a small dumbbell-shaped bone under the thumb. Footballers who've suffered a broken scaphoid use tape to protect the wrist from further injury.

✔ **Good-luck charms:** A number of famous players refuse to take to the field without a lucky sock or their bootlaces tied in a particular manner. Good-luck charms may sound silly, but the reality is that whatever makes you happy is okay — as long as the charm has no potential to incur an injury. Jewellery, including necklaces, bracelets and rings, are strictly out of bounds on the field, though some footballers are weighed down by their 'bling' away from the game!

✔ **Black armbands:** The club usually supplies armbands, worn as a mark of respect, after the death of a club identity or other dignitary.

Being on the Ball

The ball used in Australian football has specific dimensions and weight, according to the rules of the AFL. Don't be mistaken by thinking of a football as a *pigskin* — even though this term is often used to describe a football, especially by Americans. The ball used in Australian football is made of 100 per cent leather and a brand spanking new one is highly prized because of the ball's special aerodynamic qualities.

Size counts

The AFL's *Laws of the Game* stipulates that the football 'must conform to a standard size of 720–730 millimetres by 545–555 millimetres and be of a shape and standard specification approved by the Australian Football League'. The law relating to the size of the football also states: 'The dry weight of the inflated ball shall be between 450 and 500 grams.'

The ball used in Australian football is oval in shape, but I've often seen balls being kicked around the streets and parks that are as round as soccer balls. Although these old balls are fine for *scratch* matches (games with no official bearing), their official lifespan is definitely over.

The League's laws also stipulate that the home team is responsible for providing the footballs for the match. Although a friendly game only requires one ball, AFL matches require a number of balls. A new ball is used at the start of each quarter when the ground is wet or soggy and sometimes on a kick-out after a behind. Multiple balls are also needed because occasionally a spectator snaffles a ball. I've even known footballs to be kicked over the grandstand and into the street — and not everyone is honest enough to return a football worth $100 or more.

Forbidden fruit

One of the most unusual circumstances involving a football occurred in a professional match at Geelong in 1970. The game was between the Cats and South Melbourne (now the Sydney Swans). Cat forward Doug Wade was taking a vital shot for goal in the final minutes of play when suddenly a spectator threw an apple at the football.

Incredibly the apple hit the ball in mid-flight, the ball slewed off-course and South Melbourne stole a close victory. The devil in the stands was never identified! Wade wasn't allowed to retake his kick because the incident was considered outside the rules of play. Nothing like this had ever occurred before, and there was no rule covering such a freak incident. And nothing even remotely like it has occurred since, so it's still very much a grey area. However, this is just one incident in more than a century of competition. Fans' bags are now checked as they enter the grounds, so anyone wanting or being able to throw or fire weapons would be unlikely. An apple appears to be as dangerous as it gets, and you'd have to be a phenomenally accurate shot to hit the ball in mid-air, as the fan in 1970 obviously was.

Ball brands

A company called Sherrin makes the most common brand of ball used in Australian football — in fact, this company is such a huge part of the sport, the term *kick the Sherrin* has become part of football vernacular. Other popular brands include Ross Faulkner, Burley and Lyrebird, and each has its devotees. Usually, footballs are reddish-brown, although bright yellow balls are used in night matches.

Smaller footballs are manufactured for junior use. And for younger children extremely light, plastic footballs are a terrific option to help them develop their ball-handling skills.

In my playing days in Victoria, the football was either a Sherrin or a Ross Faulkner and, frankly, I was never able to tell the difference between the two — unless I looked at the brand name — and never considered the brand of a ball to be an issue. Then one day I played in a match in Western Australia using a ball made by the local manufacturer, Burley, and I discovered that various brands of footballs can feel extremely different. In this case, the ball appeared to be slightly more pointed.

Finding Where to Get in Gear

You can find specialist AFL shops in every state of Australia, and I recommend you buy from these shops, because the League approves their products. That said, you may well find what you want at a sporting goods chain shop or independent store. However, remember that, by buying approved AFL products, you're financially supporting your club.

For AFL gear, check the Web sites for each of the AFL teams (see Chapter 19) or check the AFL Web site (www.afl.com.au).

Part II
Playing the Game

Glenn Lumsden

*'... and he's climbing a stairway
to heaven ...'*

In this part . . .

Playing Aussie Rules is great fun, but first you have to know how. In Chapter 5, I explain the various playing positions and their importance to the outcome of the game. In Chapter 6, I cover the skills involved in different kicking styles, which are fundamental to the game of Aussie Rules, as well as the spectacular skill of marking. Then, in Chapter 7, I look at the other essential skills — handpassing and bouncing, either of these moves done while running with the ball at the same time. It sounds difficult but it's easily learned. I also look here at leading, defensive moves and tackling. The skills of the game are unique and may take some time getting used to, let alone perfecting, but the rewards are enormous, for spectators and players alike.

This part is where the action is — so get ready to get down and dirty!

Chapter 5

The Positions

*W*ho does what where is an important component of Aussie Rules; even if you don't intend playing the game, you should be aware of the playing positions. Not only does this knowledge make following the game's tactics easier, but you can also actually follow what's happening in a match. In this chapter, I explain the playing positions and what is required of each of them.

Making Up the Numbers

Each Aussie Rules team has 22 players, making a total of 44 players in a game. However, only 18 players from each side can take the ground at any one time. The other four players on each team are known as *interchange players*. As this suggests, these players can take the ground at any given time — *if* one of the 18 in the side leaves the ground at the same time.

Having interchange players allows the team coach to be more flexible with tactics, to cover weaknesses and build strengths, and to replace injured players.

Players can leave and take the ground at any time, as many times as they like, as long as only 18 players are on the ground at any given time. If a team captain believes the opposition has more than 18 men on the ground, he can ask the umpire(s) to *take a count* of the opposition. If the opposition is found to have more than 18 players on the ground, its score is automatically cancelled.

The *count* is an extreme rarity in football (it has not occurred in living memory at AFL level), as all players and coaches know full well the severity of the penalty. Imagine a count occurring in an AFL grand final, with just a few minutes to play. One team has a lead of, say, 60 points and is found to have 19 men on the ground, and its score is wiped out and the premiership is lost. Wow, what headlines that would create!

Lining Up the Team

Once upon a time, and it now does seem like a fairytale, the 18 players lined up in what were known as set positions; that is, every player had a designated position. In today's game, very few set positions exist and, although teams are named and announced in set positions, these very rarely apply. Rather, coaches ask players to fill a number of roles and the game has new terminology. But, to avoid moving ahead too fast, I start with the basic team positions.

Australian newspapers usually list members of football teams by their basic positions. Known as a *team line-up*, the abbreviations at the start of each line represent the following:

- ✔ **B: Backline (3 players).** The first line of defence, these players aim to prevent scoring.
- ✔ **HB: Half-backs (3 players).** The first line of defence, but often an attacking line.
- ✔ **C: Centreline (3 players).** Midfielders whose job is to drive the ball forward.
- ✔ **HF: Half-forwards (3 players).** The first line of goal scorers.
- ✔ **F: Forwards (3 players).** Usually the main goal scorers.
- ✔ **FOLL: Followers (3 players).** Follow the ball around the ground to give drive.
- ✔ **INTER: Interchange (4 players).** Substitute players who cover for injuries or the coach's tactical moves.

But just to complicate the ABC for you, variations exist to these basic positions.

A sneaky title

Although Aussie Rules teams have official positions, a few nicknames for positions also exist. For example, the full-forward, who is usually the team's specialist goal kicker, is often known as the *goalsneak*, and this has a historical background. Although most full-forwards today are big, strong footballers, this position was once filled by smaller, more nimble players whose main weapons were pace and cunning. They would place themselves close to goal so that they could 'sneak' a goal. Now, most goalsneaks are forward pockets, with Collingwood's Leon Davis the perfect example — small, nimble and extremely dangerous close to goal.

Take, for example, the backline (B). Here, the players named on the left and right of these lines are known as *back pockets*. The player in the centre is the *full-back*. Then on the half-back line (HB), the players named on the left and right are known as *half-back flankers*, with the player in the centre of this line the *centre half-back*.

And, of course, the same applies for the forward (F) and half-forward (HF) lines, except that the players to the left and right are known as *forward pockets* and *half-forwards flankers*, and those in the centre, *full-forwards* and *centre half-forwards*. The centreline (C) is slightly different, with the player in the middle (literally) known as the *centreman*. Those to the left and right are known as *wingers*. In addition, the followers (FOLL) comprise the *ruckman* (the first named player), a *ruck-rover* (the second named player) and a *rover* (the third). Plus you have the interchange players (INTER), which are known as *the bench* because, literally, these players sit on a bench until they're called into action.

Figure 5-1 shows where these positions effectively sit on the field of play.

Teams are generally named from the backline. However, South Australians name their teams from the forward line. No wonder their interstate rivals suggest South Australians do everything backwards!

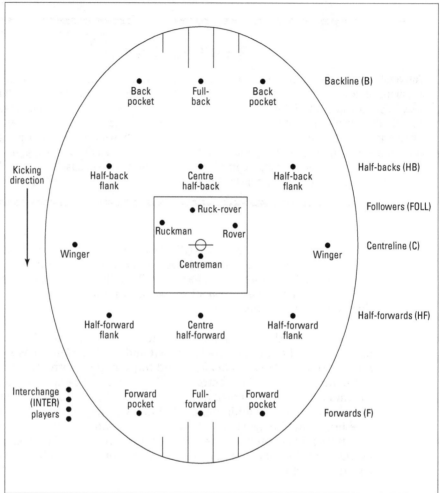

Backline (B)

Half-backs (HB)

Followers (FOLL)

Centreline (C)

Half-forwards (HF)

Forwards (F)

Figure 5-1: Where the playing positions are located on the field.

Taking Your Position

Players are no longer as restricted to fixed positions as they once were, but each position still determines that player's general role in the game, and draws on particular skills and strengths. In this section, each of the positions is discussed in depth, as well as how each player fits into the general scheme of things.

The ruckmen

Ruckmen are the most important players in any team, it often has been said — especially by ruckmen themselves! A team's ruckman is invariably the tallest player in the side and it's his duty to get his team moving forward from centre bounces, ball-ups and boundary throw-ins.

In many ways, the opposing ruckmen are like two warring dinosaurs. They grimace at each other as the umpire prepares to bounce the ball for the start of play and then leap at the ball in an effort to tap it to a teammate. This behaviour is very much like the tip-off in basketball, only much more physical.

Bounces, ball-ups or throw-ins are at the heart of the game because they are the means to start or restart play, either at the beginning of each quarter, following each goal, after scrimmages or when the ball goes over the boundary line.

The game is started by an umpire, who bounces the ball high in the centre of the ground. The ruckmen leap high and try to hit it directly to a smaller teammate or thump it forwards, sometimes as far as 40 metres. The prerequisite of height for a ruckman is obvious, but skill and courage are also required because ruckmen banging into each other 50 or more times in a match can have a devastating effect on the body.

Most clubs have at least three or four specialist ruckmen, although most have a recognised 'number one' ruckman. Clubs generally play two ruckmen per game, for a few reasons: In case of injury to the number one ruckman, to give him a breather or to allow him to take up another position for tactical reasons. Over the past few years it has become increasingly important for clubs to have *two* good ruckmen in the same side because few ruckmen have the endurance to play at the high intensity of ruck contests for an entire game. Some clubs switch ruckmen on and off the bench, whereas other clubs play one up forward while his teammate does the ruck work, and then they switch positions. For example, Geelong's Brad Ottens is a fine ruckman, but is often sent forward, where his strong marking and accurate kicking make him an extremely dangerous forward close to goal. In this way he alternates ruck duties with a teammate, usually Mark Blake.

Ruckmen are sometimes seen as characters like Lurch in *The Addams Family*, but nothing could be further from the truth. They are generally smart as well as courageous. The ruckman is responsible for pushing his team forward from bounces and throw-ins, must have good skills to win the ball around the ground, and is often seen as the protector of smaller teammates. You could say that ruckmen are big men with big jobs in the game.

The bird's-eye view of the ruckmen

Ruckmen, even from the earliest years of the game, have generally been the tallest of all footballers. However, as football has become more professional, and dietary and hereditary factors have seen the height of the average man and woman develop considerably over the past century, ruckmen are now more skyscraper than two-storey. For example, the legendary Jack Dyer, who played 312 games with Richmond from 1931 to 1949 and was one of the biggest ruckmen of his era, stood just 185 centimetres. Now, however, the average height of an AFL ruckman is 200 centimetres, with the Fremantle Dockers' Aaron Sandilands measuring 212 centimetres in his socks. Wow, that's 27 centimetres taller than Dyer. Talk about evolution!

Dyer, at 185 centimetres, was extremely mobile. In today's game he probably wouldn't even be tall enough to hold down a position like centre half-back (average height now about 191 centimetres). Yet most of today's giant ruckmen are every bit as mobile as the much shorter ruckmen of yesteryear. For example, West Coast's Dean Cox stands 204 centimetres and weighs 102 kilograms, yet covers the ground with amazing agility and runs about 12 kilometres during the course of a match. Cox is the archetypal modern ruckman, as he is brave and strong at bounces and throw-ins, is able to move quickly from one end of the ground to the other and can also take powerful marks (see Chapter 6). Also, when rested from ruck play, he can move forward to kick goals.

Rovers and midfielders

When the ruckman leaps in an effort to win the tapout from the bounce or throw-in, he aims to direct the ball to a smaller teammate, a *rover* or *midfielder*.

In many ways the term 'rover' is an anachronism, because very few genuine rovers exist these days. In years gone by, rovers were small, nippy players who could win the ball at the feet of the ruckman and other bigger opponents. They were specialists and usually light and fast on their feet. Now, however, coaches use a number of players to follow the ball around the ground to take it away from what we know as *clearances* (bounces and so on).

The old practice was for teams to have two rovers, one 'roving' around the ground and the other 'resting' in a forward pocket. When one rover tired, the other would take over. However, the game is now so fast and furious, and the players so fit, that many players never take a rest during a game and, if they do, this is spent on the interchange bench to get a complete breather.

This mattress is not for sleeping

The crash, bash role of the ruckman has forced some of these specialists to seek protection, especially for their legs. Melbourne ruckman Jeff White therefore wears special thigh and shin pads. White is considered one of the bravest ruckmen in the AFL and, because his prodigious leap is a very important element of his game, he has to protect his legs. Some unkind critics have suggested that White wears mattresses under his shorts and socks, but if his pads prevent severe bruising — or even worse — he has the last laugh.

About 20 or so years ago, coaches realised that the more rover-type players they had on the field the better, because the teams needed constant pressure around the packs. Coaches consequently developed what was described as a team's *running ability*. This, in turn, eventually led to the modern ploy of rotating midfielders. Smaller, running-type players buzz in and out of play, sometimes taking over from each other from the interchange bench, moving from a wing to the centre, from the backline to a midfield role and so on. Many of these moves are now structured so that midfielders know exactly when they have to move with the ball or drop back.

The aim is to have a group of five, six or even more players who can swap positions to generate drive from the midfield, following the ball around the ground. These players have extremely onerous tasks: Many midfielders run more than 20 kilometres every match. Playing in the midfield therefore requires enormous stamina, and many players have to be developed as midfielders. Others just don't have the aerobic capacity to run so hard for so long.

The midfielder's role is to win the ball around the packs and run, run, run, giving and receiving passes from teammates to keep their team on the move. The faster they can move the ball — by hand or foot (see Chapters 6 and 7) — the better, because quick movement to the forward line can catch the opposition outnumbered and under enormous pressure. Midfielders by nature, therefore, are highly skilled, extremely fit and the great thinkers of the game, capable of knowing exactly where to send the ball for the team's maximum benefit.

The West Coast Eagles won their 2006 premiership largely through the brilliance of their midfield group, with Ben Cousins, Chris Judd and Daniel Kerr among the best ball winners in the game. Sydney had enormous trouble containing this group, and the Eagles won the grand final by 1 point. In the previous year's grand final, Sydney may have been fortunate, as Kerr injured a leg early in the match and was sidelined for more than half the game. The Swans won by just 4 points.

Fitzroy rover Haydn Bunton (199 games from 1931 to 1937 and in 1942) was a champion rover who won three Brownlow Medals as the competition's fairest and best player. For more information on the Brownlow Medal, see Chapter 15 and, for a list of winners, see Appendix A. Today he would be described as a midfielder because he could also play on a wing or in the centre. Bunton won Brownlow Medals in his first two seasons, a feat no-one has equalled. Fitzroy initially played him on a wing but, in his era, he often was out of the play because wingers were not supposed to roam in search of the ball. Fitzroy then switched him to playing 'on the ball' and he became arguably the greatest midfielder the game has seen.

Defenders

The role of the defender is obvious. However, defenders must often play aggressively in the name of defence. Although the defender's primary role is to prevent the opposition scoring goals, the defender also adopts an essential role as an attacking player.

Until 20 or so years ago, a defender was seen as a dour stopper, someone who would run into a brick wall to stop an opposition attack. Defenders of past eras therefore not only had broad shoulders and legs like tree trunks, but also cauliflower ears and noses at right angles to their faces.

Today, because the modern game is so highly developed with its running demands and high skill levels, the defender must be able to run with the best of them, match the skills of forwards and midfielders, *and* be able to launch their own attacks. In fact, some clubs often use their best ball winners in specific roles in defence. The classic example is Sydney's Tadhg Kennelly, a wonderfully gifted midfielder with a rare knack for kicking vital goals. Kennelly, recruited from Ireland as a champion junior Gaelic footballer, reads the play superbly and is often given the rare honour of a rival club putting a *tagger* (a player who tries to negate the influence of his opponent) on him. Kennelly often gathers the ball and launches himself on a long run to drive the ball deep into attack or even bob up with a goal himself.

The half-back line

Those who play across the half-back line must have dual capabilities: Coaches want half-backs who can run off their opponents as well as nullify them. For example, a half-back is doing his job well if he can prevent his direct opponent from getting a kick and/or breaking clear. Yet the half-back should also be looking for every opportunity to run forward. If, for example, a teammate wins possession deep in defence, the half-back should be willing to break free of his opponent to dash downfield to receive a pass and then, perhaps, run deep into attack. Collingwood's Heath Shaw is so adept at this that rival coaches go out of their way to try to block his run from defences, because he is known as a goal-kicking defender.

The two half-back flankers are generally more mobile than the centre half-back, although some centre half-backs can be dangerous because of their ability and willingness to run forward. The centre half-back is often also the defensive general (such as Hawthorn's Trent Croad).

FOOTY FLASHBACK

Powered by 'Diesel'

The evolution of the midfielder is best exemplified by former champion Greg Williams, who started his career with Geelong before winning a Brownlow Medal with Sydney and a second with Carlton. As a teenager from the Victorian country city of Bendigo, Williams was twice rejected by Carlton for being too slow, before he made his AFL debut with Geelong. There, from his very first season, he was nicknamed 'Diesel' because he was the fuel on which the team ran. 'Diesel' might have been a slow runner, but he had superb skills, and his ability to judge the play saw him win the ball more than any other player of his era (1984–1997). When he played with Sydney (1986–1991), the Swans built a sensational rotating midfield around his brilliance, with Gerard Healy, Steve Wright, David Murphy and others complementing 'Diesel's' brilliance.

The backline

A team has two back pockets, the general rule being that the smaller back pocket 'minds' the smaller forward pocket and vice versa for the taller pockets.

The smaller back pocket now often wears the title of 'tagger', a player who runs with a star opposition midfielder to nullify his effectiveness. Some of these back pocket players must try to restrict the goal kicking of dangerous small forwards, such as Fremantle's Jeff Farmer or St Kilda's Stephen Milne. West Coast's David Wirrpanda is probably the best of these nullifying back pockets and has immense powers of concentration. Kicking a goal with Wirrpanda as a direct opponent is a considerable achievement.

The full-back sometimes has an extremely onerous task because he may be directly opposed to a champion goal kicker of the calibre of Essendon's Matthew Lloyd or a full-forward with a notoriously aggressive playing style such as Sydney's Barry Hall. A good full-back therefore is worth his weight in gold. For example, Carlton's fall from grace in 2002 (when it finished last for the first time in the club's long and proud history) immediately followed the retirement of champion full-back Stephen Silvagni, who was rated by the experts as 'the full-back of the century'. Full-backs are generally tall (Essendon's Dustin Fletcher stands at 197 centimetres) and strong. They must be able to match a full-forward for height, strength and pace, so a club with a quality full-back considers itself fortunate indeed.

FOOTY FLASHBACK

The full-back gold mark

Only one full-back, South Melbourne's Fred Goldsmith, in 1955, has ever won football's most prestigious individual honour — the Brownlow Medal. Goldsmith was an unusual full-back in that, instead of trying to punch the ball clear from the full-forward in aerial contests, he preferred to try to mark the ball.

This technique is anathema to a modern full-back, but Goldsmith was one of the best marks of his era. Goldsmith was on duty as a firefighter when it was announced that he had won the Brownlow Medal: He actually thought his fire brigade workmates were joking when they told him of his win!

Forwards

The main role for forwards is to kick goals. However, as with defenders, a number of forward 'types' exist. For example, the two half-forward flankers are usually quick, reasonably tall (sometimes as tall as 191 centimetres), and mobile. Highly skilled players, half-forward flankers possess that rare football quality of being able to smell an opportunity for a goal. Many half-forwards now rotate through the midfield (such as Collingwood's Leon Davis), while some are specialist goalsneaks (refer to the sidebar 'A sneaky title' earlier in this chapter), such as another Collingwood player, Alan Didak.

Centre half-forward

The centre half-forward position is arguably the most important position of them all. Good centre half-forwards come along only a little more frequently than Halley's Comet. It has often been said that a team can be built around a champion centre half-forward. A good centre half-forward also has to have great aerobic capacity because he must cover a lot of ground in his efforts to provide a target 50 metres or so from goal.

Adelaide's Wayne Carey, who spent most of his career with the Kangaroos before joining the Crows in 2003, was the perfect example of a big, powerful centre half-forward capable of turning a game in minutes. Carey, at his peak, had it all — height, immense strength, extreme mobility, superb aerial judgement and an uncanny knack for goals. He was, for years, the Kangaroos' forward general, and teammates always tried to kick the ball long and quickly to him so that he could be 'one out' with his opponent. Carey invariably won these man-on-man duels. Many are called but few are chosen, and when Carey indicated during the 2002 season that he would play elsewhere in 2003, teams scrambled frantically for his signature.

He retired in 2004 and, over future seasons, he will be the benchmark for all quality centre half-forwards. Fremantle's Matthew Pavlich arguably is the best centre half-forward of the current era and has all the qualities to make him an extremely dangerous opponent, as he is tall, solid, a strong mark, a good mover when the ball hits the ground and a long, accurate kick for goal.

I am the greatest

South Melbourne's Laurie Nash was a champion at either centre half-back or centre half-forward and, in one interstate match for Victoria against South Australia in 1934, he was moved from centre half-back to centre half-forward after half time and kicked 18 goals. Whenever Nash was asked who was the greatest footballer he had ever seen, he would reply: 'I see him in the mirror every time I shave.'

Full-forward

The other key forward is the full-forward, who usually is the team's specialist goal kicker — Essendon's Matthew Lloyd and former St Kilda and Sydney champion Tony Lockett are good examples. Players of their calibre are rare because not only do full-forwards have to be tall and strong, but they also have to be fast and an accurate shot for goal.

Allegedly, a champion full-forward, one capable of kicking 100 goals ('the ton' in the vernacular) in a season, joins a club only once every couple of decades — and sometimes never. For example, Melbourne has never had a 100-goals-a-season full-forward, although Fred Fanning kicked a club record of 97 goals in 1947, the year he kicked a League record (still standing) of 18 goals in a match against St Kilda.

Two forward pockets play alongside the full-forward, usually with vastly different styles, such as the small, quick goalsneak, like St Kilda's Stephen Milne, and the tall, high-marking type (usually a resting ruckman), like Geelong's Brad Ottens. Both types are there to kick goals — after all, that's how a team wins games.

Chapter 6

Skills of the Game: Kicking and Marking

In This Chapter

▷ Kicking terms and techniques

▷ Catching the ball with a mark

*B*ecause Australian football is so different from most other codes of football, except perhaps Gaelic football, you need to practise the skills intentionally. The more dedicated you are to your practice, the more you can improve your playing.

For example, when AFL club Melbourne recruited 18-year-old Irishman Jim Stynes from Dublin in the mid-1980s, club officials always knew he'd have to be groomed meticulously to play at the elite level. Dedication also played a huge part in Stynes' development; now it's a matter of history that he not only mastered the skills of the game but went on to win a Charles Brownlow Medal for fairest and best player in the 1991 AFL competition.

In this chapter, I discuss the kicking and marking skills needed to play Aussie Rules. (I cover other essential skills such as handpassing, running and tackling in Chapter 7.) If you're keen to excel, practise these drills regularly with a friend who also wants to become a better player.

Slam-dunking, by foot

Sydney full-back Andrew Dunkley, who retired as an AFL footballer after the 2002 season, was a rarity in Australian football because he was a notoriously poor kicker. In fact, it almost cost him his career when he was rejected by St Kilda and moved to play at a lower level in Tasmania before being signed by Sydney. Dunkley, whose other game skills were superb, camouflaged his deficiency by handpassing at every opportunity.

Getting a Kick Out of Football

Australian football is vastly different from American football (gridiron) and from both the rugby codes, simply because kicking the ball is a skill practised by all participants. American football utilises a specialist kicker. (Australia's Ben Graham, who formerly played in the AFL with Geelong, is now a designated kicker in American football.) In the rugby codes, the jobs of specialist kickers include conversions of penalties and so on. In the Australian code, every single player must be able to kick the ball well and, preferably, with either foot.

Almost every boy or girl who chooses to play Australian football is taught the skills of football from a very early age, and it's an Australian tradition for children to have a backyard kick with their father and/or siblings. For many, the skills of kicking come naturally. Others need to practise patiently over the long term. But whether you're a natural or have two left feet (could be an interesting advantage), you can have a ball trying out different kicks. In this section, I discuss the various types of kicks and how to perform them.

The punt

The *punt* kick is regarded as the ugliest kick in the game: It's little more than putting boot to ball as quickly as possible with no real attempt to make it spin correctly, bend in the air or even spiral over long distances. The plain punt kick is now very rarely used in the highly professional AFL, although it's often seen at junior levels, in which kicking skills are not fully developed. Of course, you have to start somewhere, and the punt is as good a place as any to begin a little daily practice if you've never done much kicking. Also, getting the simple punt down is a good foundation for the drop punt, which is much more frequently used.

The drop punt

The *drop punt* is a kicking style that spins in the air to make it easier to mark (catch). The drop punt is the most commonly used form of kicking in Australian football and is a must for those who wish to develop their game.

Although the punt kick was the norm up to the 1930s, Richmond's Jack Dyer developed and perfected the drop punt for accuracy in shooting for goal. It was obvious this type of kick would also be accurate around the ground, so its use became more and more prevalent. Today, the drop punt is used about 99 per cent of the time in AFL matches as the basic kicking style.

Here's how to drop punt:

1. **Hold the ball with your fingers spread evenly on each side with the thumbs almost together at a 45-degree angle to the ground, as shown in Figure 6-1.**

2. **On completion of your *run-up* (the lead-up steps before kicking the ball), lift the ball to a slightly higher angle.**

3. **Just before you kick the ball, use your right hand to guide it down and then drop it. The angle of the ball to your body at this stage should be about 60 degrees, as shown in Figure 6-2.**

4. **Make contact with the ball with your boot before it hits the ground. The ball is basically vertical at this point.**

Then, with perfect balance and a straight-leg *follow-through* (the action after contact with the ball has been made), kick the ball so that it tumbles end-on-end to its target.

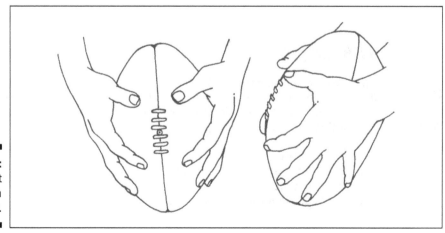

Figure 6-1:
The correct hold for a drop punt.

Figure 6-2:
Positioning
and
releasing
the ball for
a drop punt.

Don't kick directly to a teammate, because he can become a sitting duck for the opposition. Rather, aim to kick the ball about 10 metres in front of him so that he can run onto it. This technique gives your teammate the opportunity to gain a break on his opponent and therefore be able to mark cleanly without the danger of the ball being punched away or, even worse, being outmarked.

The torpedo

This kick has nothing to do with battleships but, rather, the way the ball flies through the air like a torpedo. The *torpedo* is a kick for exceptional circumstances and is best left to those who can drive the ball long distances in shooting for goal.

Torpedo kicks are difficult to mark because extra judgement is involved in the flight of the ball. In fact, only a handful of current AFL players really can 'get onto a big torp'. But, when perfected, the crowd generally roars its approval because it's a truly majestic kick.

Probably the best exponent of the torpedo is Collingwood centre half-forward Anthony Rocca who, using the style, can kick a ball 70 metres. (Refer to Chapter 5 for more information on positions.) Whenever Rocca takes a mark more than 50 metres from goal, Collingwood fans frantically urge him to 'go for the torp'. Then, if he kicks a goal with this kick, it becomes the icing on the cake. West Coast full-forward Quinten Lynch also has a huge hoof and can kick the ball 70 metres. Whenever Lynch takes a mark within 60 metres of goal, Eagle fans urge him to take a shot. He then goes back, removes a glove, and takes his kick. Eagle fans know that when the glove is off, literally, he'll try for a goal rather than pass to a teammate.

The torpedo is used almost exclusively by long-kicking forwards (and the key to kicking long is timing rather than strength) who are taking set shots for goal. Running torpedo punts are about as rare as submarines on land.

To kick a torpedo:

1. **Hold the ball at a slight angle to your body, as shown in Figure 6-3.**

   For a right-foot kick, place your left hand slightly forward and place your right hand slightly behind the lacing. For a left-foot kick, reverse your hand positions.

2. **Release the ball with your hand in the same way as a drop punt (refer to preceding section), but keep the ball at the same angle to the body throughout (as shown in Figure 6-4).**

3. **Follow your kicking leg through and make contact with the ball with your instep at a slight (about 30 degrees) angle (not with the outside of your boot).**

   This angle gives the ball a spiralling movement through the air, hence the extra distance covered with this kick.

Figure 6-3:
For a right-foot torpedo kick, hold the ball like this.

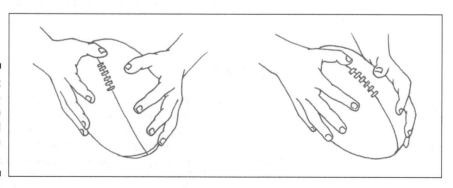

Figure 6-4:
The torpedo
kick.

Before using this kick in a match, make sure you've mastered it. Who knows — you might bring 80,000 fans to their feet at the MCG, just like Anthony Rocca has done many times in his career. Rocca's brother, Saverio, also was a huge kicker in his career with Collingwood and the Kangaroos. He retired in 2006 and immediately tried his luck in American football with the Philadelphia Eagles.

The banana kick

Yes, we have no bananas except, that is, in shooting for goal from very tight angles. The *banana kick* is a kick that curves, as shown in the example in Figure 6-5, and is an extremely difficult one to master. Forwards must make the most of every opportunity when taking a shot for goal. If you haven't mastered this difficult kick, you run a high risk of miskicking the ball and failing to score a goal. Although it was once considered outrageously bizarre, most professional forwards are now expert at the banana kick or, as South Australians call it, the *checkside punt*.

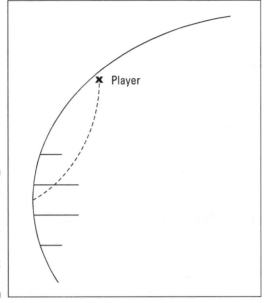

x Player

The banana kick was reputedly invented by Richmond half-forward Blair Campbell in the late 1960s. Fans gasped whenever they saw the Tiger goalsneak bend the ball through the air banana-like to score a goal from a seemingly impossible angle. Now, more often than not, any player on a tight angle is likely to attempt the banana kick.

The banana kick, like the torpedo punt, takes a lot of practice, but is nowhere near as difficult to achieve. For a right-foot kick, follow these steps (if you want to make a left-foot kick, just do the opposite):

1. **Hold the ball at a 45–60-degree angle to your body with your right hand forward on the ball, as shown in Figure 6-6.**

2. **Swing your right leg back as you guide the ball down, dropping it at an angle.**

3. **Then bring your leg through so that the ball makes contact with the right side of the ball, thereby producing a curved spin.**

Collingwood's Alan Didak is the master of the banana kick, and teammate Leon Davis has kicked many extraordinary goals from tight angles with this 'around the corner' shot on goal.

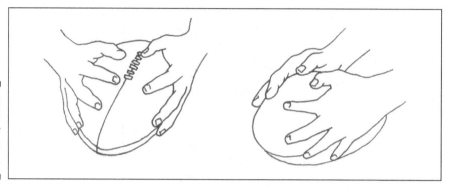

Figure 6-6:
How to hold
the ball for
a banana
kick.

Kicks gone the way of the dodo

A number of kicking styles have existed over the years, with many of them failing the test of time. For example, right up to the 1960s, drop kicks and stab passes were common. The *drop kick* was almost identical to the drop punt except that the ball actually touched the ground momentarily until contact was made with the ball on the half volley. Similarly, the *stab pass* was a form of drop kick, except that the player using it would lean back sharply to keep the ball very low to the ground, to accurately pass the ball directly onto a teammate's chest. Players no longer use these kicks because they're too risky — they can slew off the side of the boot — and, in the highly professional AFL competition, most risks have been eliminated. However, players can emulate the stab pass with a low drop punt.

Up until the 1940s, the *place kick* was often used when taking a set shot for goal. This kick was like the rugby kick for goal still used in both codes. The ball is placed on the ground, or a slight mound of earth, pointing towards the goal. The player then takes a run-up and kicks the ball from the ground to tumble through the air. This kick is now considered too time consuming for Australian football, although it's still a legal kick. These days, skills with the drop punt are so good that it's no longer necessary to use so much time taking a place kick. The last player to use the place kick at league level was Fitzroy's Tony Ongarello, who used it in some matches in the 1950s, when he lost confidence in his shooting for goal with punt kicks.

Practising your skills

Whatever type of kick you use, remember that, to become a reliable and accurate kick, you need to develop several good habits:

- ✔ **Develop a set routine of play.**
- ✔ **Grip the ball securely, but not so tightly that you have trouble releasing it.**
- ✔ **Don't push the ball from one side of your body to the other.** Keep it in as direct a line with your kicking foot as possible.
- ✔ **Guide the ball to your foot with one hand.** If you're kicking with your right foot, guide the ball to your boot with your right hand.
- ✔ **Point your toes for maximum impact on the front of your boot and keep the instep taut.** The variation on this is when you use the instep to kick a banana goal or snap for goal from a difficult angle so that you're trying to impart curve on the ball.
- ✔ **Follow through with your kicking foot.**
- ✔ **Practise as often as possible.** As the old saying goes, practice makes perfect.

In order to develop a set routine, young (and old) footballers can do no better than to watch Essendon full-forward Matthew Lloyd taking a shot for goal. The Bomber goal kicker has a set routine that never varies and, consequently, he's regarded as one of the most accurate shots for goal in the AFL.

If Lloyd takes a set shot for goal, he goes back with his eyes still on the *goalmouth* (the space between the goalposts) as he marks out his run forward. He then invariably places the ball on the ground while he pulls at his socks. These socks might already be at knee height, but the tag is part of his routine while he thinks about the shot for goal he's about to take. Lloyd then plucks shreds of grass from the playing surface and tosses them in the air to check the wind and whether its direction will help swing the ball left, right or through the centre. The wind, of course, can take the ball towards or away from the goal, and Lloyd leaves nothing to chance. In fact, he even tosses grass in the air when he's taking a shot under a closed roof at Telstra Dome. It's part of his routine and he feels comfortable with it.

And one last word of advice. Whenever you have the chance to take a kick, choose your style of kick wisely. For example, you wouldn't want to send a long torpedo kick — the most difficult to mark — if you're kicking long to the forward line, unless perhaps your team is behind in a tight finish and you want to get the ball long and as directly as possible to the forward line. Likewise, you wouldn't use a torpedo shot for goal unless trying to achieve a last-gasp win. Players who use the wrong kicking style for the situation or make poor decisions on where to kick the ball are a liability to the team and, at AFL level, find it difficult to win regular selection. Football's scrapheap is packed with players who were regarded as poor with their kicking options.

The Mark of a Footballer

Marking the ball is probably the most spectacular feature of Australian football. This skill involves catching the ball directly from the kick of another player, no less than 15 metres in distance from each other. Marks are generally taken on the chest or unopposed above the head.

The absolute essentials of marking are good judgement and clean hands. Judgement is important and comes only with practice and match play, with knowing the flight of the ball and where it's likely to drop. Clean hands mean that the ball can be grabbed without the slightest fumble. A fumbled mark is still legitimate, but even the slightest fumble can give an opponent the opportunity to knock the ball away. The best players therefore have vice-like grips, often with oversized hands.

If you've judged the ball well, the next step is actually taking the mark:

1. **Spread the fingers of both hands in order to take a bigger and stronger grip of the ball over a wider area, as shown in Figure 6-7.**

2. **Your hands should be at about a 45-degree angle and most definitely not facing the direction in which the ball is travelling.**

   The angle allows the opportunity to get the right grip, whereas front-on hands are more likely to see the ball hit the palms and bounce away.

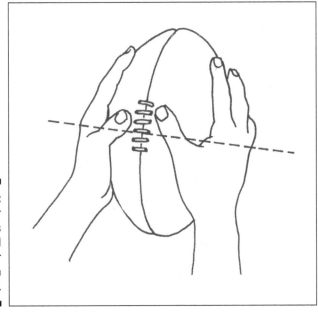

Figure 6-7:
How your
hands
should
appear
when
marking.

Sometimes you may think you can cradle the ball into your chest. This technique, however, can be dangerous because even a few extra centimetres of travel of the ball can lead to an opponent 'spoiling' the mark. So it's better to stretch out your arms in front of you to make that punch of the ball by an opponent a little more difficult.

The *high mark* involves players leaping up to a metre and a half off the ground to mark (meaning to catch) the ball while appearing to stand on an opponent's shoulder, as shown in Figure 6-8. These spectacular marks are known as *speccies* (short for 'spectacular'), for obvious reason. However, they're not the bread and butter of marking — you might be lucky to see one speccie per match.

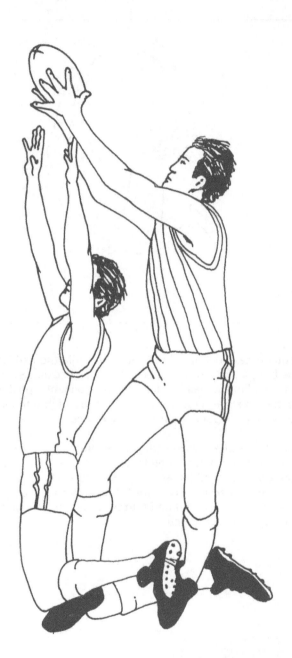

Figure 6-8:
Use good
judgement,
a decent
pace and
spring to
reach a high
mark.

A Mann with big hands

Former Collingwood ruckman Neil Mann had a hand-span so wide he could easily hold a dozen eggs in one hand. Recently retired St Kilda centre half-forward Stewie Loewe had such big hands he was nicknamed 'Buckets'.

In a pack of players, the high mark can be truly inspiring and even breathtaking, usually bringing a crowd to its feet. To achieve a high mark requires a combination of judgement, pace and spring. The main rule is to have your eyes set firmly on the ball, run at the direction from which it's travelling and then leap, sometimes using the back or rump of an opponent to get leverage, into the air. But remember that putting your hands onto an opponent's back or shoulder to get that leverage is illegal.

The golden rules for marking are:

✔ **Keep your eyes on the ball and reach only for the ball, without interfering with opponents.**

✔ **Take the ball in the hands and, if necessary, then guide it to your chest.**

✔ **Extend the fingers to create a cradle for the ball.**

✔ **Extend the arms, not only for high marks, but also for marks taken in front of the body.** In 'chest' marks, waiting for the ball to fall into the chest can be costly, because a defender can come from behind and punch the ball clear. Keeping the arms extended gives less opportunity to a defender to punch the ball clear.

✔ **Make sure your body is behind the flight of the ball.** Don't go for a mark half-heartedly with the body to one side of the flight of the ball as this makes it seem you're wary of opposition contact.

I must admit I was never a good mark when I played football. However, it wasn't through lack of trying, and probably had something to do with my eyesight being as poor as Mr Magoo's. One of my first coaches taught me how to improve my marking when at a loose end at home. He got me to kick my football as hard as I could at one of the outside walls of my parents' weatherboard home. The ball would shoot off the surface at any old angle and I learned to judge the flight of the ball, even from unexpected angles. Pity about my eyesight, though.

To practise *contested* marking, when an opponent interferes with the mark you're aiming for, get one player to stand at one end and kick the ball high into the air to two players at the other end. The aim is to improve overhead marking, so don't kick the ball to the chest. Then, if and when one player has marked the ball, he sends it by foot or hand to the player who has kicked the ball and he repeats the exercise with the next two players, and so on. The kicks need travel only 10 or 15 metres, because the aim is to help your teammates practise their contested and overhead marking.

Chapter 7

Skills of the Game: Passing, Running and Tackling

In This Chapter

▷ Handling the ball the correct way

▷ Leading for the ball

▷ Bouncing and baulking on the run

▷ Defending your teammates

▷ Tackling your opponents

*A*ustralian football employs unique skills, and the most obvious to those new to the game include handballing (passing) and the evasive skills. No other football code in the world uses handballing as a means of passing the ball. The ball is thrown in both rugby codes (union and league) and in American football, but throwing is illegal in Aussie Rules. Of course, using the hands is an outright no-no in soccer, except by the goalkeeper. If you want to play Australian football, you'll have to learn how to handball, or handpass. And, in this chapter, I show you how.

I also cover other essential Aussie Rules skills (aside from kicking and marking, of course, which I cover in Chapter 6). Both kicking and handballing are often performed while running with the ball and you need to learn how to run with the ball, how to lead for the ball and how to bounce it. Otherwise, you may as well be playing rugby.

It's illegal in Australian football to run more than 15 metres without bouncing the ball or, at least, touching it on the ground. So, if you want to take off like a jet and run past the opposition, you'd better know how to run and bounce or, in modern football terminology, *run and carry* or *run the lines* (that is, run from, say, the half-back line to the half-forward line). In this chapter I also cover defensive moves, such as baulking and shepherding, and tackling.

Pass Me the Ball, Would You?

Handballing, or handpassing, has almost always been an integral part of Australian football. At one stage during the 1930s, the Victorian Football Association (the main rival to the VFL, now AFL) decided the game would be faster and more thrilling if the ball could be thrown. Although the Association changed its rule and adopted throwing, it never caught on (if you'll pardon the pun). Australian football became more like rugby and fans detested the abandonment of one of the great skills of the game.

Handballing was an integral part of the Australian game right from the start because the game's founders specifically wanted it to be different from the rugby code. This was a stroke of genius because the Australian game is renowned for its marvellously unique handballing skills. In early eras, handpassing was used almost exclusively to get out of trouble. For example, a player cornered by an opponent and unable to kick over a distance to a teammate, would handpass instead. This pass did not have to hit a target, but, as the game developed, it became increasingly important to retain possession of the ball. Players therefore became increasingly aware of handpassing to a teammate in a better position.

In the 1960s, Western Australian Graham 'Polly' Farmer took handpassing to a new level. A ruckman, Farmer saw handpassing as a weapon rather than as a defensive tool. He therefore developed his handball skill to the point where he could direct a pass to a teammate from 40 metres. He was pinpoint perfect, and before long his style was emulated by every player. Now, footballers can handpass as well as they can kick — if not better in some cases.

Here's how to handpass Aussie Rules style:

1. **Cradle the ball with an open hand (right or left, depending on where you wish to pass the ball). Clench your other hand into a fist with your thumb outside the fingers.**

2. **Stand slightly side on with your left foot forward for a right-hand handball and vice versa for a left-handed handball.**

   Bend your knees slightly to maintain balance.

3. **When you've decided to make a handpass, direct the ball in the open hand towards the intended target.**

4. **Swing your clenched fist back and bring it forward to strike the ball at the pointed end, as shown in Figure 7-1.**

5. **After contact is made with the ball, catch your fist in your open hand.**

Figure 7-1:
Making a handpass.

Ideally, these steps result in a ball that speeds straight to its target and, if that target is just a few metres away, the ball can move like a rocket.

Many players now develop their handpassing skills so well that they can hit a target from 40 metres. Keep practising and you may achieve this. Or set your own goals, changing the target distance incrementally as you improve. A good way to practise is to handpass directly to a brick wall and catch the ball when it bounces back. Alternatively, handpass to a friend standing just a few metres from you or handpass to each other in turn.

Handpasses in the run of play

Most handpasses are performed by players standing or running. In this situation you have to be aware of the opposition around you and it may be necessary to handpass *before* you're fully balanced or fully on the run. However, some handpasses are from players who are lying on the ground, are on their knees or are falling to the ground, often because the player spots a teammate in a good position and doesn't want to waste time getting to his feet. Making a handpass from the ground or while falling to the ground requires you to handpass up to a teammate. This low ground handpass can be both spectacular and effective.

'Polly' was a cracker

Graham 'Polly' Farmer developed his handpassing skills through a training drill so unique it almost beggars belief. Farmer, during long trips as a sales representative, would stop his car and wind the window half-open.

He would then stand 10 metres away and drill handpasses through the half-open window. He rarely missed. Don't try this at home if you're just starting to train.

Shooting off a handpass is just the first part of your duty. You then have to protect the teammate to whom you passed the ball by hand. Most handpasses are made in tight situations, with the receiving teammate often just a couple of metres away. After you've sent him a handpass, you sometimes have to throw out your hands to effect a *shepherd*, a defensive action to prevent an opponent from tackling your teammate (see 'The Good Shepherd' section later in this chapter).

Drilling up for handballing

A good handpassing drill is to gather in groups of six, forming a rectangle or square. You start with one ball and handpass to the player on your right, who handpasses on to the next player and so on. Sounds easy, doesn't it? And it is! But, when you're into the swing of that play, you introduce a second ball to make the movements quicker. Then you add a third ball and a fourth and so on, up to the same number of players you have in the drill. By the end of the drill you're handpassing every second or two.

AFL clubs use this drill with players at close range and the balls move at a blur. Their reflexes and skills are exceptional. But, remember, they started using these drills as youngsters and now are reaping the benefits of constant practice. In matches, their handpassing becomes almost a reflex action, especially in tight situations.

'Diesel' power

The greatest modern exponent of handball was Greg Williams, who played with Geelong, Sydney and Carlton from 1984 to 1997. Known as 'Diesel' because he was regarded as something of a football engine, Williams often had 20 or more handpasses in a match and could send the ball up to 40 metres from either hand. He was so dangerous with his handpassing that opposition players would run alongside him to prevent him shooting out a pass to a teammate.

These tactics rarely succeeded, because Williams was a master at winning the ball and using his lightning-quick hands. He had tremendous vision and could spot a solitary teammate on the other side of the pack and invariably would rocket off a deadly accurate handpass. In today's football, the Western Bulldogs' Scott West and Brisbane's Simon Black are particularly dangerous because of their excellent handpassing skills.

Following the Leader

One of the most neglected skills in Australian football is leading for the ball. Basically, *leading* is making a dash to receive a pass from a teammate. For example, a player has the ball and starts running forward. His teammates then try to break away from their opponents to accept a pass. This play occurs all over the ground and all players must be able to know when and how to run to a position to accept a pass. And it's more difficult than it might sound.

For a start, you must know whether the teammate with the ball is more proficient with his right foot or his left foot. Leading to one side has little point if your teammate can't deliver the ball correctly to that side. Yes, all players should try to learn how to kick with either foot, but it's not a common skill in junior, suburban or country football.

You can lead for the ball from behind an opponent or from in front. Players who tend to lead from the front generally back themselves in a foot race to run away from an opponent. Speed is therefore essential. Those who lead from behind use guile, and zigzag to make the opponent guess which way they're going to lead.

The aim is to get a break on an opponent and therefore be able to run for the pass unimpeded. The master of this skill is champion Essendon forward Matthew Lloyd, who can lead from in front or from behind. There's no better way of learning how to lead for the ball than watching Lloyd. He's the master of pretending to run in one direction, only to cut back in the opposite direction, leaving his opponent flat-footed.

Leading for the ball takes a lot of practice and experience but, remember, it's a skill all players, and not just forwards, need to develop. This skill is vital for teamwork and moving the ball forward — it's almost a cardinal sin in modern football to kick the ball to a *contested* situation; that is, one in which your teammate and an opposition player have an equal chance of winning the ball. Push the odds in your favour by practising leading for the ball so you can accept a pass clear of an opponent or, at least, well in front of him.

Running with the Ball

Running with the ball is vital in Aussie Rules because the aim of the game is to get the ball to the forward line for a scoring chance as quickly as possible. All AFL teams look for *speedsters*, players who can run quickly while carrying the ball. In rugby, players tuck the ball under the arm, but this is extremely rare in Australian football, because the ball must be bounced every 15 metres. If the ball's tucked under your arm you have to move it to one or both hands for the bounce, costing valuable time in play.

The aim is to run with the ball, ready to bounce it. Some players, such as Brisbane's Jared Brennan, with his huge hands, can easily hold the ball in one hand. Alternatively, you can cradle the ball with one hand, resting it on the palm rather than holding it, or hold it with both hands. That way, when you have to bounce it, you'll experience little loss of motion.

Of course, your opposition's aim is to stop you running with the ball, and to get it from you, so evasive action is often required. This section also deals with the skill of baulking while you're on the run.

Bouncing the ball

Bouncing the oval ball so it comes back to you isn't as easy as it might sound. In this section, I offer some tips.

Hold the ball in both hands, at about a 45-degree angle, and guide or push it — do not drop it — to the ground. A well-executed bounce brings the ball back to you, because it hits the ground firmly. It's also important to bounce the ball in front of you so that it comes back to you without you breaking stride in your run.

The faster you're running, the further you need to bounce the ball in front of you.

 Don't bounce the ball in wet or heavy conditions because the ball may skid away or even get stuck in the mud. In wet-weather conditions, touch the ball on the ground instead of bouncing it. Hold the ball with both hands and, when you feel you've run close to the permitted 15 metres, bend slightly to one side and lightly touch the ball to the ground while still holding it. This move equates to a bounce and is a perfectly legal alternative.

Baulking at danger

One of the great unsung skills of Australian football is *baulking*, or *the baulk*, which is a skill whereby you sidestep an opponent. Baulking comes more easily to some, but it can be readily developed. Some players, like former Brisbane player Michael Voss, seem to have an extra sense to warn them of danger and know intrinsically when and how to sidestep. Rather than any supernatural power, years of experience have helped such players develop that skill.

Baulking is all about mobility, so clubs now have players doing training routines to help them move more nimbly in matches. These drills include running zigzag courses through obstacles so that, when an opponent bobs up to lay a tackle, the reaction is much more immediate. In other words, just as you practise what to do in case of an emergency until it becomes second nature, the more frequently you try sidestepping, the better prepared you are when the moment of danger arrives. (But don't try to sidestep tax collectors or other really important people.)

One spectacular facet of baulking is what is known as the *blind turn*. This manoeuvre occurs when a player has the ball and is being chased by an opponent. The player with the ball evades the potential tackler by suddenly swinging to one side. For example, he may hold the ball in his left hand, push his left foot hard into the ground and suddenly swing to the right. This blind turn invariably catches the opponent wrong-footed.

Another facet of baulking is the *dummy*, which all AFL players have mastered to an exceptional standard. A player in possession runs towards an opponent and moves as if to handpass to one side. This movement 'cons' the opposition player that the man with the ball is going to that side. However, the player with the ball then either runs straight ahead or to the opposite side, leaving his opponent flat-footed. Talk about Aussie Rules 'for dummies'! A change of direction can work wonders.

'King' of the Baulkers

The legendary Dick ('King Richard' to his Essendon fans) Reynolds had a great rival in another triple Brownlow medallist, Fitzroy's Haydn Bunton, during the 1930s. Both players revelled in their reputation for being brilliant at baulking, and Reynolds went to great lengths to assess Bunton. He learned that Bunton practised his baulking by weaving his way through crowds of shoppers in the department store where he worked. Reynolds therefore went to that store to spy on Bunton, and his homework eventually won him fame as the best evader of tackles in the competition.

The Good Shepherd

LEAGUE LINGO

Another great unsung feature of Australian football is *shepherding*, which basically means guarding a teammate so that one or more opponents can't tackle him, or obstructing the opposition off the ball, as shown in Figure 7-2. The classic shepherd involves running behind a teammate and using your body to block an opponent in pursuit. Players often spread their arms to enhance the blocking movement.

LEAGUE LINGO

Although most newspapers run match statistics on handpasses, kick, marks and so on, shepherds rarely get a mention. However, coaches rate them very highly and regard them as important *one percenters*, an expression used to describe the extra per cent some players put into their game to help their team win.

REMEMBER

Holding an opposition player is illegal in Australian football, but blocking an opponent is perfectly legal in most cases. You do this by putting your body between your teammate and an opponent, sometimes by spreading your arms, bird-like in flight, to make it more difficult for that opponent to get around you. However, blocking an opponent with undue force or when your teammate is going for a mark and the ball is more than 5 metres away is illegal.

Defensive play is as important to the game as racking up possessions by either kicking or handpassing. Shepherding and helping teammates in tight situations is part of the teamwork necessary for winning a game. Efforts such as shepherding or blocking an opponent can mean the difference between victory and defeat in a tight match.

Tackling the Basics

When you don't have possession of the ball, of course, your aim is to gain it by taking the ball off your opposition. In this pursuit, you need to be on the offensive.

Strangely, tackling hasn't been a highly developed art in Australian football. Players in both rugby codes (union and league) excel at tackling — probably because tackling below the waist in these codes is legal. Tackling below the knee is banned in Aussie Rules, as is tackling over or above the shoulder. The tackle therefore must be aimed at the torso, a difficult feat, especially when an opponent is moving downfield like a rhino in search of a mate.

The basic rule of tackling is to thrust your own torso behind the force of your arms to not only restrict the opponent but, hopefully, to bring him to ground. To make it even more difficult, a really good tackle also forces the opponent to retain possession of the ball because it's locked into the tackle. If an opponent can wriggle his hands free even when his motion forward has been stopped, he can still release the ball to a teammate with a handpass (refer to the section 'Pass Me the Ball, Would You?' earlier in this chapter). If you don't give your opponent the opportunity to handpass the ball, you may win a free kick.

Here's how to tackle:

1. **Go straight for the body and wrap your arms around the opponent, his arms and all.**

2. **Pin the ball to him if you can because, if he hasn't been able to get rid of the ball to a teammate during the tackle, it may be your free kick.**

Tackling is also regarded as another of the game's great one percenters, along with shepherding (refer to the preceding section 'The Good Shepherd'). Tackles are now being counted as part of the statistical reports in every major newspaper covering AFL matches.

Part III
Taking Your Game to the Next Level

Glenn Lumsden

*'Don't panic, he's only come
for your knee.'*

In this part . . .

Who knows where Aussie Rules will take you? This part gives you the information you need to go as far as you want, as player or spectator.

Chapter 8 sets out the various levels of Aussie Rules competitions — local, state and international — whether you want to just watch or join the game at some level. (Hey, you didn't really think you were going to sit out an entire part, did you?) In Chapter 9, I explain how the game has developed outside the AFL competition, through country and metropolitan competitions, and how a player can wind up drafted into the AFL level. I also provide training advice in Chapter 10, and how to avoid and deal with injuries in Chapter 11. If you're keen to coach, just turn to Chapter 12.

Chapter 8

It's a Big Football World

*A*lthough the AFL competition is by far the biggest and most important in Australian football, it's not the only competition. Hundreds of competitions exist all over Australia, from the Top End to Tasmania. Some avid fans don't even follow the AFL competition but instead follow the fortunes of their local club, or one that's far away but has sentimental appeal. In this chapter, I detail what's available locally, on a state level and internationally, as well as provide details on how you join a junior or senior competition.

Whatever club you follow, remember the one golden rule: Switching allegiance from one club to another is considered a no-no. No matter how poorly your team is performing, remind yourself that there surely must be good times around the corner. For example, St Kilda was considered out of its depth for most of its first 70 years in the VFL (Victorian Football League, now the AFL) and at times it was a laughing stock. However, Saints' fans stuck fast and were rewarded with the 1966 premiership. Me? I've stuck fast to the red and white of South Melbourne/Sydney all my life and there was no happier day — family occasions apart — than when the Swans won the 2005 grand final.

Where It All Begins: Under-Age Football

Joining a team shouldn't be too much of a problem — unless you're living in the middle of the Simpson Desert or in some parts of Queensland or New South Wales. Elsewhere, football clubs are as common as schools. In Victoria, the game's heartland, clubs exist in every metropolitan area and in most country towns. The same applies for South Australia, Western Australia and Tasmania, all regarded as 'Aussie Rules states'.

The situation is different in many parts of Queensland and New South Wales, however, because these states predominantly play rugby — union and league. However, clubs do exist in the capital cities of Brisbane and Sydney and their surrounding suburbs, and popularity is growing along some of the coastal areas, especially around the New South Wales Sapphire Coast and Queensland's Gold Coast.

You can never start playing Aussie Rules too young. And the best way for any young footballer to develop the game's skills is to join a club and play the game.

AFL Auskick: A good springboard

One of the best ways for primary-school-aged children to get into football is through the AFL's highly acclaimed Auskick program. The figures speak for themselves, with 161,159 participants in 2007 at around 2,500 Auskick centres. This represents a 21 per cent increase in three years, with an estimated 20,000 parent volunteers and 15 per cent female participation. Most Auskick sessions run through school holidays and a typical session runs like this:

- ✔ **8.50 am:** Arrive at the ground to have a kick with Mum, Dad and friends.

- ✔ **9.00 am:** Assemble in groups (organised according to age and ability) and move off to allocated areas.

- ✔ **9.05 am:** Play warm-up games — fun activities to get children ready for action.

- ✔ **9.15 am:** Learn skills, guided by the leader of each group, then facilitated by parent helpers.

- ✔ **9.45 am:** Play games incorporating the footie skills taught.

- ✔ **10.05 am:** Break up into teams (organised according to age, size and ability) and play an AFL Auskick Rules match.

- ✔ **10.30 am:** Receive encouragement awards and drinks, and then depart.

See, AFL Auskick provides a fun morning and takes less than two hours. What better and more healthy way to spend a morning!

From 2007, the AFL Auskick program was redesigned to ensure that, for each age group, children participate in activities designed to be relevant to each child's physical, mental and emotional capabilities:

- ✔ **Rookie:** Designed for children aged 5 to 8 years, this program ensures that all children develop the fundamental skills required to participate in Australian football. After completing relevant warm-up activities, children participate in skill games, further enhancing the skills introduced in sessions.

- ✔ **Pro:** Designed with a game-sense focus, the Pro program is for children aged 9 to 12. The lesson plans focus on various game-sense activities and drills, and provide participants with extended opportunities to participate in modified games.

The AFL Auskick program is run with codes of conduct, for parents and spectators and for coaches and teachers.

For parents and spectators the code of conduct is to

- ✔ Encourage children to participate regardless of ability.

- ✔ Encourage participants to always play by the rules.

- ✔ Never ridicule mistakes or losses.

- ✔ Remember that participants learn best by example. Applaud good play by all teams.

- ✔ Never publicly disagree with officials. If you disagree, raise the issue privately through appropriate channels.

- ✔ Actively discourage racial abuse.

- ✔ Recognise the value and importance of volunteer coaches.

- ✔ Remember that participants play for fun and are not miniature professionals.

- ✔ Condemn the use of violence in any form, be it by spectators, coaches, officials or players.

- ✔ Encourage players to accept the umpires' decisions.

- ✔ Demonstrate exemplary behaviour by not using foul language, or harassing players, coaches or officials.

- ✔ Respect that smoking and the consumption of alcohol are unacceptable at junior sport.

For coaches and teachers the code of conduct is to

✔ Be reasonable in your demands and consider young players' time, energy and enthusiasm levels.

✔ Avoid over-playing the talented players. The 'just average players' need and deserve equal time.

✔ Keep winning in perspective and maximise participation because children participate for fun and enjoyment.

✔ Stress safety and ensure that equipment and facilities are safe and appropriate for age and ability levels.

✔ Consider maturity levels and match up practice schedules, activities and degree of competition.

✔ Develop team respect, for opponents as well as for the judgement of officials and opposing coaches.

✔ Recognise the importance of injury by seeking and following the physician's advice concerning injured players.

✔ Keep informed, with sound principles of coaching and skill development, and development of children.

✔ Teach sporting behaviour and create opportunities to teach appropriate sports behaviour as well as basic skills.

✔ Get priorities right by ensuring skill learning and appropriate behaviour are the priorities over competition.

✔ Teach fair play and help children understand the responsibilities and implications of their freedom to choose between fair and unfair play.

Being vocal for the locals

If you live in a state or territory in which Australian football is the dominant code, take a walk to the local football ground. You may find, in the football season (late March to September), a local team in action. You may also find hardy spectators standing in the open supporting a team. They might number only in the dozens but their support is every bit as vocal as that for the AFL clubs.

Supporting your local team is a great way to follow Australian football, especially if you live a long way from the nearest AFL club. The standard of football might not be as high, but it sure can beat watching a game on television. You're right there, eating the meat pies and smelling the liniment. And why not follow your local team, even if you already support a team in the AFL?

Locating a local Aussie Rules team may be as easy as just walking around your neighbourhood and finding footballers on your local ground, either at training or in a match. Alternatively, scan your local newspaper for competition and team details. Most country football fans follow their hometown team, so that makes it even easier.

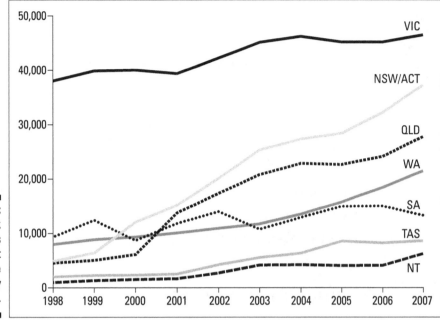

Figure 8-1:
AFL Auskick
registrations
throughout
most of the
country
have risen.

The AFL Auskick program not only teaches children the rudiments of the game, but also introduces them to the elite AFL level by giving them:

- ✔ **The chance to play Little League or AFL Auskick games during the half-time break in AFL matches.** About 25,000 children played in these matches in 2007, with match tickets supplied to 30,000 adults. The AFL provides 55,000 free tickets each year to facilitate the half-time Little League or AFL Auskick games.

- ✔ **The opportunity to attend superclinics conducted around Australia, with former Hawthorn champion Robert DiPierdomenico teaching children the game's basics.** 'The Big Dipper', as he is affectionately known, conducted 30 of these clinics around Australia in 2007.

For a registration fee of $35, your child obtains an eight-week coaching program (minimum), a backpack, a Sherrin football, a Russell Athletic cap, a CD-ROM, posters, stickers, a membership card to attend four AFL games and, in some states, insurance.

For more information or to find out your closest AFL Auskick centre, call the AFL Auskick National Hotline on 1900 945 000 or follow up the state contacts through their Web sites:

- ✔ **Australian Capital Territory and southern New South Wales:** aflnswact.com.au
- ✔ **New South Wales:** aflnswact.com.au
- ✔ **Northern Territory:** aflnt.com.au
- ✔ **Queensland:** aflq.com.au
- ✔ **South Australia:** sanfl.com.au
- ✔ **Tasmania:** footballtas.com.au
- ✔ **Victoria:** aflvic.com.au
- ✔ **Western Australia:** wafootball.com.au

Joining the junior ranks

The junior ranks usually start with around 7- or 8-year-olds and are called the Under-8s or Under-9s. Many of these very junior teams don't play matches under a formal structure, but play informal games merely to teach the game's skills and basics.

More 'serious' competition usually starts from about 9 years of age, with the Under-10s. And, depending on the size of the club, teams may also include the Under-12s, Under-14s, Under-16s and Under-18s.

Most Aussie Rules clubs around Australia have senior and junior teams, although some clubs only cater specifically for either one group or the other. For example, the AFL competition is a classic example, because the 16 AFL clubs do not have junior teams.

The 'Hawk' flew early

Former Bulldogs champion Doug Hawkins recalls that when he was about 10 years old he decided to join the local football club, Braybrook, in Melbourne's western suburbs. He remains grateful for the football skills taught to him during his developing years, and in 1978 he went straight from the Braybrook Under-18s into the senior Bulldog line-up. 'I loved my junior years and still have very fond memories of playing with Braybrook,' he says.

The junior ranks attached to senior clubs represent a good way to climb the stairs to a senior side. However, the type of club you join doesn't matter because most exclusively junior clubs have affiliations with senior clubs.

If you're a junior player having difficulty finding a club for your age group, speak to your sports teacher at school, or ask your parents to get some information for you. Most junior footballers join a particular club because their ground is near home or because they hear about it through friends.

Many schools, especially in Victoria, South Australia, Western Australia and Tasmania, have school teams for various age groups. For example, the Victorian Associated Public Schools competition is particularly strong. Several boys have played with one of the schools and in the Victorian TAC Cup (Under-18s team) and gone on to join the AFL. A recent example is Brendon Goddard, who was taken by St Kilda as the overall number one draft selection at the end of 2002. Goddard played school football with Caulfield Grammar and zone football (in the feeder Victorian State Football League competition) with Gippsland Power.

Heading off to camp

One of the best ways to further develop your football talent is to attend a special football camp or clinic. Many of these camps and clinics are organised by local and state leagues, and some involve the AFL, its clubs and players. All the AFL clubs, for example, send their players to special clinics organised by junior leagues, clubs or schools.

The NAB (National Australia Bank) AFL Pathway Program

If you're a good Aussie Rules player, you may be fodder for the NAB AFL Pathway Program. Run by the AFL, this program provides juniors with the opportunity to progress to the elite level and helps support junior clubs around Australia. The program incorporates the following:

✔ NAB AFL Under-16 Championships

✔ NAB AFL Under-18 Championships

✔ AIS/AFL Academy

✔ NAB AFL Draft Camp

✔ NAB AFL Draft

✔ NAB AFL Rising Star (the Ron Evans Medal)

For more information on the National AFL Pathway Program, go to the AFL Web site at www.afl.com.au.

Roving around

Star Brisbane key forward Jonathon Brown is a classic example of a youngster being raised in a small town and going on to play football at the elite level. Brown, who played in the Lions' 2001 to 2003 premiership sides, first picked up a football when he lived in the Otway Ranges, about 150 kilometres west of Melbourne. His father, Brian, had played with the tiny Otway Rovers club before playing 51 games with Fitzroy from 1976 to 1981. Young Jonathan played local football before joining the South Warrnambool club and then signing with Brisbane.

Football camps are entirely different from clinics, and are generally organised by specialist groups involving AFL stars and coaches. These camps often represent the best chance to have one-on-one sessions with the experts. If you can afford the tuition fee, camps are well worthwhile. Some camps are live-in and run for up to three or four days during school holidays.

Your club or school may be able to advise you of any forthcoming training camps or clinics. In addition, keep an eye on the AFL Web site at www.afl.com.au and the *Football Record*, the official AFL match-day magazine. Newspapers also help organise and promote clinics, so regularly scan your local paper (see Chapter 19 for more on AFL and the media).

Camps for the gifted junior

The best-known football camps involve elite juniors who are invited to the annual NAB AFL Draft Camp. Junior footballers eligible for the annual draft are selected to take part in these camps, where fitness, skill and physical development levels are tested. Those selected also undergo psychological testing in case they're nominated at the AFL Draft to join one of the 16 clubs.

These camps are strictly invitation only — even then, many are called and few are chosen. Most of those selected are from the elite state competitions, particularly the Victorian TAC Cup (Under-18s). These youngsters are usually identified as emerging talents at a much younger age and are guided through the promotion system through the Under-16 and Under-18 levels.

Playing the game in baby boots

Collingwood's Keith Bromage was just 15 years and 287 days old when he made his VFL/AFL debut in 1953, the youngest footballer in the competition's history. Bromage played 28 games with the Magpies to 1956 and then played 41 games with Fitzroy from 1958 to 1961.

Perseverance is the key, and aspiring footballers can take heart from several instances of players being overlooked very early, only to blossom later. For example, Carlton at the end of 2002 drafted (with the overall number 79 selection) 19-year-old Karl Norman, a youngster who emerged outside the fairly rigid selection system. Norman did not play at the elite Under-16 or Under-18 levels and, instead, played country football with Wangaratta Rovers. Carlton was alerted to his potential and he found himself in the top bracket. Wangaratta Rovers play in the strong Ovens and Murray League and Norman gave himself a chance of making the top level by switching to that competition after playing minor football with the Glenrowan club the previous season. As they say, if there's a will, there's a way. But getting up there with the best really is tough!

Most of the juniors selected to attend these camps have been assessed as potential league footballers from as young as 14 years of age. For example, they are often prepared through the NAB AFL Pathway Program, which incorporates the national Under-16s and Under-18s championships, involving every state and territory. (See the sidebar 'The NAB AFL Pathway Program' for more information.)

It's never too late to start playing Aussie Rules. In 2002, the Brisbane Lions drafted youngster Daniel Merrett after he'd played just one year of Aussie Rules. Young Merrett (at the time 17 years of age) had previously played rugby but, in his first year of Aussie Rules, was so good he ended up representing the Queensland Under-18 team. Also, Sydney recruited centre half-back Lewis Roberts-Thomson from North Shore (Sydney) after he'd played just 40 games of Australian football. He had a rugby union background through his North Shore school, but his father, Barry, had been captain of the Queensland State Australian Football team and later played with VFA (now VFL) club Sandringham. Young Lewis was an Australian football natural and, after making his Swans debut in 2003, went on to play in Sydney's 2005 premiership side.

Joining the Senior Ranks

Senior football usually means playing against men or, at least, players older than 18 or 19 years of age. However, some teams have players in their 40s and even the occasional player in his 50s. Almost all senior clubs have two teams: The *firsts* and the *reserves*. As the name implies, the firsts comprise the best players, with the rest making up the reserves.

Most footballers start in junior ranks and then work their way into the seniors. But don't worry — if you've outgrown the junior ranks but don't feel you're quite ready for topline action with a senior club, you can play in the reserves to further develop your skills. Alternatively, if you're new to the game, most teams will happily accept you in the reserves or, if you're good enough, into the firsts.

How do you find your level? The coach and the selectors do that for you. For example, if you're in the firsts and your form drops, you may be dropped to the reserves. Alternatively, if your form is good in the reserves, you may be promoted to the firsts.

Don't be disappointed if you spend a considerable time in the reserves. Many good footballers have emerged from what sometimes is referred to as the *Magoos* (rhyming slang for the Twos).

If you find the game too difficult with a particular club, you may be better off playing with a club at a lower level. Get what is known as a *clearance*, the Aussie Rules equivalent of a soccer transfer. You tell your club managers that you want to play elsewhere, and they'll provide you with a clearance form to complete. Easy!

Regardless of what level you play, the key is to enjoy the game. Even if you're playing in a club's reserves, the aim is to have fun. Although winning is fun, especially in grand finals, it all has to be kept in perspective. Unless you're playing at a very high level, the game shouldn't be taken too seriously. Part of playing is making new friends and experiencing a wonderful sense of camaraderie.

As a senior, it's important to determine exactly what you want out of playing football. Do you want to play in more powerful competitions, or do you just want to play with your mates, regardless of the standard of football? Amateur teams do exist around Australia so, if you just want a relaxed game, try to search one out. All Aussie Rules clubs welcome new members, so don't hesitate to contact your local club for more information.

Super-Rules

If you don't want to put your body on the line against younger and fitter men, but still want to be involved in the great Australian game, consider playing a game of Masters Australian Football (MAF), which was previously known as Super-Rules. Suitable for those aged 30 or over, the rules are basically the same as Aussie Rules except some have been modified to reduce the risk of injury.

MAF is played throughout Australia and associations exist in all states and territories. The masters game even has a national carnival, held annually. All that's required is a reasonable level of fitness and the time to attend one or two training runs a week.

Depending on the size of the club, MAF is sometimes broken down into the following groups:

- ✔ 30–35 years
- ✔ Superules (35 years and over)
- ✔ Masterules (40 years and over)
- ✔ Seniorules (45 years and over)

Former Fitzroy champion Kevin Murray played with several suburban clubs following his retirement from League football in 1974. Then, in his late 30s, he started playing what was then known as Super-Rules and pulled on the boots in this form of the game until in his 50s.

Check out the MAF Web site at www.maf.asn.au for more information.

Women's rules

The number of women in Australia playing Aussie Rules is increasing every year. In 2000, the first National Women's Football Championships were held in the ACT and as a consequence the association Women's Football Australia (WFA) was established. The WFA are affiliated with the AFL through the state football bodies and have their own guidelines for the game, including rules for teams, uniforms and conduct.

The main difference in the rules for the women's competition is that tackling is modified. Men are allowed to sling an opponent to the ground (as long as it's done in the play and not after the ball has been moved on), whereas this somewhat rough play is banned in the women's game. Otherwise, the rules are basically the same, with a heavy emphasis (as in the men's game) on the head being protected at all times.

The other big difference for women's games is the size of the ball, being slightly smaller than for the men's competition to help minimise hand injuries. When a Victorian metropolitan (from Melbourne) team plays an annual match against a Victorian country side, special pink balls are used. Some games are also played with fewer team members and on smaller grounds.

Here's a list of the women's state leagues that currently exist in Australia:

- ✔ Australian Capital Territory Women's Australian Football League
- ✔ Northern Territory Women's Aussie Rules Football Association
- ✔ South Australian Women's Football League
- ✔ Sydney Women's Australian Football League
- ✔ Victorian Women's Football League
- ✔ West Australian Women's Football League (Inc.)

Women also play Australian football in a number of countries outside Australia, including Papua New Guinea, New Zealand, the United States (with teams including the Denver Bulldogs, the North Carolina Lady Tigers and the Milwaukee Explosion), Canada, England and Japan. In 2007, there were 51,504 registered players, with 3,450 of these from competitions outside Australia. Recent stars in women's football include Michelle Dench, Debbie Lee and Lauren Tesorilero (Victoria), Talei Own (New South Wales), Katherine Pender (Queensland), Michele Reid (South Australia) and Nikki Harwood (Western Australia).

Breaking through

Two Victorian women, Daisy Pearce and Shannon McFerran, played in the 2007 E J Whitten Legends Match (a prostate cancer charity match named in honour of the late, great champion Ted Whitten), played at Telstra Dome. This charity match is played by former AFL stars and a handful of television celebrities, representing either Victoria or an All-Stars team from the other states. Daisy, just 19 when she played in this match, is a former Victorian Under-19s captain, and Shannon, 27, is the undoubted star of Australian women's football, having won the best and fairest award in the Victorian women's competition four times.

To find out more information on the women's football leagues and associations in Australia, check out the Women's Football Australia Web site at www.geocities.com/womensfootball. On the AFL Web site (www.afl.com.au) go to Development in the menu bar and click on Women and Girls.

The State of Play

Melburnians are fortunate because the AFL evolved from the Victorian Football League, so they have a direct link to the big league. On top of the AFL, they have their own state league, the new Victorian Football League. However, the following major competitions exist in other states and territories:

- AFL Canberra
- AFL Queensland State League
- Northern Tasmania Football League and the Southern Football League
- Northern Territory Football League
- South Australian National Football League
- Sydney AFL
- West Australian Football League

The Main teams

As a boy, I had many favourite clubs — one for just about every competition. I followed South Melbourne (now Sydney) in the VFL (now AFL) and supported my local VFA (now VFL) club Northcote (now extinct).

When I was growing up, every football fan waited for the *Sporting Globe* to arrive every Saturday night. I would pore over the Saturday afternoon results in every competition. I followed Old Paradians in the amateurs because I attended Parade College, as well as Spotswood in the Footscray District League

because many of my South Melbourne heroes (including Fred Goldsmith) had been recruited from that club, and so on. Ah, how sweet it was when most of my clubs, especially South Melbourne, were victorious. I like to think that my loyalty helps the Swans insomuch as all clubs need their supporters to stick by them in lean times. The Swans have had more lean times than most, so the good times really mean much more to Swans fans than for supporters of clubs that have known only success.

Apart from South and Western Australia, all these competitions have one major challenge: They exist in states or territories in which rugby (either union or league) is dominant.

If you're interested in any of the leagues around Australia, or the clubs involved, the best way to make contact is by phoning them directly (see your phone directory), or contact the Australian Football League on (03) 9643 1999.

Victoria

The Victorian Football Association (VFA) was formed in 1877, with eight clubs breaking away to form the Victorian Football League (VFL, now AFL) in 1897. The VFA continued in its own right until the end of the 1999 season. From there, it became an adjunct to the AFL, with several clubs joining AFL reserves combinations under the new VFL.

The clubs propsed for the VFL in 2008 are:

- Bendigo (Bombers)
- Box Hill (Hawks)
- Casey (Scorpions)
- Coburg (Tigers)
- Collingwood (Magpies)
- Frankston (Dolphins)
- Geelong (Cats)
- North Ballarat (Roosters)
- Northern Bullants
- Port Melbourne (the Borough)
- Sandringham (Zebras)
- Tasmania (Devils)
- Werribee (Tigers)
- Williamstown (Seagulls)

The VFL Web page is located on the Football Victoria Web site at vfl.footballvic.com.au.

Australian Capital Territory

AFL Canberra (www.aflcanberra.com.au) is based in the nation's capital, Canberra. The AFL Canberra clubs are:

- Ainslie (Kangaroos)
- Belconnen (Magpies)
- Canberra Wildcats
- Eastlake (Demons)
- Queanbeyan (Tigers)
- Sydney Swans
- Tuggeranong (Hawks)

When the Sydney Swans decided to field a reserves side for 2003, they elected to play in the ACTAFL instead of the New South Wales competition. Like many other competitions, this League has seen many club changes over recent years.

New South Wales

Sydney AFL (www.sydneyafl.com.au) is a new entity, replacing the old Sydney Football League. The Sydney AFL Premier Division clubs are:

- Balmain (Dockers)
- Campbelltown (Blues)
- East Coast (Eagles)
- North Shore (Bombers)
- Pennant Hills (Demons)
- St George (Crows)
- Sydney University (Students)
- University of New South Wales–Eastern Suburbs (Bulldogs)
- Western Suburbs (Magpies)
- Wollongong (Lions)

Northern Territory

The Northern Territory Football League (ntfl.aflnt.com.au) is slightly different from the other state leagues because it plays the game during the summer season (the 'Wet'), because the ground is too hard in the winter season (the 'Dry'). Clubs in this competition include:

- Darwin (Buffaloes)
- Nightcliff (Tigers)
- Palmerston (Magpies)
- St Mary's (Saints)
- Southern Districts (Crocs)
- Tiwi (Bombers)
- Wanderers (Eagles)
- Waratah (Warriors)

A number of South Australian and Western Australian footballers journey north to play in this competition during their off-season.

Queensland

The AFL Queensland State League (qfl.aflq.com.au) is considerably stronger than both the Sydney AFL and AFL Canberra. In fact, the Brisbane Lions field a reserves side in this competition. Clubs in this competition, which also has clubs coming and going from season to season, include:

- Broadbeach (Cats)
- Labrador (Tigers)
- Morningside (Panthers)
- Mount Gravatt (Vultures)
- Redland (Bombers)
- Southport (Sharks)
- Suncoast (Lions)
- Zillmere (Eagles)

Leagues are also established in the regional centres of Townsville, Cairns, Mount Isa, Ipswich, Gold Coast, Sunshine Coast, Mackay, the Darling Downs and Rockhampton.

South Australia

The South Australian National Football League (www.sanfl.com.au) was founded in 1877 and is now referred to as the Westar competition. Nine teams play in the SANFL:

- ✔ Central District (Bulldogs)
- ✔ Glenelg (Tigers)
- ✔ North Adelaide (Roosters)
- ✔ Norwood (Redlegs)
- ✔ Port Adelaide Magpies
- ✔ South Adelaide (Panthers)
- ✔ Sturt (Blues)
- ✔ West Adelaide (Bloods)
- ✔ Woodville-West Torrens (Eagles)

Don't confuse the Port Adelaide club with the AFL club of the same name, however. Although the AFL club has its roots in the old South Australian club and the two clubs share traditions, supporter bases and so on, they have separate identities. The AFL club is known as the Power and the South Australian club as the Magpies.

Although the attendance at games in this competition is nowhere near what it was pre-AFL (pre-1990), interest is considerable. The SANFL grand finals usually draw more than 30,000 fans. Many South Australians may follow the Adelaide Crows or Port Adelaide in the AFL, but they retain interest in one SANFL club or another.

Tasmania

Quite a few changes have occurred with the state Aussie Rules competition in Tassie over the last few years. In December 2000, the State Wide League (SWL), which consisted of six clubs, was disbanded and now two leagues exist: The Southern Football League (www.southernfootball.com.au) and the Northern Tasmania Football League (www.ntfl.com.au).

Three of the original clubs — the Glenorchy Magpies, Clarence Roos and North Hobart Demons — joined the SFL. The SFL Premier League now consists of eight clubs:

- Brighton (Robins)
- Clarence (Roos)
- Glenorchy (Magpies)
- Hobart (Lions)
- Kingborough (Tigers)
- Lauderdale (Bombers)
- New Norfolk (Eagles)
- North Hobart (Demons)

The other three teams — the Northern Bombers, Devonport Power (now Magpies) and Burnie Dockers — were accepted into the Northern Tasmania Football League (NTFL). The NTFL consists of 11 teams:

- Burnie (Dockers)
- Devonport (Magpies)
- East Devonport (Swans)
- Latrobe (Demons)
- Launceston (Blues)
- North Launceston (Bombers)
- Penguin (Blues)
- Smithton (Saints)
- South Launceston (Bulldogs)
- Ulverstone (Robins)
- Wynyard (Cats)

The origin of the State of Origin

In the 19th century, the powerful leagues in Adelaide, Perth and Melbourne played 'representative' matches against each other, which was known as 'interstate' football. But, in 1977, with Victoria dominant for so many years, a decision was made to adopt a new system.

Previously, if you played in the Victorian Football League (VFL) you represented Victoria, and if you played in the South Australian National Football League (SANFL) you represented South Australia, and so on. But a player who was born or started his career in a particular state represented that state under the new system. This approach meant that many South and Western Australian footballers lured to play in the powerful Victorian competition were able to represent their 'home' state.

The first of the 'State of Origin' matches was played between Western Australia and Victoria in Perth in 1977, and resulted in a 94-point win for the home state. State of Origin matches continued until 1999 when they were abandoned in favour of the International Rules matches against Ireland (see 'Ireland' later in this chapter). However, many people believe the State of Origin will return and they would love to see it again reach the popularity it did in the halcyon days of the 1980s and early '90s.

Western Australia

The West Australian Football League (WAFL) was founded in 1885, with the now-defunct team known as Rovers winning the first premiership. Nine teams play in the competition:

- Claremont (Tigers)
- East Fremantle (Sharks)
- East Perth (Royals)
- Peel Thunder
- Perth (Demons)
- South Fremantle (Bulldogs)
- Subiaco (Lions)
- Swan Districts (Swans)
- West Perth (Falcons)

As with the SANFL, many Western Australians may follow the West Coast Eagles and the Fremantle Dockers in the AFL, but they retain interest in one WAFL club or another.

For more information on the WAFL, check out their Web site at www.wafootball.com.au.

Australian Football Around the World

Despite being a largely indigenous code, Australian football is played around the world, and not only by expatriates. The tremendous growth of Aussie Rules occurred primarily in the late 1980s and early 1990s, when a number of countries, such as Canada, Denmark, Japan and the United Kingdom, formed organised competitions.

Today, Aussie Rules is established in a number of other countries including: Argentina, Brunei, Cambodia, China, East Timor, El Salvador, France, Germany, Hong Kong, Indonesia, Ireland, Israel, Malaysia, Nauru, Netherlands, New Zealand, Papua New Guinea, Philippines, Samoa, Senegal, Singapore, South Africa, Sweden, Thailand, the United States and Vietnam.

At this stage, the only real foothold Australian football has gained in Europe is in Denmark (through expatriates) and in Ireland. In this section, I detail the state of the game in those countries where it's most popular.

Denmark

The Danes follow the same eligibility rules as the competitions in Britain and the United States, and boast a team known as the Copenhagen Crocodiles. Other teams include the Amager Tigers, the North Copenhagen Barracudas, the Aalborg Kangaroos, the Farum Cats and the Arhus Bombers. A Swedish team, the Helsingborg Saints, also plays in this competition.

Ireland

Ireland also has a flourishing Aussie Rules competition, featuring such teams as the Belfast Redbacks, the Limerick Saints and the Dublin Demons. The Irish won the International Rules series in Melbourne in 2002, but this victory was not surprising because Gaelic football is similar to the Australian code, and the Irish therefore find it much easier than other European teams to swap codes. However, Australia had its revenge and won in Australia in 2005 and then in Ireland in 2006.

Gaelic football, which was developed in Ireland in the second half of the 19th century, was originally played with an oval-shaped ball and had two sets of scoring posts at each end. At the same time, Australian football was developed with an oval-shaped ball and two sets of scoring posts at each end. Coincidence? Probably not — undoubtedly some Irish influence in the Australian game, even though Gaelic football is now played with a soccer-type round ball and has only two goalposts and a net (like soccer).

Former VFL umpire and football broadcaster Harry Beitzel realised in the late 1960s that the Gaelic and Australian codes were so similar that teams from the two nations could play international matches. Beitzel twice took Australian teams to Ireland to play Test matches, which were played mainly under Gaelic football rules. The Australians astounded the Irish with their ball skills and were very well received. Then, in 1968, Beitzel invited Irish county team Meath to play matches in Australia. The 'Mighty Men of Meath' played at the MCG and were a big hit, but interest died off, mainly because these matches were seen as 'Irish rules'.

Looking like galahs

When Harry Beitzel took his first team to Ireland in 1966, he decided the Australian uniform would include a typical Down Under slouch hat, as worn by Australian soldiers. The brims of these are turned up on one side, giving a unique appearance. Beitzel went even further and had large feathers placed in the band, in club colours for individual players. For example, Carlton's Alex Jesaulenko wore blue and white feathers in his slouch hat to signify his club. Critics had a field day and suggested the Australians looked like galahs. Rather than being offended, Beitzel officially named his team 'the Galahs'. Australia's pink and grey cockatoo earned its reputation as a somewhat dumb species mainly because of its antics of hanging upside down from tree branches — a silly galah — hence the Aussie habit of describing a person supposed to be slow-witted as a galah.

Beitzel was an entrepreneur who had paid all expenses for the two tours of Ireland, and now found it impossible to continue. The concept therefore faded into the background until the Gaelic Athletic Association invited an Australian team to tour Ireland in 1984, under what was described as 'compromise rules'. The game was played with the round Gaelic ball, but with behind posts and limited tackling (this is not allowed in the Gaelic code). Western Australian John Todd was appointed coach, and it's now a matter of history that Australia not only adapted to the 'compromise rules', but defeated Ireland 2–1 in the three-match series.

Since then there have been numerous tours to Ireland, with the Irish making their first visit to Australia in 1990. The most recent series was played in Ireland (one match in Galway and the other in Dublin) in October 2006. Now known as International Rules, the two matches proved enormously popular with Irish fans. A crowd of 30,000 watched Australia win the first Test at Galway, with a massive 82,127 at Dublin's Croke Park for the second Test, which Australia also won. International Rules now looks as if it is here to stay. See 'Moving to International Status' later in this chapter for more information.

Rules? What rules?

I was sent to Ireland by the *Australian* newspaper in 1984 and 1987 to cover the two series against Ireland, and fell in love with the concept. Yet it had taken a stroke of genius by Australian coach John Todd, in 1984, to establish this hybrid code. The Australians had been humiliated in a trial match at Cork and were branded 'hopeless'. Todd used this criticism to have his players seek revenge in the first Test at Cork and, fired up, the Australians continually broke the rule of not tackling.

This naturally upset the Irish, and the biggest brawl in football history erupted. Players from both nations swapped punches, and even the officials got into the action. The donnybrook created headlines across Ireland for all the wrong reasons but, from then on, the Irish wanted to see these big, tough Australians, and whether their own men could stand up to them. They did, but Australia won that first series and Todd's leadership made a big impression on this football scribe.

New Zealand

Aussie Rules was played in New Zealand almost from the start, in the late 19th century and, in fact, the Kiwis sent a team to the 1908 Carnival in Melbourne and defeated New South Wales and Queensland. Unfortunately, World War I and the VFL clubs' parochial interests almost killed off the game in the Shaky Isles until a resurgence in the 1970s. Although Aussie Rules is still a minor sport in New Zealand, a number of clubs thrive there, including the Takapuna Eagles, the University Blues and the Hutt City Tigers. Matches are played in Auckland, Wellington and Canterbury.

The New Zealand AFL Web site has a range of interesting information, including information on International Rules. The site is at www.nzafl.co.nz.

South Africa

The AFL, in partnership with the South African government and Costa Logistics, is now applying its substantial expertise to develop and grow Australian football in South Africa.

Aussie Rules was played in South Africa in the late 19th century, mainly by Australian miners in Johannesburg. One of the organisers was Charles Moore, a former Essendon footballer who went to South Africa with the Fourth Victorian Imperial Bushmen's Contingent in the Anglo–Boer War. Moore was killed in action in 1901, but by that time there were a number of clubs all over South Africa. Unfortunately, World War I strangled the game in South Africa and only now is interest stirring in the game again.

The South African government is currently keen to adopt Australian football as 'the new sport for the new South Africa'. Because soccer has been the sport of black South Africans, and rugby union the sport of white South Africans, the government has been searching for a new game that has widespread appeal and combines the skills of both codes. The AFL's push into this new market has grown quickly, with the employment of 19 full-time staff and the education and training of a further 700 volunteers and teachers across four provinces.

In 2007, AFL South Africa launched 'FootyWild', South Africa's version of NAB AFL Auskick, with the support of Costa Logistics. FootyWild, a unique skill-development program that has a South African 'look and feel', has been widely embraced by the community, with its all-inclusive mass-participation opportunities for boys and girls aged 8–13 years. The FootyWild program has been developed by South African staff and focuses on teaching the core elements of Aussie Rules, including the skills of kicking, marking and handballing, as well as evasive and defensive skills. In 2007, over 5,000 South Africans participated in FootyWild, 2,000 in primary school competitions and a further 3,000 children and adults in community football competitions.

It is envisaged that by 2010 over 30,000 South Africans will be playing Australian football.

United Kingdom

Aussie Rules is a major international competition in the United Kingdom. The British Australian Rules Football League (BARFL), for example, is well organised, and some matches attract as many as a thousand fans — even if most of them are homesick Aussies!

Teams in this league include the West London Wildcats and the Sussex Swans. All teams must consist largely of British-born players.

The most famous game played in Britain was the exhibition match in November 1916 between two teams of Australian servicemen. The match was between the Third Division and the Training Units and featured a number of VFL stars, with South Melbourne's Bruce Sloss, Richmond's Les Lee and Fitzroy's Jack Cooper later killed in action. The match attracted 8,000 fans, including King Manuel of Portugal and the Prince of Wales (later Edward VIII). British interest died until expatriates in and around London formed several clubs.

You can find out more about BARFL by checking out their Web site at www.barfl.co.uk.

United States

Four years ago, only two cities in the United States played the game. Today Aussie Rules is played in over 30 cities. The United States Australian Football League (USAFL) has over 35 member teams, with over 1,000 people playing the sport. Teams include the Chicago Swans, Los Angeles Crows, Orange County Bombers, St Louis Blues and the Western Pennsylvania Wallabies.

There are four regional leagues: The California Australian Football League, the Mid American Australian Football League, the Arizona Australian Football League and the South-Eastern Australian Football League. 'Local' players must be included in teams, although a substantial sprinkling of expatriate Aussies can be found among the ranks.

Many Americans have adopted the game through coverage on pay television, and many follow the AFL through the Internet. (See Chapter 19 for more information on football media.) And the game is even infiltrating schools. In Chicago, over 20 schools include Australian football in their physical education curriculum.

For more information on the USAFL, check out their Web site at www.usfooty.com.

Moving to International Status

With Aussie Rules gaining popularity all over the world, a move is being made by the AFL to promote it even further. In May 2001, the International Australian Football Confederation (IAFC) was formed to bring together the people, organisations, clubs and leagues who play or are involved with Australian football internationally. Since then, the AFL has formally taken responsibility for developing the game internationally.

In 2002, the Australian Football International Cup was played in Melbourne, with sides comprising nationals of the United States, Canada, Great Britain, Denmark, Ireland, South Africa, Japan, New Zealand, Nauru, Papua New Guinea and Samoa. The series final was played at the MCG — and won by Ireland, begorrah! The second International Cup was played in Melbourne and Wangaratta in 2005 and won by New Zealand. To mark the 150th aniversary of the first game of Australian football, in 1858, a third International Cup is being played in Melbourne and Warrnambool in 2008.

Chapter 9

From the Bush to the Big Time: Moving through the Levels of Play

In This Chapter

▹ Spreading the football gospel

▹ Understanding the draft system

▹ Playing rookie

W*herever you go in Australia, from Melbourne to Melville Island, from desert to rainforest, one universal feature stands out in the landscape — a set of posts rammed into the dust or turf. This multitude of spindly goal and behind posts signifies the level of worship to the modern god of Australian football.*

As the elite football competitions took shape in the major cities, other competitions popped up around the country — in the suburbs, the bush and in schools — and continue to bloom today. The AFL is the controlling body of the main competitions (see Chapter 14) but, as I explain in this chapter, many other levels of Australian football exist and are enjoyed by thousands upon thousands of people each winter.

Ovals All Over

Australian football originated in Victoria, with the earliest recorded game in 1858, and spread quickly to Tasmania, South Australia and Western Australia and more slowly to New South Wales and Queensland. Due to the enormous distances involved, the game developed at a different pace from state to state.

Football competitions are organised in every town with a population of more than 500 and a few with less (including the cats and dogs). Outside of New South Wales and Queensland, where rugby union and rugby league remain dominant (for the time being), no self-respecting town or suburb is without an Australian football team. If a town is too small to support a team, the locals unite with neighbouring towns to form a football club and, more often than not, the area's winter social calendar is built around that club.

More than 2,618 football clubs exist in Australia, with matches played at every level from seniors to Under-8s. The massive web of competition is constantly evolving as various clubs are forced to move from one competition to another as a result of, for example, the need to play at a lower level or because of the tyranny of distance.

Rural rivalry

Football played in country areas generates tremendous local interest to the degree that one town may have rivalry of a ferocious nature with another town just 20 kilometres down the highway. And that rivalry can even be generated by teams in the same town. For example, in the powerful Hampden Football League in western Victoria, three teams from the same town — Warrnambool, South Warrnambool and North Warrnambool — battle it out for the honours each year.

One of my favourite players is Sydney's Wayne Carroll (1979–1985), who first played for the exotically named New South Wales country team Mangoplah–Cookardinia United. Sydney teammate Brett Scott (1981–1988) was recruited from The Rock–Yerong Creek club.

Country football clubs usually recruit team members from the local population, but ring-in players from outside the town are often recruited. Clubs in the country pay close attention to staff appointments at local schools, hospitals, police stations and so on, because a club never knows when a class footballer is going to be transferred into or out of the area. Because transfers such as these are so important to a club, the occasional string is pulled to make sure the 'right' transfer decisions are made.

The larger country clubs in the more powerful competitions are able to pay top players, but because relatively small sums are usually involved — up to $400 per match — the practice can in no way be called even part-time professionalism. In past decades, country clubs were often able to entice league stars to the bush to captain and coach the locals with offers that included free housing, a job and a considerable stipend. Today, this practice doesn't exist because the AFL competition is now highly professional and the top-quality players stick with the money.

Melbourne full-forward Fred Fanning is an example of a top city player being lured to the country. After kicking a League record of 18 goals in a match against St Kilda in 1947, 25-year-old Fanning accepted the position of captain and coach at the Victorian country club Hamilton on a wage of 20 pounds a week (the basic wage in those days was about 6 pounds). In contrast, Melbourne had been paying him just 3 pounds a week!

City kickers

Football is played at every possible level in the city and includes amateur and semi-professional competition. In Melbourne, for example, one of the most powerful competitions is the Victorian Amateur Football Association, which, as the name implies, is a strictly amateur organisation. Despite this amateur tag, the competition's standard is extremely high, and AFL players regularly abandon professionalism to play in the amateur association's competition.

Every major Australian city has semi-professional competitions, with payments to players ranging from the lucrative to the ridiculous. For example, a number of clubs pay top players $800 or more a match, whereas other clubs present a tray of meat to the best player of the match (vegetarians be warned!).

The majority of Australian football clubs — country or suburban — have several teams, including seniors, reserves and under-age teams. In fact, many football associations insist that member clubs field a specified number of teams to make sure clubs develop junior footballers. This excellent training concept means that the clubs involved share the responsibility for the development of Australian football.

Class acts

Australian football is also played at school level and although inter-school competitions are no longer as common as they were 20 or 30 years ago, most schools in the southern states have Australian football teams. In Victoria, for example, a number of inter-school competitions thrive, including the highly rated Associated Public Schools. The standard played by the Public Schools teams is so high that AFL talent scouts are regular visitors to the matches.

Draft Craft

Although football is played at a range of levels, a footballer can only reach the AFL level through the League's draft system.

The 16 AFL clubs are each allowed to have 38 players plus a number of veterans aged over 30. At the end of each season each club has a number of vacancies for the following reasons:

- Players are dropped after being judged not good enough for the team.
- Players are forced to retire as a result of injuries.
- Players simply pass a use-by date and retire, later to thrill or bore grandchildren with tales of playing football at the elite level.

A club fills vacancies using the strict AFL draft system and then balances the team's talent using a trading system. You can find out exactly how the system works in this section.

Swap till you drop

At the end of each season, the 16 clubs submit player lists to the AFL and then spend several allotted days at a selected venue (usually Telstra Dome) haggling over possible player trades.

For example, the Brisbane Lions may need a small, mobile player to balance out the team, whereas the West Coast Eagles may require a tall player. In the case that the opposing clubs have the required players, the clubs use the official *trading* days to make a swap.

Each club has what is known as a 'football department', usually comprising the football manager, the coach, his assistants, selectors and recruiting staff. This group makes the decisions on players to draft, on the recruiting staff's recommendations. However, in many instances the coach has the final say, as he might require a particular type of player.

In terms of trades, a player can reject a move, and this does occasionally happen. For example, Essendon wanted to trade Justin Blumfield to Brisbane at the end of 2002, but he refused to move interstate and, instead, was traded to Melbourne. At the end of the 2005 season, Hawthorn ruckman Peter Everitt wanted to be traded to Sydney but, because he still had a year of his contract to run and the two clubs could not reach agreement, Everitt remained with the Hawks in 2006. However, he was traded to the Swans at the end of that season and made his debut with Sydney in 2007.

Some players flourish after a swap, as they may have been held back at their original club because another player was filling the position he wanted to play. For example, James Clement was a star in defence at Collingwood after being traded from Fremantle.

Most players want to be known as a 'one-club' footballer, but some are happy to move around to better their careers. It makes no difference, because fans quickly accept a player from a rival club, and football history is dotted with names of famous players who achieved fame at a second or even third club.

Trade till you fade

The clubs are also allowed to trade at the annual national draft, which is usually held in November.

The order of the draft takes place in the reverse of team positions at the end of a season. For example, a team finishing last on the ladder has first choice at the draft, with the top team having the final choice. Several rounds occur, and once the first round has been completed, the process starts again.

The national draft is a make-or-break time for ambitious young footballers. The system works on a strict order of merit, and no player can be listed by an AFL club unless he is first nominated at a draft or through what is known as the *rookie draft* (see the section 'Rookies and Crookies' later in this chapter).

In 1986, the League adopted the American football and basketball system of a national draft, for the following reasons:

✔ To give the preceding season's less successful clubs first choice of the available players

✔ To give clubs the option of exchanging draft choices for experienced players

The *annual national draft* now operates under the following system:

1. **When a club has less than eight wins over two seasons it has what is known as a *priority pick*, or *compensatory selection*, ahead of all other selections.**

2. **The club finishing last on the ladder then has the next choice (if there *is* a priority pick) and the second last club has the next choice in the draft of players.** (Refer to Chapter 2 to see how the ladder works.)

3. **The order of choice by teams continues up the ladder, with the premier team having the final choice.**

4. **After every club has made a player selection, the system starts again, with the bottom club having first choice and so on.**

   Note: Priority picks (see Step 1) apply only in the first round of choices.

5. **The draft is completed when all clubs have finalised playing lists.**

   The system includes the proviso that a club may elect to be a player or two (or even three) short until the club makes further choices at the pre-season draft. (See the section 'Rookies and Crookies' later in this chapter.)

FOOTY FLASHBACK

Life was like a box of chocolates (till 1968)

Until 1968, Victorian Football League clubs (now the AFL) were able to nominate one player from any or all of the separate suburban zones. For example, the Collingwood zone included the suburb of Collingwood and a number of outer areas such as Heidelberg, Rosanna, Montmorency and so on. In addition, all clubs competed on equal terms for any player in country areas.

Until 1968, country areas of Victoria were 'open' recruiting zones and country players were able to sign for any of the clubs. From 1968, clubs were allocated specific country zones and could select players only from their own zones. This system operated until 1986, when the draft was introduced.

Clubs were not allowed to offer a potential recruit any monetary inducement and instead had to convince a player why he should sign for that club rather than a rival club. As a result, recruiting staff not only had to judge whether a player was talented enough to make the grade, the staff also had to be as smooth-talking as snake-oil salesmen.

To bypass the rule forbidding wage negotiation, club officials invented a plethora of ruses. One of the most common ploys was to hand the mother of the potential recruit a chocolate box containing a wad of bank notes. Not everyone

was so lucky — Richmond legend Royce Hart, a Tasmanian, signed for the Tigers in the mid-1960s after being offered a suit, shirt and tie.

Victorian Football League clubs were also limited to just two signings from interstate clubs each season. To achieve the signings, the clubs were given what were known as *Form Fours* and recruiting decisions were made very carefully. The Form Four system was devised to prevent the drain of talent from other states and, for many years, clubs were not allowed to recruit any players from the developing football states and territories unless the player concerned was legitimately transferred in his job.

For example, North Melbourne signed Canberra youngster Alex Jesaulenko on a Form Four, but was unable to win his release from the 'developing territory' rule. As a result, when North's two-year hold on Jesaulenko expired, Carlton signed him on another Form Four, having somehow managed to arrange a public service job transfer to Melbourne for Jesaulenko. He went on to become one of the greatest players the game has known.

After 1968, the Victorian Football League (now AFL) allocated the clubs separate country zones in Victoria and southern New South Wales for exclusive player development.

The national draft is sometimes televised live because it creates enormous interest, with fans eager to discover who has been signed to which team. Traditionally, several of the players who are expected to be among the first to be nominated are present for television interviews during the draft, with interest specifically focused on which player becomes the number one nomination. Club officials sit around a quadrangle of tables and nominate or select a player in turn (as described earlier).

I attended the 2000 national draft as a sports journalist and heard gasps of surprise when Richmond, with the overall number 41 selection, nominated 17-year-old Andrew Krakouer, the son of former Kangaroo champion Jim Krakouer. Young Andrew, from Western Australia, had at that time only played colts (junior) football, and his nomination became headline news. Richmond never regretted the choice — Andrew Krakouer made his senior debut for the team in 2001.

Although most of the footballers nominated at the national draft are from the elite under-age competitions, any footballer can nominate. You can be somewhat overweight or over the hill and still seek entry to the AFL ranks but, because every club has an army of talent scouts, your chances of finding a spot are going to be slimmer than your waistline.

The AFL, for the sake of family continuity at a particular club, has an exception to the general draft pecking order known as the *father–son rule*. The rule means that the son of a footballer who has played 100 (50 until 2003) or more games with a particular club is eligible to automatically join that club. To nominate a player under the father–son rule, the club has to sacrifice a selection in the draft.

Freshen up for the new season

Although the annual national draft is the AFL clubs' main recruiting initiative, clubs have a fresh chance to top up on players before the start of a new season. This system is known as the *pre-season draft*. Clubs take advantage of this draft if the team still has one or two vacancies left and wants to have the maximum of 38 players plus veterans at the beginning of the season. To decide which players to choose, these clubs often invite rejected players to train with the team over the summer as a trial for the pre-season draft.

The pre-season draft is a lot smaller than the national draft and generates a lower level of interest because few known outstanding talents remain to be chosen at this stage. However, every now and then a club snares a young player through the pre-season draft who develops into a star footballer.

For example, in 2005, Carlton nominated small forward Eddie Betts as a pre-season draft selection and he has since been an invaluable player for the Blues.

Rookies and Crookies

The only other ways for a footballer to be placed on an AFL player list are the following two methods:

- ✔ To be selected at the annual rookie draft, which follows the pre-season draft. (To be eligible for the rookie draft, players must be under 23 years of age and can then only play at AFL level if later promoted to the senior list.)
- ✔ To be promoted because a listed player is temporarily or permanently removed from the list as the result of a long-term injury or retirement.

Several quality players have moved up to AFL football through the rookie draft, including Essendon's Damien Peverill, Adelaide's Nathan Bock, Brisbane's Colm Begley (recruited from Ireland) and Sydney's Brett Kirk, among many others.

One of my abiding memories of Sydney's 2005 grand final triumph is of Swan defender Tadhg Kennelly being presented with his premiership medallion. Kennelly was so excited he performed an impromptu Irish jig.

The pluck of the Irish

In 1999, Sydney recruited 19-year-old Tadhg (a Gaelic name for Tim) Kennelly, a champion Gaelic footballer with the Irish club County Kerry. Sydney held a special training camp in Ireland and selected him as the player with the most potential to play Australian football. In 2000, the club placed Kennelly on the rookie list to learn the skills of the Australian game and he surged ahead so quickly that he was promoted to the senior list and made his AFL debut in 2001, less than two years after arriving in Australia. He is now rated one of the most exciting players in the game and played in Sydney's 2005 premiership side. He has since been joined by Brisbane's Colm Begley, who made his AFL debut in 2006, and Collingwood's Martin Clarke, who debuted in 2007.

Chapter 10

Training: The Ins and Outs

*A*ussie Rules is a physical game — no beg-pardons exist for heavy bumps and even the occasional bone-shaking collision. The game also requires top fitness, especially at the higher levels. A good footballer is a prepared footballer. This chapter can help you develop the physical capabilities for playing one of the world's most demanding ball games.

Getting Physical for Footy

Most youngsters living in the Aussie Rules parts of this big, brown land start handling a football almost from the time they can walk. Indeed, many a father has presented his newborn with a ball and a club scarf or beanie at birth. These children grow up with a football being almost an extension of their limbs.

If this experience isn't one you had, don't worry — you're not behind the eight ball. In this section, I detail the important elements of a training routine that will get your skills and body in top order.

Warming up and cooling down

Before every training session, you need to warm up. Warming up typically involves five to ten minutes of light activity, such as jogging and some stretching routines.

Stretching not only reduces the risk of injury but also builds your flexibility and reduces muscle tension. Figure 10-1 shows a simple warm-up routine that you can use to stretch major muscles and joints.

Figure 10-1:
A simple
warm-up
routine.

When you're stretching, try to

✔ Stretch alternate muscle groups.

✔ Stretch slowly and gently.

✔ Hold your stretches for 10 to 20 seconds.

✔ Never stretch to the point of pain.

✔ Always breathe slowly and easily.

In addition to those exercises shown in Figure 10-1, you need to spend a bit more time stretching the hamstring muscles to avoid any tears or strains. The hamstring is the long muscle running at the back of the leg from the buttock to the knee. Hamstring injuries are particularly common in Australian football because of the explosive speed required when taking off for the ball. (See Chapter 11 for more information on injuries.)

Suitable stretching exercises for the hamstring include the following:

✔ Sit on a chair with one foot on the floor and the other leg extended on a chair in front of you. Keep your back and knee straight. You should feel a stretch behind your knee and up towards your buttocks. Hold for 20 seconds and repeat with your other leg.

✔ Prop your leg up on a railing or chair, or even just in front of you on the floor. Try to extend your leg so that it's straight. You may feel tension in the back of your leg. Pull your toes towards your body to enhance the stretch. To advance this stretch further, simply reach your hands towards your foot, maintaining your upper body position. Hold the stretch for 20 seconds and repeat with your other leg.

✔ Stand with one foot crossed over the other. Bend at the hips, reaching towards the floor and keeping the knees slightly bent. Repeat with the opposite foot crossed in front.

✔ Lie on your back with your back flat and eyes focused upwards. Grasp the back of one thigh with both your hands and (leg bent) pull that thigh into a 90-degree angle to the floor. Then slowly straighten your knee. To increase the stretch, get a friend to lean against your leg. Hold the stretch for 20 seconds and repeat with your other leg.

Cooling down after your training session is really important, too. An effective cool-down consists of gradually reducing activity levels for five to ten minutes, such as a slow jog or walk followed by gentle stretching, along the lines of the exercises suggested in Figure 10-1.

Practising drills

If you really want to master the game's ball skills, start by handling the football as often and for as long as possible. Flick it from hand to hand, kick it to yourself, bounce it against a wall and catch it. Get the 'feel' of the ball.

After you feel confident in handling the ball, involve yourself in drills with your teammates or friends, either at formal training sessions or at impromptu get-togethers.

Try this drill to develop your ball handling and hand-to-eye coordination:

1. **Form a circle about 1 to 2 metres in diameter with a few friends or teammates.**

2. **Handpass to each other as quickly as possible.** See Chapter 7 for an explanation of this term.

3. **Use several footballs (if available) and move them from one to another as quickly as possible.**

4. **Try to get the balls moving at lightning speed.**

You can do the same exercise for kicking, only make the circle much bigger by standing about 20 to 30 metres apart. Again, use several footballs, if available, and kick to each other, while focusing on speed and accuracy.

For another good routine, try the following:

1. **Form two groups standing 20 metres apart.**

2. **One person from one group has a football and runs forward to handpass to a teammate coming from the opposite direction.**

3. **Then, when that person has the ball in the middle of the two groups, he runs forward to handpass to someone coming the other way.**

4. **Repeat for anything up to ten minutes to help achieve a high level of handling skill.**

AFL teams often do this routine in their on-ground warm-ups, so watch them perfect this drill and follow their example.

FOOTY FLASHBACK

Practice makes perfect (or close to it)

Cliché, but true — practice really can make perfect. Take, for example, the ball-handling skills of Sydney's talented Irishman, Tadhg Kennelly. The Swans star had never handled an Australian football before he was recruited by the Swans straight from playing the round-ball Gaelic code of football. Kennelly then spent ten hours a day handling the ball, kicking it and handpassing it until it became second nature for him to make the oval-shaped ball all but sing and dance. Kennelly is now regarded as an expert ball handler, simply because he practised until he knew he could control the ball in almost any match situation.

Collingwood's Martin Clarke, who also was recruited from Ireland, made his AFL debut in 2007, just 12 months after first handling an Australian football. He now is regarded as an expert at handballing. Some players develop bad habits very early and it's believed Kennelly, Clarke and another Irishman, Brisbane's Colm Begley, are so fluent with handpassing that they did not develop these bad habits as boys, but learned the game's crafts from scratch. It has nothing to do with the luck of the Irish and little wonder all AFL clubs now have talent spotters in the Emerald Isle.

Watching what you eat

When you're training, you need to ensure you have sufficient fuel to maintain your weight and provide enough energy for your requirements.

Although everyone has different dietary requirements, if you play a game such as Aussie Rules you need to have an increased intake of carbohydrates. Focus on meals that consist of carbohydrates, such as rice, pasta or potatoes, and protein, such as chicken or fish.

All AFL clubs employ dietitians to ensure players watch what they eat. Players not only need carbohydrates to maintain energy levels; they also need to keep their weight down.

Players are subjected to regular assessments of their weight, which usually take the form of a skin-fold test. This test involves the club's medical staff using pincer-type instruments to measure the depth of the player's skin fold on their hips. These tests give a fair indication how much body fat a player is carrying, so woe betide any player who returns from the summer break having eaten too much Christmas pudding!

Gone forever are the days when players ate big steaks on the morning of a match. Most players eat heaps and heaps of carbohydrate-laden food in the lead-up to a match. This is usually in the form of pasta, especially the night before a match.

Former Geelong champion Bob 'Woofa' Davis, who was non-playing coach of the Cats' 1963 premiership side, wrote in his autobiography *Woofa* that he ate a steak lunch on his way to his debut match against Fitzroy in 1948. No player in his right mind now would even entertain such a pre-match diet.

Staying hydrated

When you're training, you must ensure that you keep up your liquid intake to replace the fluid you sweat out and to avoid dehydration, especially on hot days.

The AFL over recent years has had pre-season matches in Darwin and Cairns, where the weather has been so hot that it has been estimated that some players lost 5 or 6 kilograms in that time. Basically, this lost weight is water and it must be replenished. (The AFL now takes extreme care in scheduling matches away from the hottest weather in tropical climates.)

Even on days when the temperature is a more comfortable 20 degrees Celsius you'll see water boys carrying drinks to players. This practice is an accepted and necessary part of the game.

Always make sure you have a drink — preferably water — before, during and after your training session. Thirst is not a sign of dehydration because you can get dehydrated before you actually feel thirsty, so keep your fluids up.

Grasping How the AFL Footballers Train

Numerous levels of Australian football exist, from junior teams for players as young as 8 years of age, right through amateur suburban and country competitions to the elite AFL level. (Refer to Chapter 8 for more information on each of these different levels.)

Each level has different training needs. Some clubs expect their players to attend training sessions only once or twice a week. The professional AFL footballers, however, are expected to train almost every day pre-season (four months before the start of a season) and up to four or five times a week during the season (when games are played). In this section, I detail the AFL training workload.

Working out pre-season

Many AFL veterans admit to hating pre-season training, even though it's water and oxygen to their professional careers. Without pre-season work, a footballer is most unlikely to see out a full season. In fact, many injured players blame a lack of preparation for their injuries.

Some players may not be able to complete a pre-season campaign because of injury from the previous season or an unexpected injury setback during the pre-season period. More often than not, these players struggle to reach top form during the following season. A good pre-season campaign is therefore essential.

AFL footballers have a break of at least two months at the completion of a season and then gather for four months of solid sweat and grind to become physically prepared for the next season. In the past, it was common for footballers to have four or even five months 'off the track'. They would return to training just a month before the new season and try to reach full fitness in a short period. However, this approach was in the semi-professional era of 30 years ago, when all footballers also had full-time jobs.

In the late 1960s, Richmond coach Tom Hafey started preparing his team much earlier than usual, and the Tigers consequently gained a fitness break on their rivals. Hafey set the trend and others followed, to the extent that footballers now train almost every day pre-season and sometimes even twice a day. This work involves running sessions to get the legs ready for match play, training drills with footballs to develop handling skills, and plenty of weight work. These weight sessions are often held in the early morning, with skills or running work in the afternoon.

Football at AFL level makes enormous demands on the body, so a footballer with little bulk is going to find it difficult to cope with the physical battering. Weights are used to build body strength, which is also important in holding off opponents. The trick is to 'bulk up' without losing leg speed or mobility. All AFL clubs employ weights specialists who prepare individual programs for their players.

Considerable debate exists as to whether junior footballers should use weight training, so young players need to seek expert advice before commencing such a routine.

Most AFL clubs also have special pre-season camps, sometimes at military bases. These camps run for three to seven days and involve not only normal training, but special military drills, such as obstacle courses that may involve rope-climbing, abseiling and so on. These camps not only help develop fitness, strength and endurance, but are also considered excellent for team bonding. Collingwood, before each of the 2006 and 2007 seasons, went to the United States for altitude training, the theory being that it added to the players' aerobic capacity. St Kilda in 2006 went to South Africa for specialised training and bonding away from the glare of the Australian football media.

Warming up pre-match

All players need to prepare themselves for a match, so all AFL footballers have set pre-match routines. They not only have 'rub-downs' by club masseurs, but also have their joints taped by training staff to help prevent injury, and take part in team warm-ups. (See Chapter 11 for information on taping.)

One type of warm-up, started only about three years ago by then Western Bulldogs' coach Terry Wallace (later Richmond coach), involves players taking the ground about 30 to 40 minutes before a match and having ball drills (refer to 'Practising drills' earlier in this chapter). Some players even have goal-kicking practice.

Drills are important to get the feel of the ball and of the ground surface. Players also kick balls to each other in the change rooms. Players stand 10 to 15 metres apart and kick the ball hard, straight to a teammate.

On the wrong tram

Footballers sometimes try to cut training corners, especially when the going is tough. When Tom Hafey was coach of Richmond in the late 1960s, one of his favourite drills was making the players run 10-kilometre timed circuits of the Tan, an area surrounding Melbourne's Botanic Gardens. One player, the bulky Brian 'The Whale' Roberts, used to take a shortcut and Hafey could never understand how this 110-kilogram giant could run so fast in training, but not in a match. Also, when Ron Barassi was coach of Carlton around the same time, player Adrian Gallagher caught a tram back to the training ground after the squad was sent on a run. Gallagher soon figured out that there were no shortcuts under Barassi — he and teammates had to do push-ups as punishment for training misdemeanours.

Set-piece sessions are part of the training drills at each of the 16 AFL clubs. (See Chapter 13 for details on each of the clubs.) These set-piece routines may be handball work in circles or criss-cross drills in which players run from 45-degree angles rather than in a straight line to handpass to each other. This set-piece drill is extremely demanding, not only in terms of ball skills, but also of concentration.

The most important part of the warm-up is stretching, which is guided by a team official or a physiotherapist. (All AFL and semi-professional clubs have physios, whereas lower level and junior clubs usually make do with qualified trainers.)

Cooling down post-match

About 20 years or so ago teams would finish a match and head straight for the after-match function to down a few refreshing ales. No longer! Research has shown that alcohol can hinder the healing process from bruising, so players are now encouraged instead to consume energy drinks brimming with electrolytes and other goodies. Players also eat fruit and, believe it or not, lollies such as jelly snakes, which are full of glucose and therefore good for recovering energy. Most players also look like pack mules after a game as they have niggling injuries 'iced up' to prevent internal bleeding and therefore help recovery.

After a game has been completed, the players are called into a huddle in the dressing rooms and go through a five-minute series of exercises, similar to those practised pre-match (refer to preceding section). These exercises are considered essential to help prevent the stiffening of muscles and limit whatever damage may have been caused to tissue. After they've completed these exercises, players head for the coach's room to be congratulated — or blasted. Ah, the vagaries of football!

I must admit to having been the world's worst football trainer. I played for a team (Hartwell Presbyterians, who were mainly Catholics) of mostly University of Melbourne law students and, because of our studies, never trained. Remarkably, we made the grand final one year and decided to train on the Thursday night before the big match. It was our one and only training session of the season, and we then went to the pub to drink and pick the team. Needless to say, we were beaten!

Training, taskmaster-style

About 35 years ago, enforcing heavy 'match conditions' training early in the week was almost a club tradition. Players would pair off and play virtual practice matches. Being 'punished on the track' was also traditional for a team that had disgraced itself the previous Saturday. Coaches would make them train long and hard to remind them of their shortcomings and of what they could expect if it happened again.

Surprisingly, this 'punishment training' re-emerged in 2002, with several coaches, including former Kangaroos and Carlton coach Denis Pagan, putting players through these old-fashioned mud-and-guts training sessions.

The normal practice now is for teams to have a swim or a very light run the day after the match and have skills sessions the following day. Another skills session follows, perhaps two days later, and a final light run the day before a match. Some weight sessions may be included and some players may wish to do extra work, like taking practice kicks for goal.

AFL footballers now are virtually full-time professionals, and training usually is in the morning or afternoon. In the semi-professional era, all training was held in twilight or under lights. Players formerly held down full-time positions and it was common for them to turn up to training in overalls or business suits after work. Footscray's (now Western Bulldogs) 1954 premiership captain and coach Charlie Sutton worked for the local council and used to take his horse and dray to the Western (now Whitten) Oval for training. It was a common Footscray joke to unhitch the horse from a rail and 'hide' it and the dray from Sutton.

Chapter 11

Injuries and How to Deal with Them

*I*njuries have been part of football ever since it was invented, and not just necessarily in Aussie Rules. Because Australian football is an impact sport, injuries are unavoidable. Sure, some players might go through their career with hardly a knock, but others can have one injury after another.

For example, when Heath James was on Sydney's list from 1999 to 2002, he had no less than eleven hamstring tears. And, just when he appeared to be over these problems, he severely injured a knee at a football clinic for schoolchildren. Gavin Brown had a range of injuries over his career, including seven concussions and three groin operations. On the other hand, Richmond's Kevin Bartlett hardly missed a game through injury in his 403 games with the Tigers from 1965 to 1983. Sydney's Jared Crouch played 194 games from his debut in 1994 to 2006, when he was finally forced out with severe shoulder and ankle injuries. He then tore a hamstring in 2007 and had to wait until the penultimate round match against Collingwood to reach his 200-game milestone.

To keep you on top of your game, in this chapter, I detail the common types of injuries to look out for, as well as ways to avoid injury and treat any that you may experience.

Common Types of Injuries

Research has found that lower limb injuries are most common in high-level competition players, whereas upper limb injuries are prevalent among children and community-level participants. Overall, however, the most common injury in Aussie Rules is a hamstring strain or tear, which most footballers experience at one time or another. Groin and anterior cruciate injuries follow closely behind.

In addition, players break bones, strain their muscles and receive all sorts of cuts and abrasions. Figure 11-1 highlights the most common injuries. Of all the major football codes played in Australia, Aussie Rules has the highest percentage of injuries per player in a season, so injuries are part of the game, unfortunately.

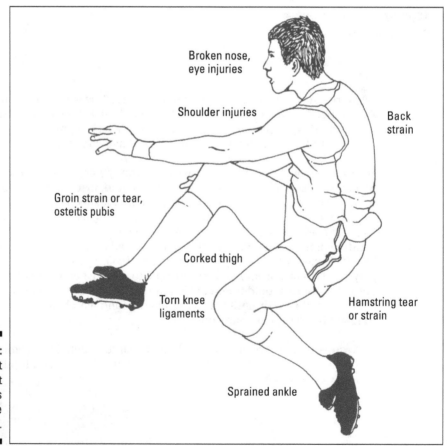

Broken nose, eye injuries

Shoulder injuries

Back strain

Groin strain or tear, osteitis pubis

Corked thigh

Torn knee ligaments

Hamstring tear or strain

Sprained ankle

Figure 11-1: The most frequent injuries in Aussie Rules.

Zing went my hamstrings

The song might go 'zing, zing, zing went my heartstrings', but for Australian footballers it's more likely to be the quaintly named hamstring, which refers to three muscles in the back of the thigh that stretch from the buttocks to the knee.

A strained or torn hamstring is the most common form of injury in Australian football because the amount of sprinting involved in the game subjects this muscle to high-tension loads. It's also the hardest of the Aussie Rules injuries to diagnose.

Recurring hamstring injuries have wrecked many a career, including that of champion Melbourne midfielder Stephen Tingay, who finally had to retire in 2001 because of his inability to shake off hamstring woes. However, some footballers are more prone to these injuries than others, because hamstring strains can be related to back problems. A back complaint or poor back flexibility may put pressure on the muscles at the back of the leg.

Former Collingwood captain and champion midfielder Nathan Buckley missed most of the 2007 season with chronic hamstring problems, but made a triumphant return in the round-21 match against Sydney at the MCG. Also, Essendon full-forward Matthew Lloyd tore a hamstring so severely in the third round of the 2006 season that he missed the rest of the season.

Breaks of an unlucky kind

The term 'break a leg' might be a good-luck call for actors, but it's definitely not good news for footballers. Unfortunately, broken legs are part and parcel of the game, although statistics reveal that on average only three or four AFL footballers each season run into this type of injury. Of course, players also endure broken collarbones, arms, fingers and hands, as well as facial fractures.

The most common break affects one of the lesser known parts of the anatomy — the *scaphoid* bone in the wrist. This small dumbbell-shaped bone at the base of the thumb is often broken when a footballer spreads his hand to lessen the impact of a fall. The jarring of the hand, and especially of the thumb, breaks the scaphoid. Sometimes the break fails to heal because the bone is so small, being just a couple of centimetres in length, and has a poor blood supply.

For example, Ted Whitten, known as 'Mr Football' and one of the greatest of all Australian footballers, broke the scaphoid bone in his left wrist early in his career and played for many years with this wrist heavily strapped. A broken bone could not stop this champion.

Stone the Crowes!

In 1958, Carlton ruckman Bob Crowe slipped and fell as he ran onto the ground for the start of a game. He rolled an ankle and was unable to play, but couldn't be replaced in the selected squad because he had already been listed on the team sheet, as required by the AFL's *Laws* *of the Game*. Sydney's Lewis Roberts-Thomson ruptured an Achilles tendon as he was about to take the field for a match against Carlton in 2004 and could not be replaced because his name had already been included on the team sheet.

A nose for trouble

Any Australian footballer who has played the game for any lengthy period will have had at least a bloodied nose, if not a broken proboscis. Because of the impact, often head on head, of colliding footballers, facial injuries are sometimes unavoidable. For example, in 2002, Essendon captain James Hird was seriously injured when his head accidentally took a heavy blow from the knee of teammate Mark McVeigh in a match against West Coast in Perth. It was a sickening collision, with Hird suffering facial fractures. The courageous Hird returned to action six weeks later wearing a protective mask that made him look like the Phantom of the Opera.

Fortunately, however, such serious facial injuries are rare, although North Melbourne (now Kangaroos) ruckman Noel Teasdale wore a protective pad over his forehead after an accidental head clash with teammate Ken Dean in 1964.

Nothing soft about these injuries

The term *soft-tissue injury* sounds deceptively harmless. In fact, a soft-tissue injury can put a footballer out of action for up to two months, depending on its severity. Soft tissue refers primarily to muscles, tendons and ligaments, but it can also refer to nerves, arteries, veins, capillaries, organs and glands. Injuries to soft tissue include:

✔ **Dislocations:** This type of injury occurs when a bone is displaced from a joint, and can affect the nerves and blood vessels. Some players have joints that dislocate easily due to either a congenital condition or weak ligaments stretched by previous repeated dislocations.

✔ **Strains:** This sort of problem occurs when too much load is placed on muscle tissues.

✔ **Sprains:** This kind of minor injury occurs when too much motion is applied to ligaments.

✔ **Bruising:** Bruising is bleeding of damaged blood vessels beneath the surface of the skin.

In Aussie Rules, the most common forms of soft-tissue injuries include a 'corked' thigh (which is mild to severe internal bruising to the thigh muscle) and a sprained ankle, as well as calf and thigh strains.

Keeping your knee out of it

Whenever an AFL footballer goes to ground clutching a knee, fans fear the worst. More often than not, the injury is no more serious than a sprained *medial ligament* (inside the knee), sidelining the player for a couple of weeks. However, the fear is that the footballer has ruptured a *cruciate ligament*, which crosses over the middle of the knee to give it stability. If this is the case, the player has no lateral stability in his knee. He might be able to run in a straight line, but twisting and turning, even slightly, is out of the question. This type of injury plagued a number of players during the 2001 and 2002 seasons, but occurred less often over the 2005–2007 seasons. Knee injuries like these are simply a random occurrence.

Former Melbourne key forward David Schwarz and former Adelaide and Hawthorn ruckman Shaun Rehn, both of whom retired in 2002, had three knee reconstructions each. Both fought against almost overwhelming odds to continue their AFL careers.

Going, going, groin

One of football's most serious injuries is a *groin strain* or tear, which occurs when muscles in the groin are strained by stretching the legs too far. Players can sometimes play with this type of injury, depending on how serious it is.

For example, Sydney ruckman Jason Ball strained a groin muscle during pre-season training in 2002 and tried to return to action several times. However, the injury kept recurring, so he eventually had surgery and missed the entire season. Also, Brisbane's Jason Akermanis went into the 2002 grand final against Collingwood with a slight groin strain, only to aggravate the injury early in the big match. Akermanis later explained he was in agony, even when he kicked the sealing goal with just seven minutes to play.

The new football injury swear words

Don't utter the words *osteitis pubis* around a football club: It's the modern football injury that cuts down a large number of players each year. Osteitis pubis is a bone stress injury of the pubic bone in front of the pelvis. Extremely debilitating, this injury causes inflammation and swelling to the extent that some affected footballers can't even walk.

The increase in osteitis pubis has been put down to current modern training regimes that focus on developing extreme levels of fitness and place increased pressure on the pubic bones of the pelvis.

This injury is especially prevalent among young players who may not be fully developed physically. For example, Hawthorn's Luke Hodge (who turned 18 during the 2002 season) had a delayed start to his AFL career in 2002 because of osteitis pubis, after he was named as the overall number one selection at the 2001 national draft. St Kilda's Luke Ball and West Coast's Chris Judd were also severely affected by groin problems in 2007. Both showed enormous courage in continuing to play, even though both were rested at times during the season.

Back to basics

Some footballers develop back problems due to the game, but for others such injuries can be genetic. Playing in the ruck with a continuous crashing of body on body can cause back problems, particularly lower back strain.

St Kilda's Justin Koschitzke, for example, won the 2001 Rising Star Award as the best young player in the AFL, but then missed most of the 2002 season with a back injury. Koschitzke bravely tried to continue playing, but the Saints wisely decided they had such an invaluable football commodity that they ordered their young star to have complete rest.

A cold can last weeks

AFL clubs commonly hide the injuries of the players from the general public. For example, I remember being told as a football writer about 15 years ago that a certain star player was out of action because of a viral infection.

The player actually was out of action for six weeks. Some viral infection! He had a fractured jaw but the club didn't want the opposition to know because it feared that particular part of his anatomy would be targeted.

Avoiding Injuries

If any footballers know how to avoid injuries, they should spread the news. A football player has no guarantee that he'll get through any match unscathed. However, keeping fit and taking every precaution helps. In this section, I address the various ways you can prevent injury.

Always warm up and cool down

A number of injuries can be put down to a lack of or insufficient warm-up before exercise, particularly hamstring and soft-tissue injuries. Warming up your body helps to increase or maintain flexibility and muscle suppleness.

A proper warm-up entails stretching of all the major muscles and joints and five minutes of cardiovascular work to increase the heart rate. (Refer to Chapter 10 for more information, including a range of suitable exercises in Figure 10-1.)

Likewise, cooling down after your game is important to reduce muscle stiffness and soreness and avoid dizziness, which is sometimes caused when you stop physical exercise suddenly. To cool down, gradually decrease the intensity of your exercise by doing five minutes of cardio and finish the session with stretching.

Taping where need be

Taping is a very detailed and precise procedure that acts to protect and stabilise a particular part of the body. The correct taping of ankles can help prevent ankle sprains or even breaks. The same goes for shoulder, wrist and thumb bandaging. If a footballer has a suspect joint, it should be taped to help prevent bending or breaking.

The most common material used for taping is leukoplast tape, which is a rigid adhesive tape. Determining how to tape a player depends on his needs and varies from player to player, and ultimately needs to be decided by an expert. For example, one player may have a problem with the inside of the ankle, whereas another may have a problem on the outside. Also, shoulder injuries vary enormously.

Don't attempt to do your own taping: Taping is a job for an expert. Trainers need to know what they're doing and follow correct procedures. If you have any queries on taping, contact the AFL.

Getting into the right gear

Protective gear can save you from injury, and a number of footballers elect to wear it. The better gear is custom-fitted for you, of course, but beginners can save themselves a lot of pain if they invest in even the stock brands of protective wear and use it regularly.

Leg guards

A very simple kind of protection are shin guards and thigh guards (sometimes called pads), which, when properly fitted, act as a barrier to minor leg injuries, such as bruising, cuts and welts. Shin guards and thigh guards are usually made of plastic and fitted and adjusted with velcro straps. If they're not fitted properly, the guard can slip and be more of a hindrance than a help.

Don't mistakenly assume a mere shin guard or thigh guard makes you invulnerable on the field; you can still get a broken leg if you're playing a rough game.

An army of trainers

If you take a good look at an AFL match you'll notice many extra people on the ground at any given time. Apart from the 18 players on each side, plus the field, goal and boundary umpires, you'll see water boys and trainers. Each AFL club has a veritable army of trainers who assist the club doctor and physiotherapist(s). If a player even looks as if he's injured, trainers run out to him. Then, after examining the injury, they may signal (crossed forearms at eye level) that the doctor or physio is needed.

Mouthguards

The best way to make sure you get false teeth is to play the game without a mouthguard! All footballers need to wear mouthguards. Aussie Rules is a contact sport and the risk of a blow to the head or face is high. Mouthguards act as a shock absorber for the teeth and jaw and reduce the risk of concussion.

You can choose from three types of mouthguard available on the market:

- **Stock mouthguards:** You can buy these mouthguards in pharmacies and sports stores. Offering a false sense of protection, these mouthguards are made of rigid plastic, are quite uncomfortable and don't secure firmly in the mouth.

- **'Boil-and-bite' mouthguards:** Made from thermo plastic material, these mouthguards soften when placed in hot water. You then place the mouthguard in your mouth and bite down to mould it to your teeth. Unfortunately, their shape deforms easily and they often don't fit well.

- **Custom-fitted mouthguards:** The best of the lot, these mouthguards are designed by a dentist to fit to your mouth perfectly. They're made from a special shock-absorbing material and allow for natural breathing and speech.

Helmets

Helmets are more common in junior football than at AFL level. Nevertheless, a couple of AFL stars over recent years have believed in the theory that a helmet offers the best protection from head injuries. Former St Kilda midfielder Nathan Burke started wearing a helmet after suffering recurring headaches, and Brisbane's Shaun Hart (who was named Norm Smith medallist for best on the ground in the 2001 AFL grand final) always wore a helmet.

The luck of the Irish

Melbourne's Jim Stynes was regarded as a 'lucky' footballer because the Irishman played an AFL record of 248 consecutive games. However, Stynes believed mental strength was all-important: He even overcame a serious knee injury in 1994 during his run of consecutive games. His run ended in 1998 when he was forced out with a broken hand.

Some players wear helmets on a temporary basis. For example, Sydney's Jude Bolton had his head gashed in an accidental collision in the 2005 grand final against West Coast and finished the match in a helmet to protect the wound. Then, as the Swans posed for celebratory photographs, he forgot he was wearing it. He later threw it to the crowd and someone collected a marvellous souvenir of one of the greatest grand finals of them all.

You can find a range of different styles of helmets available. Hart (who retired in 2004) wore one that covered the forehead completely and had full padding on the sides of the head. It was held in place by a buckled strap under the chin. This basic style of helmet is usually made of rubber or polystyrene, covered by leather or soft plastic. The one Bolton wore in the 2005 grand final looked like a World War II bomber crew helmet.

Other helmets used over the years resemble bicycle helmets. For example, when Phil Narkle played for St Kilda from 1984 to 1986 and then with West Coast from 1987 to 1989, he wore a half-egg-shaped helmet. This design gave tremendous protection to the top of the head, but offered no protection over the temple area.

In 2002, Essendon captain James Hird suffered facial fractures in an accidental collision with teammate Mark McVeigh. He returned to action a month later wearing a special facial guard that covered his forehead and parts of his fractured cheekbone.

Treating Injuries: RICER

The common way to treat soft-tissue injuries is RICER: Rest, Ice, Compression, Elevation and Referral. Usually, this treatment is all you need to get back on your feet, depending on the injury, particularly if you RICER diligently for the first 48 hours after an injury.

✔ **Rest:** Stop doing activities that aggravate your injury. (If you sprain your ankle, don't try to 'walk it off'.) Rest can often mean the difference between an injury that heals right away and one that nags you for months. But don't use your injury as an excuse to quit exercising altogether. Simply choose an activity that doesn't hurt. If you pull a hamstring, there's no reason to stop upper-body weight training.

✔ **Ice:** Ice reduces swelling and deadens pain by constricting blood flow into the injured areas. Apply ice for 15 to 20 minutes three or four times a day for as long as you feel pain. You can apply ice with a pack, a plastic bag full of cubes or a packet of frozen vegetables. Just don't allow the ice to rest directly on your skin; otherwise, you're inviting a whole new list of problems such as ice burns. Figure 11-2 shows the application of an ice treatment.

✔ **Compression:** Put pressure on the injured areas to keep the swelling down. Wrap a damp bandage around the injury, or buy a special knee, elbow or wrist wrap or brace (see Figure 11-2). Wrap tightly enough so that you feel some tension but not so firmly that you cut off your circulation or feel numbness.

✔ **Elevation:** Elevating your injured body part reduces swelling by allowing fluids and waste products to drain from the area, much like water runs downstream. (Waste products are bits of broken blood cells and other inflammatory agents hanging around the injury.) If your ankle is injured, you don't need to raise it so high that it's perpendicular to the ground. Propping it up on a couple of fluffy pillows will do. Elevation works best when used in conjunction with the rest of the RICER treatment.

✔ **Referral:** If pain persists, always refer to a doctor for a proper check-up before undertaking further exercise.

Figure 11-2:
Two important steps of RICER: The application of ice (left) and compression (right).

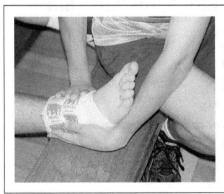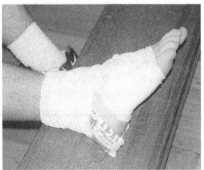

After 48 hours the objective is to

- ✔ **Heal:** You need to let your body do this naturally. In addition, you can assist the process by applying heat or lightly massaging the area.
- ✔ **Stretch:** Basically, you just have to move the injured area with the aim of regaining full flexibility. Physiotherapy can help here.
- ✔ **Strengthen:** As stretching increases your mobility, gradually reintroduce weight-bearing exercise. Let pain be your guide here and don't push yourself too much.

Head injuries need to be taken seriously. If you or a fellow player has a head injury, stop playing and see a doctor immediately. Additionally, you shouldn't train for at least seven days after the injury occurred. The policy held by most of the AFL clubs is that if a player suffers a head injury, he is to miss at least one match because there could be delayed symptoms, such as bleeding inside the head and brain injury. Every injury should be treated seriously. Even the smallest of injuries can lead to a lengthy absence if it isn't given the right attention.

When Sydney's Jared Crouch played his 194 consecutive games from his debut in 1994 to during the 2006 season, he carried many niggling injuries into most games. When asked about his remarkable durability, Crouch said he was a firm believer in the power of ice. He became known as Sydney's 'Ice-man' because of his faith in its powers to help rejuvenate the body and restrict injury damage to tissue.

The Aussie Rules ice machine

AFL change rooms have more ice than you would find in the world's largest bar — and none of it goes in drinks. As soon as any footballer reports a soft-tissue injury or bruise, ice is applied. A player may spend time on the interchange bench with a knee or thigh wrapped in ice before the medical staff allow him back onto the ground. Ice is also applied to any injuries immediately after the match.

Remember though that you should always get any injury checked out by a professional.

Handling Common Injuries

Every injury requires its own treatment, with broken bones requiring setting, ruptured cruciate ligaments and other severe injuries requiring surgery and hamstring strains requiring rest. The following is a general guide on how to handle those injuries common to Aussie Rules.

Every injury is different, so you need to consult your doctor for professional help.

✔ **Hamstring strains and tears:** RICER (refer to preceding section) followed by stretching and strengthening exercises as permitted by a physiotherapist. Usually, recovery takes 21 days for a hamstring strain. Hamstring tears are altogether different — a player can be sidelined for two months.

✔ **Ankle injuries:** RICER and follow up with physiotherapy and heat. In extreme cases, or when quick recovery is essential, AFL clubs use a *hyperbaric chamber*. This approach allows the injury to have an increased flow of oxygen, helping the recovery process. Carlton's Fraser Brown used a hyperbaric chamber and was able to play in the 1995 grand final after severely twisting an ankle the previous week.

✔ **Dislocated fingers:** The usual treatment is to pull the joint back into place. A compound dislocation — when the joint breaks the skin — is much more serious and surgery is sometimes required. Footballers also fear finger ligament damage. West Coast's Daniel Kerr, for example, was sidelined late in the 2007 season after injuring a finger in a match against Richmond, and he had to have immediate surgery to repair the ligament.

✔ **Corked thigh:** Ice is the best treatment for this deep-seated bruising of the thigh muscle (apply 15–20 minutes each hour initially). Recent evidence suggests that stretching the muscle immediately after the injury reduces bleeding and minimises muscle shortening. See your physiotherapist for ongoing treatment.

✔ **Dislocated AC joint:** The *AC (acromioclavicular) joint* is a shoulder joint, near the collarbone. Depending on the severity of the dislocation, a player can be sidelined for anything from one week to four. It's a nasty and painful injury, but far better than breaking a collarbone or dislocating the shoulder altogether. The latter are long-term injuries, with complete rest required. Or, in a worst case scenario, shoulder reconstruction surgery may be required. (Shoulder reconstruction surgery involves tightening the ligaments around the shoulder and is often done over summer.)

- ✔ **Broken nose:** Unless the break is severe, few players are sidelined by this type of injury. At AFL level, players who have had a nose broken during the season have post-season surgery. Many footballers also have nasal reconstructions following retirement.

- ✔ **Knee injuries:** A ruptured cruciate ligament means a total knee reconstruction. At best, a footballer can return to action 6 to 8 months after surgery, but full rehabilitation can take 12 months or even longer. A medial strain is far less serious; a player with this type of injury may miss just a couple of matches. In previous eras, damage to the knee cartilage was regarded as extremely serious and could have meant a 12-week or even longer lay-off. Now, however, cartilage tears can be repaired with keyhole surgery and a player may miss just one match.

- ✔ **Broken bones:** Some players can return to the field with a broken finger or even a broken hand. A broken leg, however, is a very serious injury that can sideline a player for anything from four weeks to a season, depending on the severity of the break. A small fracture of the fibula may mean a month out of the game, but serious fractures can occur. For example, Sydney's Jamie Lawson broke a leg early in a match against Richmond at the MCG in 1994 and never played again, following complications. Richmond's Nathan Brown broke a leg in a match early in 2005 and the television footage was so graphic that viewers were advised to close their eyes if they didn't want to see the leg snap. Brown courageously returned to action for the start of the 2006 season, but it took almost two years for him to fully recover.

Carlton's Les Witto has the dubious distinction of being the only footballer to have died from injury in a VFL/AFL match. Witto, a recruit from Broken Hill, broke an arm in a match against Geelong in 1926, in just his sixth game for the Blues. Tetanus set in and he later died in a Geelong hospital. The Carlton club then ran a testimonial to help Witto's widowed mother.

Ready yourself for a return to the fray only when you know with certainty that your injury has healed completely. When you do return to the field, listen to what your doctor, physio or trainer tells you. Miracle cures don't exist; if you return too soon after injury, you may run into even worse problems.

Check out these Web sites for more information on injury prevention and management:

- ✔ **Sports Medicine Australia (**www.sma.org.au**):** Australia's peak national umbrella body for sports medicine and sports science. You can find links to various programs and projects.

- ✔ **Smart Play (**www.smartplay.net**):** A well-designed site hosted by the South Australian branch of Sports Medicine Australia, full of clearly presented information specifically to educate children playing sport, including information on sports injuries and prevention. A site worth adding to your favourites, because it regularly presents new material.

Chapter 12

So, You Want to Coach

*T*he standing joke in football is that anyone who wants to coach at AFL level not only needs to be an amateur psychiatrist to analyse the players in his (and increasingly her) team but should also see a psychiatrist. Coaching causes heartburn and anguish because the pressure is intense. This tension is illustrated by another football joke: Only two kinds of coach exist, those who've been sacked and those who are about to be sacked. Of course, this joke mainly refers to coaches for the AFL, where the turnover rate (usually three or four a year) is high.

Coaching is often a thankless task and those who fail may feel figuratively hanged, drawn and quartered. Every coach, even the most successful, has critics. Criticism goes with the job. However, coaching can also be enormously rewarding, and not only in terms of premierships. Coaching gives you the opportunity to put something back into the game.

In this chapter, I cover the essentials for successful coaching. Parents, families and fans must remember that winning games is not necessarily the measuring stick for success. In junior football it's all about teaching the skills of the game and having fun. In more senior ranks, even at AFL level, coaches can be enormously successful without winning premierships or even getting their team into the finals. For example, they can help in the development of mediocre players and encourage younger players to take the next step on the path to football stardom.

McHale and hearty

Collingwood's James 'Jock' McHale holds the record as the VFL/AFL's longest serving coach. McHale held the Collingwood job from 1912 until his retirement at the end of the 1949. McHale coached Collingwood for 714 games and this record seems certain to last for many years yet, if not forever. Ironically, the man selected to replace him didn't last even one game. Bervyn Woods resigned just one week into the job after disgruntled Magpie fans jeered him pre-season in 1950, and he was replaced by Phonse Kyne.

Former Richmond player Kevin Sheedy coached Essendon in 635 games to the end of the 2007 season after being appointed coach in 1981. Sheedy's 27-season tenure therefore is the second-longest in VFL/AFL history. Just think of how long Sheedy coached the Bombers: Many members of the 2007 squad weren't even born when he first coached Essendon. He also has the unusual achievement of coaching champion Bomber Tim Watson *and* his son Jobe.

Licensed to Coach

In years gone by, virtually anyone could coach a football team. No coaching qualifications were available or deemed necessary and, by and large, coaches were appointed on playing experience and seniority. Now, however, most clubs want qualifications. AFL coaching qualifications are approved under the Australian Sports Commission's National Coaching Accreditation Scheme (NCAS). See the Australian Sports Commission's Web site at www.ausport.gov.au for more information on NCAS.

Three AFL accreditation levels are currently available:

✔ **AFL Level 1 (AFL Auskick) Certificate:** The entry level for coaching children between 5 and 12 years of age. The course generally takes 14 hours over a number of sessions. Subjects include planning, teaching the game's basic skills, team play, tactics, safety issues and organisation. This course is particularly suitable for parents who want to assume a coaching role. If you're successful and agree to abide by the AFL's code of conduct, you receive a certificate and your name is registered on the AFL coaches' database and with the NCAS.

This database lists all accredited coaches so that any club wanting to appoint a coach can contact the AFL to determine whether an applicant has completed a coaching course. Currently more than 25,000 coaches are registered with the AFL. Specific versions of the AFL Level 1 course are available for coaches of youth (ages 13–17) and senior (open age) teams.

✔ **AFL Level 2 Certificate:** The AFL's accreditation for coaches who want to coach at a higher level. Around 30 hours of coursework is involved, including a weekend workshop. Subjects include planning; sports psychology and communication; fitness; the coach and umpiring; and principles of physical preparation. You're assessed 'on the job' at training and on match days. If successful and you agree to abide by the AFL's code of conduct, you receive a certificate and your name is registered with the AFL and the NCAS.

✔ **AFL Level 3:** The highest possible training level available, this course is designed for those who are dealing with footballers at a professional (AFL) or semi-professional level (such as state league). Held as a week-long residential course, the subjects are almost identical to those for the Level Two Certificate but are studied in much greater depth, while also covering issues such as emerging technology and media relations. Coaches at this level must have an ability to study videotapes of the opposition, examine statistical data and understand sports psychology. In addition, coaches at this level must be able to deal with press queries and post-match press conferences.

For further information on these courses, or if you want to enrol, visit the Coaching section of the AFL Web site (`www.afl.com.au`) or contact the AFL National Coaching Manager on (03) 9643 1859.

Keys to Successful Coaching

To be a successful Aussie Rules coach, you have to act in some ways like the general of an army. Depending on the level at which you're coaching, you may or may not have lieutenants. At AFL level, you have several assistants, such as a defence coach, an attacking coach, a skills coach and so on. However, if you coach a junior club, you may be the sole coach, without lieutenants.

Some piano teachers aren't maestros, but they can and do produce prodigies. The same can be said of football coaches, because even the greatest champions start somewhere. Basically, a good coach

✔ Knows the game inside and out.

✔ Appreciates the players' skills.

✔ Comprehends the opposition.

✔ Corrects technical problems.

✔ Acts as an amateur psychologist.

- ✔ Conveys eternal optimism.
- ✔ Knows how to motivate and extract every drop out of the players.

Coaches must be confident of their own abilities. After all, coaches who aren't confident of being able to do the job are sure to have their negativity rub off on their players. Be firm, be positive, be a winner.

Know the game inside and out

Obviously, coaching Australian football requires a sound knowledge of the rules of the game, and experience playing helps. The greater your knowledge, the better you're likely to be.

Most coaches learn the game as players, although some coaches have never played the game but are very observant fans. Most coaches at AFL level have played at this elite standard, although former Carlton coach Wayne Brittain (2001–2002) never played at AFL level. He started coaching in Queensland after a successful career playing at the lower levels of the game. He watched and learned, eventually impressing the Brisbane club during a stint with Queensland Football League club Windsor–Zillmere. He moved from Brisbane to become a Carlton assistant coach in 1996 and then was appointed the Blues' senior coach when David Parkin retired at the end of the 2000 season. Brittain is a classic example of a coach who has studied the game, its skills, its tactics and its management. You can develop some of these skills through the coaching courses outlined in the preceding section, 'Licensed to Coach'.

FOOTY FLASHBACK

This coach was a Smartie

About 35 years ago, a well-known player complained during a match that he felt listless and could not 'fire up'. He asked his highly respected coach if there was a simple solution, like a pick-me-up tablet. Of course, performance-enhancing drugs are absolutely taboo in football, but the coach handed the player a small red pill and told him to swallow it with a gulp of water. He winked and told the player it would 'work wonders'. The footballer played the game of his life, but later found out that the coach had slipped him a red Smartie. That's clever football psychology.

The Coaches Code of Conduct

The old-fashioned rant-and-rave coach is out of favour. When I played football, coaches verbally abusing players was common, and this was done sometimes through curses, sometimes through insults, sometimes both. There were also instances of coaches asking players to perform tasks well beyond the rules. In the 1960s, for example, most league clubs had players known as 'enforcers'. These players sometimes were in the side only to put a star player from the opposition out of action.

Now, however, coaches follow a code of conduct that frowns on bad language, insulting players and illegal tactics. The code also provides a reference point for clubs, parents, athletes, schools and employers to expect that a coach will demonstrate appropriate standards of behaviour.

In addition to signing the Coaches Code of Conduct as part of the accreditation requirements of the AFL, potential coaches may be required to sign a code of conduct or ethics with their club. Contact the AFL on (03) 9643 1999 for more information.

Of course, coaching juniors at 8 or 9 years of age is vastly different to coaching at AFL level. But if you can't kick, handpass or understand team positions and tactics, you probably aren't yet prepared to teach the youngsters the basics of the game.

Coaching at the junior level necessitates far more skills training than with senior footballers. The skills of the game are generally learned at under-age levels, so the coaches of these teams must be able to impart one-on-one knowledge. They usually teach their young charges how to kick correctly, how to handpass, how to mark, how to tackle and so on. (Refer to Chapters 6 and 7 for information on the skills needed for the game.)

Know your players

Everyone is an individual and deserves individual attention, even when you're coaching a team. A good coach remembers that no two players are the same, and you need to work with each player's strengths and abilities. Twins Chris and Brad Scott, who played for Brisbane, are good examples. Chris was considered slightly more skilled than his twin, and is super-aggressive and a ferocious tackler. Brad's career was slower to develop and he actually played with Hawthorn in 1997, before joining his brother the following year. Brad may not have been quite as talented as Chris, but was a reliable defender whose courage could never be questioned. If you're coaching a young charge who can thump the ball a country mile but has poor ball-handling skills, you want to work on that junior's weakness to make him a better all-round player.

However, coaches also use the knowledge of their players as individuals to mould them into a team by selecting each footballer for the right playing positions. Obviously, a tall youngster is likely to be the team ruckman. But if he's a strong mark overhead and an accurate kick, he may be assigned to play as a key forward. If a particular player is good at running in straight lines, without fear of being bowled over by an opponent, and sticking with her opponent, a defensive position might be the correct role.

Also, a coach needs to know every player's individual temperament. For example, one player may react powerfully and positively to what is euphemistically called 'a rocket up the backside'. Another player may shrivel and lose confidence. The coach must know which players can react positively to criticism and which players lift only when praised.

Know the drills

Coaching also means knowing how to train. Anyone can ask players to run laps or kick the ball to each other from one end to another, but to be a good coach you need to know a variety of training drills and vary them to avoid boredom. (Refer to Chapter 10 for drills that you can incorporate into your coaching routine.)

Even at the AFL level, coaches ask players to walk or run to a different beat at times, sometimes ordering indoor activities or even a light-hearted game of soccer to break the routine.

The intensity of skills training at AFL level is very high. Most AFL footballers have excellent kicking, handballing, marking and tackling skills. Moreover, all of the AFL clubs employ specialist skills coaches to further develop these skills. For example, an AFL player may be an excellent kick and handpasser but not be good taking overhead marks, so he's given special assistance to help him overcome this weakness. At AFL level, nothing is overlooked. Senior AFL coaches generally don't involve themselves in trying to iron out skill problems but, rather, would tell the player of the problem and order him to have specialised training with the skills coach. The AFL coach has much bigger fish to fry (tactics, team development and so on) and has lieutenants to look after the relatively minor aspects.

The beauty of coaching kids

Coaching juniors is a tremendous way to interact with a younger generation, and the joy of teaching juniors the skills of the game can bring a glow to any coach's soul. Some coaches never aspire to taking over at senior level and just want to work with 'the kids'.

For example, former Coburg (Victorian Football Association, now Victorian Football League) champion Ray Jordon coached at junior levels for many years and won a reputation as the best developer of football talent in Australia. All AFL clubs had Under-19 teams until 1991 and Jordon at various times worked with the Richmond, Melbourne and North Melbourne (now Kangaroos) juniors. He developed a number of stars and was largely responsible for turning Melbourne's Jim Stynes into a champion.

Stynes was recruited from Ireland without ever seeing a game of Aussie Rules and started his development in the Melbourne Under-19s under Jordon. A tough taskmaster, Jordon worked on every aspect of Stynes' game and the Irishman went on to win a Brownlow Medal as the fairest and best player in the AFL in 1991. That triumph gave Jordon enormous satisfaction.

In teaching basic skills at the junior level of Aussie Rules, you need not be such a perfectionist, but coaches may want to let parents know what skills the young players need help with so they can practise on their own. Perhaps most importantly, junior-level coaches want to ensure that players don't develop any bad habits in their basic skills but learn the skills correctly from the start.

The Role of the Coach

AFL clubs fall over themselves to secure the best coaches, and offer big bucks to those who prove worth their efforts. Some have incomes well in excess of $500,000 because they know the game inside out and work hard for the benefit of the team. But, even if you're just a volunteer coach for a small under-age team, you need to be dedicated and keep an eye on the big picture.

The work of a coach is like an iceberg — 90 per cent of it's unseen by the football public. If you wish to coach — at any level — you must be prepared to work hard. Even at the junior level, the workload can be demanding. For example, most junior clubs train twice a week, say every Tuesday and Thursday, from about 5 pm. This training can last for two hours, depending on the age group and the level at which the team is training. At the semi-professional level, training may be three or even four nights a week, with additional responsibilities, such as maintaining players' body-weight levels, ensuring they adhere to dietary demands and providing extra weight and skills training.

Tactics in days gone by

Coaches before the 1970s had a very limited perspective on tactics. Football was far less professional than it is today and coaches worked only part time, often for low wages. They didn't have the time or the opportunity to study rival strengths and weaknesses in any great depth. Rather, coaches told their players that a certain rival may be a poor tackler or a dangerous player when left unguarded, and pretty much left it at that. Some coaches may have shifted players around to improve team performance or set players specific tasks to restrict opposition players, but, by and large, tactics were not considered as important as knowing where to place players for maximum benefit.

Then, in the 1970 grand final, Carlton coach Ron Barassi realised he'd have to do something drastic if the Blues were to overcome the 44-point half-time lead held by Collingwood. Barassi ordered his players to handpass at every opportunity. He realised that the deficit was so large that his team had to move the ball as quickly as possible to give themselves time to haul in the margin. Barassi's tactics worked: The Blues won by 10 points. Ever since, coaches have been trying to hoodwink each other with tactics.

Coaching at AFL level

All coaches acknowledge that the hard work for a season starts immediately at the end of the previous season. Even as Brisbane celebrated its 2002 AFL premiership, coach Leigh Matthews talked of planning for 2003. When West Coast won the 2006 premiership, coach John Worsfold said his immediate thoughts were of how to prepare for the following season. At AFL level, coaching starts with the pre-season trade period each October, when players and draft positions are swapped. Some players may have retired and others may want to move to another club. In November, the AFL holds its annual draft, with a far less important draft held in December. Then, and only then, do AFL coaches know which players they'll have available for the new season.

At lower levels, recruits often come and go through a season, and rules are far less formal because these competitions are usually amateur or, at best, only semi-professional. When a coach has most of his squad assembled, the hard work starts. The coach prepares his pre-season training program — at

AFL level, this is truly gut-wrenching. At the elite levels, the coach devises the program with the advice of fitness experts, including dietitians. At lower levels, there is still a lot of work to be done and it's common in Australia for entire team squads to run together along a beach, through streets or up hills to strengthen the legs for the hard running each game requires.

Devising and conveying tactics

Some of the modern tactics involve set-plays. Coaches devise playing instructions for particular situations and the players must carry out the coach's instructions. There are far too many set-plays to describe even a handful, and coaches are always coming up with new ones. The most basic is the ruckman tapping the ball to a midfielder at centre bounce, and that midfielder then handpassing to a teammate running past.

Specific tactics also exist for particular game situations. For example, in his first year with the Swans in 1996, Sydney's Rodney Eade developed a brilliant system that became known as 'the flood'. He instructed his players that, when the opposition had possession of the ball, they should run back to 'flood' their rivals' forward line and congest play. Then, when the Swans won possession, they would 'flood' forward to create opportunities for themselves.

This tactic required great levels of fitness, but the Swans were so successful that they made the 1996 grand final for the first time since 1945. They were eventually defeated by North Melbourne (now the Kangaroos), but almost every other club also started using Eade's 'flood' tactics. So much so, in fact, that its inventor was caught out himself in 2002. Playing lowly St Kilda, which was missing 11 senior players through injury, the Swans ran into what was called a 'super-flood'. The Saints had almost every player run to the Swans' forward line to block almost every scoring opportunity. The Saints relied on quick breakaways themselves and, despite the odds, led for almost the entire match. The Swans managed to overcome St Kilda's tactics only in the final few minutes and scrambled a draw.

Other common tactics include transferring the ball from one side of the ground to the other where a teammate has broken clear, or having a big player, usually a ruckman, fill a position in front of the opposition's star key forward to help hinder his leading for the ball (refer to Chapter 7 for more on leading and running skills) and force him to overcome two rivals.

Adelaide coach Neil Craig and Sydney counterpart Paul Roos also introduced 'tempo' football, slowing down the game to suit their teams' need. For example, if Adelaide or Sydney's rivals have kicked three quick goals, the Crow or Swan players then deliberately slow down the tempo of the game so they can draw breath and avoid being blown away. This tactic has long been used in basketball and it's no coincidence that both Craig and Roos have studied other sports and codes.

This very tactic was used against the Crows in one match with Richmond at Telstra Dome. Tiger coach Terry Wallace set out to frustrate the Crows with man-on-man tactics and to reduce the pace of the game. The Crows became frustrated with Richmond's mainly negative matches and, in a low-scoring game, Richmond triumphed.

Most coaches have their own special tricks as well. For example, former Kangaroos coach Denis Pagan (who later coached Carlton) devised a system specific to his team's capabilities. Because he had one of the best centre half-forwards the game has seen in Wayne Carey, he instructed his players to kick long into an open area on the forward line for Carey to run into to win possession. This tactic was dubbed 'Pagan's Paddock', and it helped the Roos win the 1996 and 1999 premierships.

AFL coaches spend countless hours studying the opposition, and most have back-up staff whose job it is to provide video replays of rivals. These video experts often take note of particular player quirks, team tactics and even set-plays. Every coach knows which players are weak on the left or right foot, which have trouble handpassing to the left or right and which are likely to succumb to pressure. Everything is noted.

Players are even instructed on where to run in a match, ready for a teammate to deliver the ball to a particular position. There also are set-pieces, especially close to goal. Two classic examples were displayed during the 2005 finals series. Sydney ruckman Jason Ball was drilled to tap the ball over his head for a smaller teammate to win possession close to goal. Ball did this in the second semi-final against Geelong, and teammate Nick Davis was the beneficiary, kicking the winning goal for the Swans with just a few seconds to play. Then, in the grand final, Ball repeated the set-play, this time tapping the ball to Amon Buchanan, who goaled to give the Swans the lead over West Coast. Sydney held on to this lead over the final 12 minutes of play, so this set-piece was worth all the planning and practice.

Unfortunately, junior and amateur coaches don't have the luxury of professional videos (though taking your own digital videos to study is a good idea if you've got the gear), back-up staff or the time to practise set-pieces, and therefore must study the opposition through actual game play. A good coach picks up rival strengths and weaknesses through observation, and plans his tactics accordingly.

A tactical move helped Adelaide win the 1997 grand final against St Kilda. Adelaide coach Malcolm Blight switched midfielder Darren Jarman to full-forward to take advantage of his speed against St Kilda full-back Jamie Shanahan. Jarman was far too nimble for the much bigger Shanahan and kicked five goals in the final quarter and finished the match with six goals. Adelaide won by 31 points, after trailing by 11 points at half time, and Blight was hailed a football genius.

Coaching on the Internet

As with any topic, the Net has a range of useful sites on coaching. For a start, check out the AFL Web site (www.afl.com.au) — go to Development in the top menu bar, and then click on Coaching. Other coaching sites dedicated to Aussie Rules include:

✔ **Coach AFL** (www.coachafl.com): This Web site provides coaching advice for coaches and players, as well as research and other information, including in-depth interviews with professional coaches and players. The site also has a coaches' forum, and one of the researchers is former Melbourne coach Mark Riley.

✔ **Swooper Coach** (www.swooper.com.au): In order to get the training aids on offer — which include audiovisual and printable material — you need to become a registered member. After you register, you can access the Australian Football World Coaching Manual online at any time. This Web site features former star Richmond half-forward John Northey, who was known as 'Swooper' because of his habit of — yes, you guessed it — swooping on the ball. Northey, who played with Richmond from 1963 to 1967, coached Sydney, Melbourne, Brisbane and Richmond.

Part IV
The Australian Football League

Glenn Lumsden

'I take it he was one of their better players.'

In this part . . .

Interested in the 16 AFL clubs, their histories and their heroes? Turn to Chapter 13, where you'll find a comprehensive listing of each team. Of course, Aussie Rules itself has a rich and colourful history. In Chapter 14, I detail this history, including the game's international influences and diverse background. I also cover how the game is now controlled and the structure of the AFL.

And to round the part off, you can find details of the various awards on offer in Chapter 15 and information on the fields of dreams — the venues for AFL football — in Chapter 16.

Chapter 13

Club Cultures and Stars

*T*he AFL is made up of 16 clubs with at least one club in each mainland state of Australia. Many of the clubs were original members of the League in 1897, whereas the other clubs joined the competition over the past century. Despite the difference in longevity with the League, no club is regarded as being more important or more powerful than any other club — except for bragging rights.

The 16 clubs have individual traditions and cultures, with a number of the clubs being more conservative than other clubs. For example, whereas certain clubs revere individual heroes, other clubs prefer to celebrate team glory. At the same time, some clubs have a rich tradition of premiership success, whereas others have yet to win even a single premiership. Regardless, supporters love the clubs they barrack for and would rather consider living on Mars than switching loyalties to another team.

This chapter looks at the teams that the avid fans follow, team by team in alphabetical order. I also name some of the stars of each team — past and present — along with their achievements and awards (see Chapter 15 for details of some of the AFL awards and Appendix A for lists of winners).

Adelaide

Adelaide is one of the AFL's youngest clubs, but in the past decade the club has proved to be more than capable of trouncing the opposition, and has a reputation for being a ferocious competitor with tremendous pride in the team's performance.

- **Club colours:** Navy blue guernsey with red and gold hoops; navy blue shorts; and navy blue socks with red and gold hoops
- **Founded:** 1991
- **Home ground:** AAMI Stadium
- **Nickname:** The Crows
- **Premierships:** 1997 and 1998

The Adelaide club was formed in 1991 as part of the expansion of the AFL to become a truly national competition. The club was formed under the auspices of the local South Australian league and from the start has been extremely competitive, coming close to competing in the 1993 grand final after just three years in the competition.

In 1997, the Crows achieved the ultimate reward for the club's determination to succeed by defeating St Kilda in the grand final. The following year, the club won a second premiership by defeating North Melbourne (now Kangaroos) in the grand final.

Adelaide supporters are regarded as among the most vocal and parochial in the national competition. Don't believe me? Go and watch a Crows match at AAMI Stadium — but beware of wearing anything that even resembles the opposition's colours unless you're up for a challenge.

When the Adelaide club was launched prior to the start of the 1991 season, it was universally accepted in South Australia that the club should take the official state colours of navy blue, red and gold. Had the Adelaide club been established before World War II, however, the picture would look a lot different because the state's colours were originally chocolate brown and turquoise.

Stone the crows!

For more than a century, South Australians have been referred to as Crow-eaters. The phrase for the questionable old culinary habit of eating the big black birds was, fortunately, abbreviated to the Crows as a natural choice at the time the club was founded.

Crows, by the way, are found on every continent except for South America and Antarctica and, as Adelaide fans well know, crows are one of the most intelligent species of birds (so, go crow about that!).

Star players to have represented Adelaide include:

- ✔ **Brett Burton:** Known as 'The Birdman' because of his ability to leap high for marks, Burton started with Adelaide in 1999 and quickly established himself as a Crow hero.

- ✔ **Simon Goodwin:** One of the best midfielders in the competition, he started with Adelaide in 1997 and played his 200th game during the 2007 season.

- ✔ **Ben Hart:** A dashing defender who started with the club in 1992 and played in the Crows' 1997–1998 premiership sides. He retired in 2006 and played a club record of 311 games (since broken by Mark Ricciuto).

- ✔ **Andrew Jarman:** A hard-working centreman with genuine flair. He played 110 games with the Crows from 1991 to 1996.

- ✔ **Darren Jarman:** Andrew's brother, a highly skilled *utility* (a player who can fill many different roles in a team, playing in any number of positions). He started with Hawthorn in 1991 and moved to the Crows in 1996, playing in premiership sides with both clubs.

- ✔ **Chris McDermott:** Adelaide's first captain, who played 117 games with the Crows from 1991 to 1996. A hard, tough midfielder.

- ✔ **Tony McGuinness:** A quick, skilled rover who started with Footscray (now Western Bulldogs) before moving to Adelaide in 1991. He played 113 games with the Crows to 1996.

- ✔ **Andrew McLeod:** Regarded as one of the best players in the AFL, McLeod is blessed with sensational skills. He made his debut in 1995 and is a regular 'All-Australian' selection (for which a panel of former players and experts choose the best players of the season). He won Norm Smith Medals as best player on the ground in both the 1997 and 1998 Adelaide grand final wins.

- ✔ **Tony Modra:** One of the Crows' most popular players, Modra was famous for his huge leap and goal-kicking ability. He played 118 games with the Crows from 1992 to 1998.

- ✔ **Shaun Rehn:** A hugely talented ruckman whose career was hampered by three knee reconstructions. He played 134 games for the Crows from 1991 to 2000 before moving to Hawthorn.

Lleyton Hewitt's other love

One of Adelaide's greatest fans is Wimbledon tennis champion Lleyton Hewitt, who was raised in this city. Hewitt scans the results and news of the Crows wherever he is in the world, and the club sent him its congratulations after he won the 2002 Wimbledon singles crown. His father, Glyn, played in the AFL (then VFL) with the Richmond club.

- **Mark Ricciuto:** Regarded as one of the toughest players in the AFL, Ricciuto made his debut with the Crows in 1993 and was appointed club captain in 2001. He held this position until his retirement at the end of the 2007 season. His round-22 game against Collingwood at Telstra Dome was his 311th for the Crows and equalled the record of 311 held by Ben Hart. Ricciuto, who went on to break the record the following week, made football history in 2003 when he became the first Adelaide player to win a Brownlow Medal. He tied with Sydney's Adam Goodes and Collingwood's Nathan Buckley.

- **Nigel Smart:** A gifted defender who was the epitome of reliability. Made his debut in 1991 and played 278 games until his retirement in 2004.

To find out more about Adelaide, check out their Web site at www.afc.com.au.

Brisbane Lions

Brisbane Football Club was launched in 1987 and was known as the Bears. Brisbane plodded up and down the Australian football ladder over the years but, since making the finals series in 1995 and then merging with the Fitzroy Lions in 1997, the team has become a force to be reckoned with by all comers. The Brisbane Lions won consecutive premierships from 2001 to 2003 and then was gallant in defeat by Port Adelaide in the 2004 grand final.

- **Club colours:** Maroon guernsey with a gold lion emblem on the chest, a blue yoke and gold and white trim; maroon shorts; and maroon socks with gold and blue hoops below the knee
- **Founded:** 1987
- **Home ground:** The 'Gabba (Brisbane Cricket Ground)
- **Nickname:** The Lions
- **Premierships:** 2001, 2002, 2003

The Brisbane club was founded in 1987 as an early expansion of the national competition, and used the Carrara Oval on the Gold Coast as the team's home ground. Originally known as the Brisbane Bears, the team struggled so much on and off the field that the team became known as the Bad-News Bears, finishing on the bottom of the ladder in both the 1990 and 1991 seasons.

Careful building of the team and a move to the 'Gabba ground in Brisbane helped to lift the club from the cellar and the Bears made the finals series in 1995. Since then, the club has been regarded as one of the most consistent sides in the competition.

More than a koala can bear!

The Brisbane club was originally named the Brisbane Bears for alliteration purposes. However, the club's original guernsey featured a stylised koala and the media quickly pointed out at the 1986 launch of the club that the koala isn't a bear.

On merging with Fitzroy for the start of the 1997 season, Brisbane adopted the Lions as the team's nickname. Had the clubs merged earlier, however, Brisbane may well have been known by another name, because Fitzroy was originally known as the Maroons and then in the 1940s and 1950s as the Gorillas.

In 1997, the club merged with the Melbourne-based Fitzroy Lions to become the Brisbane Lions and inherit Fitzroy's rich tradition. (Fitzroy was an original member of the Victorian Football League in 1897 and won eight premierships — the last in 1944 — before falling on hard times in the 1990s.)

When the Brisbane club was founded in 1987 as the Bears, the club's colours were gold and magenta. After merging with the Fitzroy Lions in 1997, Brisbane adopted a guernsey design similar to the one used by Fitzroy, with the exception that the large FFC (Fitzroy Football Club) logo and small gold lion on the chest were replaced with the larger lion emblem. Over the years, the Fitzroy club colours changed numerous times from maroon and gold to dark maroon and navy blue to dark maroon, navy blue and white and, finally, in the 1970s, to light maroon, blue and gold.

Star players to have represented the Brisbane Lions include:

- **Jason Akermanis:** A very quick midfielder with tremendous natural flair. Made his debut in 1995 and played in the 2001–2003 Lions premiership sides. Won the Brownlow Medal in 2001. Moved to the Western Bulldogs in 2007.

- **Simon Black:** Dashing winger–midfielder who won the 2002 Brownlow Medal and played in the 2001–2003 premiership sides. Made his debut in 1998.

- **Jonathan Brown:** Regarded as the best centre half-forward in the competition. Big, strong and fearless, he played in the 2001–2003 flag sides. A superb mark and a long kick. Started with Brisbane in 2000 and his father, Brian, played with the Fitzroy Lions (1976–1981).

- **Justin Leppitsch:** Brilliant key position defender who excelled as centre half-back. Strong mark and a triple premiership player (2001–2003). Made his debut in 1993.

- **Alastair Lynch:** A Tasmanian who started his career with Fitzroy in 1988. Moved to Brisbane in 1994 and was regarded as one of the best goal kickers in the competition. Also a triple premiership player, he retired at the end of the 2004 season.

- **Michael Voss:** A hugely talented midfielder with incredible strength, Voss won a Brownlow Medal in 1996 and led the Lions to premiership glory from 2001 to 2003.

Find out more about the Brisbane Lions at their Web site at www.lions.com.au.

Carlton

The Carlton club has a rich tradition of success and refuses to tolerate anything resembling failure. As proof of the club's determination to be the leader of the pack from the day the League came into being, Carlton is tied with Essendon for winning the most premiership games, with 16 apiece.

- **Club colours:** Dark navy blue guernsey with a large white CFC (Carlton Football Club) monogram on the chest; dark navy blue shorts; and dark navy blue socks
- **Founded:** 1864
- **Home ground:** Princess Park is the club's training and administrative base, and home games are played at the MCG or Telstra Dome.
- **Nickname:** The Blues
- **Premierships:** 1906, 1907, 1908, 1914, 1915, 1938, 1945, 1947, 1968, 1970, 1972, 1979, 1981, 1982, 1987 and 1995

The Blues won consecutive flags in 1906, 1907 and 1908, and then won premierships on a regular basis. The club has also boasted a swag of the greatest players the game has seen, including:

- **Craig Bradley:** Retired at the end of the 2002 season after making his debut in 1986. A brilliant midfielder, he captained the Blues from 1998 to 2001.
- **Horrie Clover:** One of the best centre half-forwards of all time, Clover played 147 games for Carlton from 1920 to 1931.
- **Bert Deacon:** Was Carlton's first Brownlow Medallist, in 1947. A champion centre half-back, he played 106 games with the Blues from 1942 to 1951 and later served Carlton as club secretary.

- ✔ **Bruce Doull:** A great Carlton favourite and a magnificent defender over 356 games from 1969 to 1986.

- ✔ **Brendan Fevola:** The enigmatic Fevola won the John Coleman Medal as leading AFL goal kicker in 2006 after starting with the Blues in 1999.

- ✔ **Alex Jesaulenko:** Regarded as one of the most skilful players of all time, Jesaulenko could play in almost any position and is the only Carlton player to kick 100 goals or more in a season (115 in 1970). He was captain-coach of Carlton's 1979 premiership side.

- ✔ **Stephen Kernahan:** A Carlton legend who topped the club goal kicking every year from 1986 to 1996. A champion key position forward, Kernahan captained the Blues from 1987 to 1997.

- ✔ **Anthony Koutoufides:** 'The Golden Greek' started with the Blues in 1992 and quickly established himself as one of the most athletic big men in the competition. Although 190 centimetres tall, he played mainly as a midfielder, but could also hold down a key position. Captained the Blues from 2004 to 2006 and retired in 2007.

- ✔ **John Nicholls:** An extremely solid ruckman, Nicholls played 328 games with Carlton from 1957 to 1974 and was captain-coach of the Blues' 1972 premiership team.

- ✔ **Stephen Silvagni:** Son of another Carlton favourite in Sergio, Silvagni is regarded as one of the game's greatest full-backs. He made his debut in 1985 and played 312 games with the Blues until his retirement in 2001.

- ✔ **Greg Williams:** a master centreman with unsurpassed handball skills, Williams joined Carlton after stints with Geelong and Sydney and won a Brownlow Medal with the Blues in 1994.

The Carlton club was founded as an adjunct of the Carlton Cricket Club in 1864, using a scrap of gravel-pocked scrubland on the brow of a hill near the corner of Royal Parade and Gatehouse Street for the team's first matches. Carlton enjoyed considerable success in the early Challenge Cup competitions, and a later series of triumphs in the Victorian Football Association competition won the club an invitation to join the Victorian Football League in the 1897 breakaway competition.

Carlton originally wore navy blue guernseys with a white yoke. However, the yokes were usually made of leather and turned orange in the wash. The club adopted the famous CFC (Carlton Football Club) logo early in the 20th century and, for one season in the 1920s, included white trim on the collars of the team's guernseys.

Visit the Carlton Football Club's Web site at www.carltonfc.com.au for up-to-date information and news.

Singing the Blues

For many decades, Carlton has been known as the Blues because of the club's traditional dark navy blue guernseys. However, in Carlton's earliest years, the club was known as the Butchers because the team at that time wore navy blue and white hooped socks (in days gone by, no self-respecting butcher was seen without a boldly striped blue-and-white apron tied smartly over his working whites).

For a brief time in the 1940s, a number of people referred to Carlton as the Cockies because of a famous cockatoo, which sat in the grandstand and loudly cheered for Carlton.

Collingwood

The Collingwood club was one of the founding members of the Victorian Football League in 1897. By 2002, the team had won 14 premierships, eclipsed only by the Carlton and Essendon clubs.

- **Club colours:** Black guernsey with white vertical stripes on the torso and horizontal stripes on the sleeves; black shorts with white trim; and black socks
- **Founded:** 1892
- **Home ground:** The training base and club headquarters are located at the Lexus Centre in Olympic Park. Home games are played at the MCG or Telstra Dome.
- **Nickname:** The Magpies
- **Premierships:** 1902, 1903, 1910, 1917, 1919, 1927, 1928, 1929, 1930, 1935, 1936, 1953, 1958 and 1990

The Collingwood club was founded in 1892 at a meeting at the Grace Darling Hotel, Collingwood, with the specific intention of applying to join the Victorian Football Association. Most of the football fans at the historic meeting belonged to the junior Britannia Football Club. The crowd agreed at the meeting to form a club to supersede the junior club and that the new club was to be called Collingwood.

The Collingwood club enjoyed immediate success and became one of the original members of the Victorian Football League in 1897. Known as the Magpies, the club won a league premiership in 1902 and quickly established themselves as one of the power clubs of the competition.

Birdwatching

Collingwood has always been known as the Magpies, partly because of the club's signature black-and-white colours and partly because of the presence of so many magpies at nearby Dight's Falls.

Trivia buffs may care to note that the good old Aussie magpie is unrelated to the species of magpie found in North America and Eurasia . . . and a good thing too, as those feathered friends are members of the crow family!

The mid-1920s saw Collingwood soar to the top of the ladder and the club played in both the 1925 and 1926 grand finals, losing first to Geelong and then, the next year, to Melbourne.

The following year, the club established a still-standing record when the team won four consecutive premierships from 1927 to 1930. The Magpies of this era boasted stars of the quality of Gordon and Syd Coventry and Harry and Albert Collier. Later champions include:

- **Nathan Buckley:** A marvellous midfielder regarded as the heartbeat of Collingwood almost from the time he joined the Magpies from Brisbane in 1994. He won a Brownlow Medal in 2003 and was appointed club captain in 1999. Won the Norm Smith Medal as best player on the ground in the Magpies' 2002 grand final loss to Brisbane.

- **Peter Daicos:** One of the most magically gifted footballers to have played the game. A forward with great goal sense, Daicos played 250 games with Collingwood from 1979 to 1993.

- **Peter McKenna:** Hugely popular full-forward with a cult following. McKenna kicked 838 goals with the Magpies from 1965 to 1975, with a season's best tally of 143 goals in 1970.

- **Peter Moore:** Richly talented ruckman who could also fill a key position. Won a Brownlow Medal with Collingwood in 1979.

- **Jack Regan:** Known as 'the prince of full-backs', Regan was a marvellous defender who played 196 games for the Magpies from 1930 to 1946.

- **Lou Richards:** The 'clown prince' of football who captained Collingwood to the 1953 premiership as a champion rover and later became the game's best loved commentator.

- **Bob Rose:** Champion rover who played 152 games with the Magpies from 1946 to 1955.

- **Len Thompson:** Giant ruckman who won a Brownlow Medal in 1972 and later became a club committee man.

- ✔ **Ron Todd:** Prolific goal kicker who shocked Collingwood by walking out in 1940 to play with VFA club Williamstown.
- ✔ **Marcus Whelan:** Brilliant centreman who won a Brownlow Medal in 1939.

Unlike many other clubs that have played chameleon over the years, Collingwood has always worn black and white stripes; however, the club from which the team was founded, Britannia, wore the patriotic colours of red, white and blue.

For more information on the Collingwood Football Club, visit their Web site at www.collingwoodfc.com.au.

Essendon

The Essendon club started out on top by winning the Victorian Football League's first season in 1897 and has maintained the team's strength over the years, right up to 2000, when the team yet again took out Australian football's top honours.

- ✔ **Club colours:** Black guernsey with a red sash; black shorts with red trim; and black socks with red hoops
- ✔ **Founded:** 1873
- ✔ **Home ground:** Essendon Recreation Reserve (known as Windy Hill). Essendon uses this venue as its training and administrative base, but plays its home games at the MCG and the Telstra Dome.
- ✔ **Nickname:** The Bombers (sometimes also known as the Dons)
- ✔ **Premierships:** 1897, 1901, 1911, 1912, 1923, 1924, 1942, 1946, 1949, 1950, 1962, 1965, 1984, 1985, 1993 and 2000

The Essendon club was founded in 1873 at a meeting of football fans with horseracing and agricultural ties at the Ascot Vale home of Robert McCracken. The club enjoyed immediate success and was a founding member of the Victorian Football Association in 1878 and then the Victorian Football League in 1897.

The club's name comes from the area where the team was founded, but games were played for decades at the East Melbourne Cricket Ground (adjacent to the Jolimont railway yards). In 1921, the club moved to the Essendon Recreation Reserve, which is known as Windy Hill.

Donning a new nickname

The Essendon club was once known as the 'Same Old' because fans often said 'the same old' team was up there winning the flag. The club is also sometimes now known as the Dons.

Since World War II, the club has been known as the Bombers because of the close proximity of Essendon Airport to Essendon's former home ground of Windy Hill, which is still the club's training and administrative headquarters.

Essendon won the inaugural Victorian Football League premiership of 1897 and has tasted success on a regular basis ever since. Essendon's greatest era was from 1946 to 1951, when it played in six consecutive grand finals for three premierships. Essendon champions over the years include:

- ✔ **Jack Clarke:** Champion centreman who played 263 games with Essendon from 1951 to 1967 and later coached the club.

- ✔ **John Coleman:** One of the greatest full-forwards of all time. He starred from 1949 to 1954 but had his sensational career ended by a serious knee injury.

- ✔ **Terry Daniher:** Brilliant key position player who captained the Bombers to the 1984 and 1985 premierships.

- ✔ **James Hird:** Brilliant utility who was appointed club captain in 1998 and won a Brownlow Medal in 1996. Played in the 1993 and 2000 Essendon premiership wins and won the 2000 Norm Smith Medal as best player on the ground in the grand final win over Melbourne. One of the game's greatest champions, Hird retired at the end of the 2007 season.

- ✔ **Bill Hutchison:** Champion rover who won Brownlow Medals in 1952 and 1953.

- ✔ **Matthew Lloyd:** A great full-forward who is idolised by Essendon fans. Joined the team in 1995 and was appointed club captain in 2006.

- ✔ **Simon Madden:** Champion ruckman who played a club record of 378 games with Essendon from 1974 to 1992.

- ✔ **Graham Moss:** Western Australian ruckman who won a Brownlow Medal in 1976.

- ✔ **Dick Reynolds:** Essendon's greatest identity, who won three Brownlow Medals (1934, 1937 and 1938) and coached the club from 1939 to 1960.

- ✔ **Tim Watson:** Brilliant ruck-rover who captained the club from 1989 to 1991 and was idolised by Bomber fans.

Essendon proudly boasts that the team has always worn a black guernsey with a red sash. However, during the mid-1970s, the team broadened the sash and, for a brief period, switched from black to red shorts. The Bombers then broadened the sash even further as an alternative guernsey from 2007. This sash is so wide that the guernsey is more red than black.

For more information on the Essendon Football Club, check out their Web site at www.bombersfc.com.au.

Fremantle

The Fremantle club was the second team from Western Australia to join the AFL after West Coast. One of the 'babies' of the AFL, Fremantle debuted in the Australian football national competition in 1995.

- ✔ **Club colours:** Purple guernsey with one red and one green chest panel separated by a white anchor; purple shorts; and purple socks with green, red and white hoops below the knee
- ✔ **Founded:** 1995
- ✔ **Home ground:** Subiaco Oval
- ✔ **Nickname:** The Dockers
- ✔ **Premierships:** None — so far!

The Fremantle Dockers were founded under the auspices of the West Australian Football League. Since the beginning, the team has struggled to rise up the rungs of the AFL ladder past 12th position, which the team reached in 1997 and 2000. Fremantle fans needn't despair, though, as North Melbourne (now the Kangaroos) took 50 years to achieve premiership success and the Dockers believe the team can achieve stardom in a lot less time than that.

Launching the Dockers

The Fremantle club held a public forum to decide on the team's nickname before entering the AFL in 1995. The suggestions put forward by the public included the Sharks, the Pirates and a number of other names with a nautical theme.

After much debate, club officials settled on the Dockers tag because of Fremantle's heritage as a seaport and because dockers (wharf labourers) have a reputation for being hard working and making sure the job is done well and on time.

Quality players who have represented the Dockers include:

- **Ben Allan:** A hard-working midfielder who was one of Fremantle's earliest stars and captained the club from 1995 to 1996.

- **Peter Bell:** A courageous rover who was club captain from 2002 to 2006. Bell won club best and fairest awards in 2001, 2003 and 2004. A great leader.

- **Troy Cook:** Hard-hitting midfielder who won club best and fairest in 2001. He was with the Dockers from 2000 and retired at the end of the 2007 season.

- **Jeff Farmer:** A lively forward, Farmer started his career with Melbourne, but joined Fremantle in 2002. A Docker favourite.

- **Peter Mann:** Ruckman and key position player who captained the Dockers in 1997 and 1998.

- **Tony Modra:** Flamboyant full-forward who earlier had been a champion Adelaide goal kicker.

- **Shane Parker:** A solid and reliable key position defender, he was the first Docker to play more than 200 games for the club.

- **Matthew Pavlich:** Started his AFL career with Fremantle in 2000 and quickly established himself as one of the best centre half-forwards in the game. Appointed club captain in 2007.

The Fremantle Dockers chose purple as the team's basic colour because no other AFL team uses this colour. The red and green panels on the team's guernseys represent the port (red) and starboard (green) navigation lights used on ships and harbour entrance beacons.

For more news on the Fremantle Football Club, visit their Web site at www.fremantlefc.com.au.

Geelong

One of the oldest football clubs in Australia, Geelong holds the record for winning 26 consecutive games without being defeated. The team's finest years were in the early 1950s, but Geelong fans were buoyed in 2007 when it won 15 games straight.

- ✔ **Club colours:** Navy blue guernsey with white hoops; navy blue shorts with white trim; and navy blue socks with white hoops
- ✔ **Founded:** 1859
- ✔ **Home ground:** Skilled Stadium (formerly Kardinia Park)
- ✔ **Nickname:** The Cats
- ✔ **Premierships:** 1925, 1931, 1937, 1951, 1952, 1963 and 2007

The Geelong club was founded in 1859 by members of the Corio Cricket Club and became an instant force in football. Original members of the Victorian Football Association, Geelong won a hat trick of premierships from 1878 to 1880 and again from 1882 to 1884 before becoming inaugural members of the Victorian Football League in 1897.

The first League premiership won by the Cats was in 1925 and then the team enjoyed a truly golden era in 1951 and 1952, when Geelong won two premierships. Under the coaching of the legendary Reg Hickey during the 1951 to 1952 era, the team went 26 games without a defeat — an achievement that's still a League record. The Cats had competed in four grand finals since the 1960s (1989, 1992, 1994 and 1995) before a resounding premiership win in 2007, the first since 1963.

Over the years, the Geelong club has signed on several of the great champions, including in the early years Henry Young and Peter Burns. In later times, Geelong's stars of the game have included:

- ✔ **Gary Ablett Junior:** A wonderfully talented midfielder and forward who joined the Cats in 2002.
- ✔ **Gary Ablett Senior:** One of the greatest players the game has seen, he started with Hawthorn, but became a Geelong champion. Started as a winger, but developed into an outstanding full-forward after crossing to Geelong. He played just six games with Hawthorn in 1982, and 242 with Geelong from 1984 to 1996. Known to Geelong fans as 'God' because of his freakish ability.

- **Jimmy Bartel:** Brilliant midfielder who won the 2007 Brownlow Medal and played in the Cats' premiership side that season.
- **Paul Couch:** Champion centreman who won a Brownlow Medal in 1989.
- **Bob Davis:** Great club identity who was a star half-forward in the 1950s and was non-playing coach of the 1963 Cats premiership side.
- **Graham 'Polly' Farmer:** Champion Western Australian ruckman who became a Cats legend in the 1960s.
- **Fred Flanagan:** Brilliant centre half-forward who captained Geelong to the 1951 and 1952 flags.
- **Bill Goggin:** Champion rover of the 1960s and later coached the Cats.
- **Edward 'Carji' Greeves:** Centreman famous as the first Brownlow Medal winner (1924).
- **Reg Hickey:** Brilliant defender who was captain and coach of the 1937 Cats flag side and later was non-playing coach of the 1951 and 1952 flag sides.
- **Gary Hocking:** Hard-hitting utility who played 274 games with the Cats from 1987 to 2001.
- **Alistair Lord:** Brilliant centreman who won a Brownlow Medal in 1962.
- **Ian Nankervis:** Played a record 325 games with the Cats from 1967 to 1983 and was a wonderfully reliable back pocket.
- **John 'Sam' Newman:** One of the game's most colourful characters, he was a top ruckman and centre half-forward who played 300 games for Geelong from 1964 to 1980. Now one of the game's most popular media identities.
- **Peter Riccardi:** Speedy winger who played 288 games with the Cats from 1992 to 2006.
- **Bernie Smith:** Dashing back pocket who won a Brownlow Medal in 1951.
- **Doug Wade:** Solid full-forward who topped the club goal kicking 11 times from 1961 to 1972, missing out only in 1965.

FOOTY FLASHBACK

Top Cats

The city of Geelong was regarded as the 'pivot' of Victoria in the 19th century. As a result, the football club was known as the Pivotonians — until fate intervened. Legend has it that in a 1923 match Geelong was trailing behind the opposition when suddenly a black cat walked across the Corio Oval turf and the club immediately took on the new identity.

Geelong has always worn the team's signature colours of navy blue and white. Situated close to the sea, the blue is symbolic of the water and the white represents the ever-present seagulls.

To find out more about the Geelong Football Club, visit their Web site at www.gfc.com.au.

Hawthorn

The Hawthorn club joined the Victorian Football League in 1925, but didn't make the grade as a formidable team until the 1960s. After winning four premierships in the 1960s and 1970s, Hawthorn was regarded as the team to beat throughout most of the 1980s.

- **Club colours:** Brown guernsey with gold vertical stripes on the front and back; brown shorts with gold trim; and brown socks with gold hoops
- **Founded:** 1873
- **Home ground:** Glenferrie Oval was the Hawks' training and administrative base until 2006, when it moved its headquarters to the old and redeveloped VFL Park, Waverley. The club plays its home games at the MCG and the Telstra Dome.
- **Nickname:** The Hawks
- **Premierships:** 1961, 1971, 1976, 1978, 1983, 1986, 1988, 1989 and 1991

The Hawthorn club was founded in 1873 as a junior team known as Booroondara. The team's record was so insignificant that the club didn't even bother to apply to join the senior Victorian Football Association or Victorian Football League competitions for many years.

In the early 1900s, the club became known as Hawthorn, becoming linked with the Hawthorn Cricket Club, and was admitted to the Victorian Football Association in 1914.

In 1923, Hawthorn made the finals for the first time, and the club's officials then agitated to join the league as a club representing Melbourne's eastern suburbs. The bid was successful and Hawthorn joined the league in 1925; however, the team endured years of failure and humiliation until legendary coach and former club captain John Kennedy guided the Hawks to the 1961 flag.

Hawthorn has remained a power club of the competition ever since that first premiership and the Hawks team has produced many champions, including:

- **Graham Arthur:** Clever half-forward who was Hawthorn's first premiership captain, in 1961.
- **Dermott Brereton:** Brilliantly flamboyant centre half-forward who helped inspire the Hawks to the 1989 premiership after being injured early in the grand final.
- **Shane Crawford:** Dashing midfielder who won a Brownlow Medal in 1999 and was club captain from that year until 2004. Has been playing with Hawthorn since 1993.
- **Peter Crimmins:** Classy rover who captained the club from 1974 to 1975 before tragically succumbing to cancer.
- **Robert DiPierdomenico:** Ferocious winger who won a Brownlow Medal in 1986.
- **Jason Dunstall:** Champion full-forward who kicked 1,254 goals in 269 matches from 1978 to 1993.
- **Peter Hudson:** Champion full-forward who kicked 150 goals (equalling Bob Pratt's League record) in 1971.
- **Peter Knights:** High-marking centre half-back who played 264 games from 1985 to 1998.
- **Leigh Matthews:** One of the greatest players of all time, Matthews could rove or play in a key position. Captained the Hawks from 1981 to 1985 and later coached Collingwood and Brisbane to premierships.
- **David Parkin:** Dashing back pocket who captained Hawthorn to the 1971 flag and later coached the Hawks and Carlton to premierships.
- **John Platten:** Brilliant South Australian rover who won a Brownlow Medal in 1987.
- **Michael Tuck:** Incredibly endurable ruck-rover who played a League record of 426 games with the Hawks and captained the club to four premierships (1986, 1988, 1989 and 1991).

In the early days, when Hawthorn was known as Booroondara, the team's colours were pale blue and white, but this combination was later changed to blue and red. Since joining the Victorian Football League and subsequently the AFL, Hawthorn has worn brown and gold.

Check out Hawthorn's Web site at www.hawthornfc.com.au for more information.

Hatching of the Hawks

The Hawthorn team was known in the early years as the Mayblooms, after the hawthorn bush of that name that traditionally bloomed in the Northern Hemisphere's spring. For a brief period in the 1930s, the Hawthorn players wore yellow guernseys with a brown vee and became known as the Mustard-pots.

In 1942, the legendary Roy Cazaly (who played Australian football until the amazing age of 48) took over as coach and demanded a more ferocious tag and called on alliteration to give Hawthorn a new identity — the Hawks.

Kangaroos

The Kangaroos is one of the newest names in Australian football, but, under the names of Hotham and North Melbourne, the club has been around since 1869. The game's legendary Ron Barassi came out of retirement to coach North Melbourne in the 1970s and pushed the team to premiership victory for the first time in 1975.

- ✔ **Club colours:** Royal blue guernsey with white stripes; royal blue shorts with white trim; and royal blue socks
- ✔ **Founded:** 1869
- ✔ **Home ground:** The Kangaroos' training and administrative base is the Arden Street Oval, North Melbourne, but the club plays its home games at the MCG and the Telstra Dome.
- ✔ **Nickname:** The Roos
- ✔ **Premierships:** 1975, 1977, 1996 and 1999

Known as North Melbourne until 1999, the Kangaroos were founded under the name of Hotham in 1869. Disbanded no less than three times in the club's earliest years, the club was briefly known as North Melbourne before it amalgamated with the Albert Park club and retook the name Hotham in 1876 and became a founding club of the Victorian Football Association the following year.

In the early 1900s, the club switched back to being North Melbourne and proceeded to dominate the Victorian Football Association competition for a number of years. All was well until a bid to join the Victorian Football League resulted in the team being temporarily expelled from Association competition in 1907.

The Shinboners' shenanigans

North Melbourne was known as the Shinboners throughout their early years in the League, allegedly because of the North players' reputation for aiming kicks at the opposition players' shins. The name made such an impact that when North won the team's first grand final in 1950, local butchers decorated their shop windows with ox bones.

In 1954, North officials decided the Shinboners tag was unflattering and adopted the kangaroo emblem, thus giving the team a new nickname.

On returning to the field, North Melbourne continued to win premierships, and club officials became convinced the team belonged in the stronger League competition. As a result, the club made an abortive attempt to merge with Essendon in 1921 and was again expelled from the Victorian Football Association. Undeterred, North Melbourne again rejoined the Association in 1922 and, finally, three years later, was admitted to the Victorian Football League.

North Melbourne struggled for many years in the stronger competition but, after 50 years in the League, the club finally won a premiership match under the eagle eye of legendary player and coach Ron Barassi. The Roos enjoyed enormous success in the 1970s and again in the 1990s under the coaching of Denis Pagan.

Roos stars over the years have included:

- **Glenn Archer:** Named the 'Shinboner of the Century' in 2006, in recognition of his wonderful career with the Roos. Established a new club record number of games (310) with the Roos in 2007. A ferociously competitive defender.

- **Allen Aylett:** Champion rover who played 220 games for the Roos from 1952 to 1964 and later served as club and VFL (now AFL) president.

- **Malcolm Blight:** Brilliant South Australian forward and utility who won the Brownlow Medal in 1978 and later coached Adelaide to two flags.

- **Wayne Carey:** Known as 'The King', the champion centre half-forward captained the Roos to the 1996 and 1999 flags.

- **Barry Davis:** The Roos' first premiership captain, in 1975, Davis starred as a half-back flanker after moving from Essendon.

- **David Dench:** Arguably the best full-back of his era, Dench captained the Roos and played 275 games for the club from 1969 to 1994.

- **Les Foote:** A superbly gifted centreman, Foote won three club best and fairest awards and captained the club from 1948 to 1951.

- **Ross Glendinning:** A champion key position player from Western Australia, Glendinning won a Brownlow Medal in 1983.

- **Keith Greig:** Brilliant winger who played 294 games for the Roos from 1971 to 1985 and won Brownlow Medals in 1973 and 1974.

- **John Longmire:** Star full-forward who topped the club goal kicking in consecutive seasons from 1990 to 1994.

- **Mick Martyn:** Tough full-back who played 287 games with the Roos from 1988 to 2002.

- **Wayne Schimmelbusch:** Super-courageous winger who played a then club record 306 games and later coached the Roos. His games record was broken late in 2007 by Glenn Archer.

- **Adam Simpson:** Prolific ball winner who was appointed club captain in 2004.

- **Jock Spencer:** Champion full-forward who topped the club goal kicking seven times between 1949 and 1956.

- **Anthony Stevens:** Courageous midfielder who captained the club from 2002 to 2003.

- **Noel Teasdale:** Big-hearted ruckman who captained the club from 1964 to 1967 and won a Brownlow Medal in 1965.

The Roos club has always worn royal blue and white, with variations in the design of the guernseys, shorts and socks. In the earliest years in the Victorian Football League, the Roos wore royal blue with a white vee and at one stage wore royal blue with a white NMFC (North Melbourne Football Club) monogram on the chest.

For more information on what's happening with the Roos, visit their Web site at www.kangaroos.com.au.

Melbourne

The oldest football club of them all, Melbourne was founded in May 1859, just weeks ahead of the founding of the Geelong club. The club's greatest era was from 1954 to 1960, when Melbourne played in seven consecutive grand finals for five premierships.

- **Club colours:** Navy blue guernsey with a red yoke; navy blue shorts with red trim; and red socks

- **Founded:** 1859

- **Home ground:** MCG

- **Nickname:** The Demons

- **Premierships:** 1900, 1926, 1939, 1940, 1941, 1948, 1955, 1956, 1957, 1959, 1960 and 1964

Range of different Hughes

Because of the Melbourne club's blue and red colours, the team was tagged the Fuchsias, a flower of the same colours. The club was also known as the Redlegs because of the players' red socks but, when Frank 'Checker' Hughes took over as coach in 1933, he demanded his players use more aggression and suggested the footballers 'play like demons'. The name stuck.

The Melbourne club was founded as an adjunct to a cricket club, with Messrs T Wills, H Harrison, T Hammersly, G Bruce, T Marshall and the Rev. A Brown forming the club's first committee.

The committee's first meeting was held at the Parade Hotel (now the MCG Hotel) in Wellington Parade, just across the road from the Melbourne Cricket Ground. Melbourne was a powerful club from the team's earliest years and was an inaugural member of the Victorian Football Association in 1877 and the Victorian Football League in 1897.

Although Melbourne never won a Victorian Football Association premiership, the club won a Victorian Football League flag in 1900 and has achieved periodic success ever since. The Demons won three consecutive premierships from 1939 to 1941, but the club's greatest era was from 1954 to 1960, when the team played in seven consecutive grand finals for five premierships (including three consecutive flags from 1955 to 1957). The Demons' golden era in the 1950s was under the coaching of the legendary Norm Smith, a fiery redhead known as 'The Red Fox'.

The Melbourne club has produced many champions over the years, with rover Fred McGinis one of the earliest League superstars. Other Demons stars through the years include:

- **Ron Barassi:** The son of a Melbourne player (Ron Snr), ruck-rover Barassi became synonymous with the Demons as club captain 1960–1964, before moving to Carlton. Coached Carlton and the Kangaroos to premierships.

- **John Beckwith:** Dour back pocket who captained the Demons in the 1957 and 1959 flag wins.

- **Denis Cordner:** Champion ruckman or key defender who captained the club from 1951 to 1953.

- **Don Cordner:** Denis's brother, Don also was a champion ruckman and won a Brownlow Medal in 1946.

- **Fred Fanning:** Burly full-forward who holds the League record for the most goals in a match, 18 against St Kilda in 1947.

- **Robert Flower:** Superbly gifted winger idolised by Demon fans over a club record 272 games from 1973 to 1987.

- **Jack Mueller:** Strong full-forward who played 216 club games from 1934 to 1950.

- **David Neitz:** In 2007 became the first player to notch 300 AFL games with Melbourne. Also holds the record for the most goals by a Demon. Was appointed club captain in 2000.

- **Norm Smith:** Wily full-forward who played 210 games for Melbourne from 1935 to 1948 and then coached the club to six flags.

- **Jim Stynes:** Irishman who developed into a champion ruckman. Won a Brownlow Medal in 1991.

- **Ivor Warne-Smith:** One of Melbourne's earliest heroes, the all-rounder won Brownlow Medals in 1926 and 1928.

- **Shane Woewodin:** The Western Australian centreman had a stellar 2000 season to win the Brownlow Medal, but was traded to Collingwood before the 2003 season.

The Melbourne team initially wore all white, but in 1862 a maroon stripe was added to the guernsey and, in 1864, a blue cap was added to the official uniform. The maroon was switched to red in 1868 and, soon after, the club started wearing blue and red.

Check out Melbourne's Web site for more information at www.demons.com.au.

Port Adelaide

Another of the 'baby' AFL clubs, Port Adelaide joined the competition in 1997 and made the finals just two years later. The Port Adelaide club was founded in 1870 and played in the South Australian competition (the South Australian National Football League). However, the club sought and won a licence to join the AFL from 1997 as the second (after Adelaide) South Australian club in the competition. Port played in the SANFL under the nickname of the Magpies and this separate body still plays under this name in the SANFL. Port Adelaide supporters therefore have two teams to follow, although they have separate identities.

- **Club colours:** Black guernsey with white lightning stripes and teal chest panels; black shorts with teal trim; and black socks
- **Founded:** 1997
- **Home ground:** AAMI Stadium
- **Nickname:** The Power
- **Premierships:** 2004

The Port Adelaide club, known as The Power, was admitted to the competition to allow South Australia to have two AFL clubs, joining the Adelaide Crows, with whom the team shares a keen rivalry. Whenever Port and the Crows clash, South Australian football fans are whipped into a frenzy by an excited media and the matches are known as *The Showdown*.

Although Port Adelaide is a new AFL club, the team sprang from the loins of the old Port Adelaide, easily the most powerful team in the South Australian competition. Two Port Adelaide clubs exist, with one competing in the AFL and the other, under virtually the same umbrella, involved in South Australian football.

Port's AFL champions include:

- ✔ **Peter and Shaun Burgoyne:** The Burgoyne brothers are among the AFL's most prolific midfielders and spell double trouble for all rivals.

- ✔ **Chad and Kane Cornes:** More double trouble for rivals. The Cornes brothers are extremely versatile and are the sons of former South Australian champion Graham Cornes.

- ✔ **Stuart Dew:** A powerful midfielder with a thumping kick, he played 180 games for The Power from 1997.

- ✔ **Brendon Lade:** Big-hearted ruckman who was named in the 2006 'All-Australian' side (the best players of the season, chosen by a panel of former players and experts from all players in the competition).

- ✔ **Brett Montgomery:** Midfielder who originally played with the Western Bulldogs, Montgomery won Port's best and fairest in 2000.

- ✔ **Matthew Primus:** Giant ruckman who started with Fitzroy, Primus was club captain from 2001 to his retirement in 2005.

- ✔ **Warren Tredrea:** Strong marking key forward who has been the Power's leading goal kicker over recent seasons.

- ✔ **Gavin Wanganeen:** Wanganeen won a Brownlow Medal with Essendon (1993) before joining Port for its inaugural AFL season in 1997. Club captain from 1997 to 2000.

Power to the Port

When the Port Adelaide club was admitted to the AFL in 1997, the team was forced to shed the club's traditional image as the South Australian Magpies because Collingwood had been using the feathered image for more than a century. A group of officials, visiting the United States before the club was launched, was impressed by American team nicknames such as the Orlando Magic. Port then chose 'The Power' to reinforce the team's image as a successful and dynamic force.

When the Port Adelaide club entered the national competition in 1997, the AFL banned the team from wearing the team's traditional colours of black and white because of the clash with Collingwood's uniform. The Power didn't duck the issue (er, sorry) and added the teal colour. However, it was allowed to wear the old traditional black and white stripes in a Heritage Round match in 2007 (refer to Chapter 4 for an explanation of these matches).

Port Adelaide surprised the football world when it won the 2004 premiership in only its eighth season. It defeated Brisbane in the grand final to spark emotional scenes in South Australia.

You can find out more about the Port Adelaide Football Club by visiting their Web site at www.portadelaidefc.com.au.

Richmond

The Richmond area has been synonymous with football since the 1860s. Proving how formidable the Richmond club has been over the years, the team has won an impressive ten premierships since joining the Victorian Football League in 1908.

- ✔ **Club colours:** Black guernsey with a yellow sash on the front only; black shorts with yellow trim; and black socks with yellow hoops
- ✔ **Founded:** 1885
- ✔ **Home ground:** The Tigers' training and administrative bases are at the Punt Road Oval, Richmond, and its home games are played at the MCG and the Telstra Dome.
- ✔ **Nickname:** The Tigers
- ✔ **Premierships:** 1920, 1921, 1932, 1934, 1943, 1967, 1969, 1973, 1974 and 1980

A Richmond Australian football team played in various competitions around inner Melbourne from the 1860s, but the present Richmond club was formed at a meeting at the Royal Punt Hotel, Richmond, in 1885.

As with most football clubs, the Richmond club was founded to keep cricketers fit during the winter months. The club won just two Victorian Football Association flags (in 1902 and 1905), but was such a consistent performer that the Victorian Football League, seeking expansion in 1908, admitted the Richmond and University clubs.

Putting a Tiger in the tank

When Richmond was admitted to the League in 1908, the club was occasionally referred to as the Wasps or the Yellow and Black Angels. However, in the early 1920s, a supporter watching the Richmond games from a tree just outside the Punt Road Oval often bellowed 'come on Tigers' because of Richmond's yellow and black colours. The name stuck.

Trivia buffs may care to note that the tendency for the Tigers to be merciless on the field is supported in the line by playwright George Bernard Shaw: 'When a man wants to murder a tiger he calls it sport; when a tiger wants to murder him he calls it ferocity.'

As well as a high level of playing strength, the Richmond club had one other great advantage for the Victorian Football League — close proximity to public transport, as the club's Punt Road ground was located opposite a railway station.

The Tigers won the Victorian Football League flag in 1920 and came up trumps again in the following season, mainly as a result of the brilliance of players Barney Herbert, Clarrie Hall and former Collingwood player Dan Minogue. The Tigers have been intermittently successful since the 1920s, reaching true greatness under the coaching of Tom Hafey from 1967 to 1974, when the club won four premierships.

Great Tigers stars over the years include:

- **Kevin Bartlett:** Champion rover who played a club record of 403 games from 1965 to 1983. Prolific goal kicker. Later coached the club.
- **Francis Bourke:** Courageous winger and defender who played 300 games for the Tigers from 1967 to 1981 and later coached the club.
- **Wayne Campbell:** Brilliant midfielder who assumed the captaincy in 2001 and retired in 2005 after playing 297 games with the Tigers.
- **Roger Dean:** Talented back pocket specialist who captained the club to the 1969 flag.
- **Jack Dyer:** Richmond's greatest identity, Dyer played 312 games for the club from 1931 to 1949 and was captain from 1941 to 1949. 'Captain Blood' was one of the most feared ruckmen in the game.
- **Royce Hart:** One of the greatest centre half-forwards the game has seen, Hart captained the Tigers to the 1973 and 1974 flags.
- **Stan Judkins:** Clever winger who won a Brownlow Medal in 1930.
- **Matthew Knights:** Hard-working midfielder who captained the Tigers from 1997 to 2000. Appointed coach of Essendon for the 2008 season.

- **Bill Morris:** Brilliant ruckman who won a Brownlow Medal in 1948.

- **Matthew Richardson:** Big, strong full-forward whose father, Alan, played for the Tigers. Played his 250th game for the club in 2007.

- **Michael Roach:** Lanky full-forward renowned for spectacular marking skills. Topped Richmond's goal kicking seven times, with a best of 112 goals in 1980.

- **Kevin Sheedy:** Ferocious defender who captained Richmond in 1978 and later became master coach of Essendon.

- **Ian Stewart:** A highly skilled centreman who won a Brownlow Medal with the Tigers in 1971 after winning two (1965 and 1966) with St Kilda.

- **Fred Swift:** Dashing full-back who captained Richmond to the 1967 premiership, the club's first in 23 years.

- **Jack 'Skinny' Titus:** Lightly framed full-forward who played 294 games from 1926 to 1943 and topped the club goal kicking 11 times, with a best of 100 goals in 1940.

- **Dale Weightman:** Brilliant rover known as 'The Flea', Weightman played 274 games for the Tigers from 1978 to 1993.

- **Roy Wright:** Champion ruckman who won Brownlow Medals in 1952 and 1954 and captained the club from 1958 to 1959.

The Richmond club's original colours were black, yellow and blue, but the blue was dropped when the club was admitted to the league in 1908. In the early days of the league, Richmond switched to play in yellow and black striped guernseys, but adopted the current design of black with yellow sash in 1914.

Find out more about the Richmond Football Club by visiting their Web site at www.richmondfc.com.au.

St Kilda

The St Kilda club was invited to join the Victorian Football League because the team had an excellent ground and was near excellent public transport. The team's struggles during the early years in the League proved, however, that location, location, location isn't always the be all and end all!

- **Club colours:** St Kilda's guernsey has a black and red back and, on the front, a red yoke with a black cross on a white and red bodice. On the left breast sits the club's crest and the neckband is white with a black stripe (phew!) The shorts are black with red and white trim, and the socks are black with red and white circles under the knee.

✔ **Founded:** 1873

✔ **Home ground:** The Saints' training and administrative bases are at the Moorabbin Oval, but the club plays its home games at the MCG and the Telstra Dome.

✔ **Nickname:** The Saints

✔ **Premierships:** 1966

The St Kilda club grew from a club representing South Yarra in the late 1860s. In 1873, the South Yarra club needed additional support and approached several St Kilda footballers with the idea of forming a new football club — and St Kilda was born.

Although the Saints struggled through the team's years with the Victorian Football Association, the club was invited to join the Victorian Football League in 1897 as the team's excellent ground, the Junction Oval, was close to public transport. St Kilda, however, struggled terribly in the first years with the Victorian Football League and often languished on or near the bottom of the ladder until making the 1913 grand final, eventually losing to the Fitzroy club.

The Saints then took another 42 years to play in another grand final, only to go down to Essendon. The following year, 1966, saw the Saints break the premiership drought by defeating Collingwood in the grand final by 1 point. The victory remains the Saints' only flag triumph and, since that 1966 premiership, the team has made only two other grand finals, losing to Hawthorn in 1971 and to Adelaide in 1997.

Although the Saints have struggled over the years, the club has produced a number of the greatest champions the game has known, including:

✔ **Darrel Baldock:** Brilliant Tasmanian centre half-forward with marvellous skills, Baldock captained the Saints to their only flag, in 1966.

✔ **Trevor Barker:** Dashing full-back renowned for spectacular marking. Played 230 games for St Kilda from 1975 to 1989.

✔ **Barry Breen:** Famous for kicking the winning point for St Kilda in the 1966 grand final win over Collingwood. A classy centre half-forward, Breen played 300 games for the Saints from 1965 to 1982.

✔ **Nathan Burke:** Dashing midfielder and defender who started with the Saints in 1987 and won three club best and fairest awards. Played a then club record 323 games from 1987 to 2003.

✔ **Roy Cazaly:** One of the most famous names in football, Cazaly played 99 games with the Saints and captained the club in 1920 before moving to South Melbourne.

- **Vic Cumberland:** One of St Kilda's early heroes, Cumberland was a ruckman who played 126 games for the Saints from 1903 to 1915, his career interrupted by World War I.

- **Danny Frawley:** A champion full-back, Frawley captained the Saints from 1987 to 1995 and was appointed Richmond coach in 2000.

- **Fraser Gehrig:** Kicked 103 goals with St Kilda in 2004. Big burly full-forward who is fourth on the club's all-time goal-kicking list.

- **Brian Gleeson:** A ruckman, Gleeson won a Brownlow Medal in 1957, but injured a knee in a practice match the following year and never played again.

- **Robert Harvey:** Prolific midfielder who won Brownlow Medals in 1997 and 1998 and four club best and fairest awards. Captain from 2001 to 2002 and in 2007 played his 350th game, a club record.

- **Verdun Howell:** A champion full-back, Tasmanian Howell won a Brownlow Medal in 1959.

- **Tony Lockett:** The most prolific goal kicker the games has seen, Lockett kicked 898 goals for the Saints from 1983 to 1994 before moving to Sydney. He won a Brownlow Medal in 1987.

- **Stewart Loewe:** Strong-marking centre half-forward who played 321 games with the Saints from 1986 to his retirement at the end of 2002.

- **Bill Mohr:** Champion full-forward who topped St Kilda's goal kicking every year from 1929 to 1940.

- **Neil Roberts:** Dashing centre half-back who won a Brownlow Medal in 1958.

- **Ross Smith:** Courageous rover who won a Brownlow Medal in 1967 and later coached the Saints.

- **Ian Stewart:** Champion centreman who won Brownlow Medals with the Saints in 1965 and 1966 before winning another one with Richmond in 1971.

- **Colin Watson:** A highly gifted centreman, Watson won a Brownlow Medal in 1925.

- **Nicky Winmar:** The first Aboriginal player to record 200 League games, this highly skilled half-forward played 230 games with the Saints from 1987 to 1998 before a brief stint with the Western Bulldogs.

The St Kilda club has worn red, black and white for all but a short period during World War I. During that time, the team switched to red, black and yellow because red, black and white were the colours of the German flag.

Find out more about the St Kilda Football Club by visiting their Web site at www.saints.com.au.

The Saints come marching in

Because St Kilda is a seaside suburb, the football club was originally known as the Seagulls. During the 1950s, however, a number of people tried, unsuccessfully, to change the team's tag to the Panthers. The team is now extremely happy with the more logical nickname of Saints.

Sydney Swans

The Sydney club started out in life as the South Melbourne club and then, in 1982, moved north to New South Wales. The move was surrounded by controversy and initially the team fell on hard times. Perseverance, however, paid off and Sydney is now one of the national competition's most respected clubs.

- ✔ **Club colours:** Sydney's guernsey has a red back and a white front with a red yoke and features a white cut-out of the Sydney Opera House; red shorts with white trim; and red socks.
- ✔ **Founded:** 1867
- ✔ **Home ground:** Sydney's training and administrative base is the Sydney Cricket Ground and the Swans play most of their home games there, with some at Telstra Stadium.
- ✔ **Nickname:** The Swans
- ✔ **Premierships:** (As South Melbourne) 1909, 1918, 1933 and (as the Swans) 2005

The Sydney club was transplanted from Melbourne's southern suburbs. The club's origins date back to the 1860s and the Albert Park and Emerald Hill clubs, which amalgamated in 1867 to become South Melbourne.

One of the most powerful teams in the Victorian Football Association, South was one of the instigators in the breakaway to form the Victorian Football League in 1897, but the team took until 1909 to win a premiership. The team followed that win with flags in 1918 and 1933, but then fell on truly hard times and, after going down to Carlton in the 1945 grand final, did not play off for the premiership again until 1996, when it went down (as Sydney) in the grand final.

The Swans' struggles through most of the 1970s and early 1980s threatened the club's existence and, in 1982, the club headed north to become the Sydney Swans. The move to Sydney wasn't an immediate success and, after two ownership consortiums and a rescue from financial problems by the AFL, the club eventually came of age in the harbour city in the mid-1990s. The Sydney team is now regarded as one of the most stable clubs in the competition and, in 2005, won the club's first premiership since 1933. The breaking of this 72-year flag drought had many of its old South Melbourne fans in tears. There were wild scenes near the club's old home ground of the Lake Oval as the club celebrated the four-point victory over West Coast in the grand final. The team then was given a parade through the streets of Sydney the following Friday.

I never thought, or dared even dream, my beloved Swans would one day win a premiership. I admit I shed a quiet tear after the final siren of the grand final, just like thousands of others who had followed the club through so many lean years. I feared I would have a terrible hangover the next morning, but I had just one beer after the big match — a quiet one with Swans player Nick Davis and his father Craig (former player with Collingwood, Carlton, the Kangaroos and the Swans) in the rooms before heading to the official celebration at the Crown Casino, where I had just one glass of wine. Who needed alcohol?

The Swans have always had a tradition of producing champion footballers, including:

- **Leo Barry:** Short for a full-back, but a wonderfully reliable player. And who could forget his breathtaking mark to deny West Coast in the final seconds of the 2005 grand final?
- **Peter Bedford:** Brilliant centreman or half-forward who won a Brownlow Medal in 1970.
- **Vic Belcher:** A powerful ruckman, Belcher is the only man to have played in two flag sides in the red and white, in 1909 and 1918.
- **Warwick Capper:** A full-forward renowned for his spectacular marking, Capper topped the Swans' goal kicking from 1984 to 1987, with a best tally of 103 goals in 1987.
- **Dennis Carroll:** Dashing half-back who captained the club from 1986 to 1992.
- **Ron Clegg:** Brilliant key position player who won a Brownlow Medal in 1949 and captained the club from 1953 to 1954 and again from 1957 to 1960.
- **Fred Goldsmith:** Champion full-back who won a Brownlow Medal in 1955.

✔ **Adam Goodes:** A champion utility who can play in a key position or as a midfielder. Won Brownlow Medals in 2003 and 2006, and played in the Swans' 2005 premiership side. Therefore one of the club's most decorated players.

✔ **Barry Hall:** Champion key forward who, as club co-captain (with Leo Barry and Brett Kirk), accepted the 2005 premiership cup with coach Paul Roos.

✔ **Gerard Healy:** Brilliant ruck-rover who joined the Swans from Melbourne and won a Brownlow Medal in 1988.

✔ **Paul Kelly:** 'Captain Courageous', Kelly was regarded as the bravest player of his era and won a Brownlow Medal in 1995. He captained the club from 1993 to his retirement at the end of 2002.

✔ **Brett Kirk:** The Swans' co-captain from 2005, always has epitomised total commitment. He never stops working for his team in the midfield.

✔ **Tony Lockett:** Champion full-forward who joined the Swans from St Kilda in 1995. Second (behind Bob Pratt) on the club's all-time goal-kicking list.

✔ **Herbie Matthews:** Champion centreman who won a Brownlow Medal in 1940.

✔ **Laurie Nash:** A champion key position player regarded as one of the best of any era. Played in the 1933 premiership side and also played Test cricket for Australia.

✔ **Michael O'Loughlin:** Set a new club games record in 2007, when he played his 261st AFL game. Also third (behind Bob Pratt and Tony Lockett) on the Swans' all-time goal-kicking list.

✔ **Bob Pratt:** Arguably the greatest full-forward of them all. Kicked 681 goals from 1930 to 1939 and 1946, including a League record (shared with Hawthorn's Peter Hudson, 1971) of 150 goals in a season.

✔ **Ricky Quade:** Super-courageous ruck-rover who captained the club from 1977 to 1979 and was the club's first coach in Sydney (1982–1984).

✔ **John Rantall:** Dashing half-back who played a club record of 260 games with the Swans from 1963 to 1972 and 1976 to 1979.

✔ **Barry Round:** Big-hearted ruckman who won a Brownlow Medal in 1981 and captained the club from 1980 to 1984.

✔ **Bob Skilton:** The club's greatest identity, the champion rover won three Brownlow Medals (1959, 1963 and 1968) and captained the club from 1961 to 1968 and 1970 to 1971.

✔ **Graham Teasdale:** High-marking ruckman who joined the club from Richmond and won a Brownlow Medal in 1977.

✔ **Greg Williams:** Champion centreman who won a Brownlow Medal in 1986 and won another with Carlton in 1994.

Top billing

South Melbourne was known as the Southerners, the Bloods and the Blood-stained Angels until the early 1930s. The team then embarked on a massive recruiting drive, with football writer Hec de Lacy suggesting that so many Western Australians played for the team, the club should be known as the Swans. The nickname was so popular, the word stayed with the team for the move to Sydney in 1982.

The South Melbourne club's original colours were blue and white, but were switched to red and white in 1880. The guernsey design has changed frequently over the years from red and white stripes to white with a red sash, red with a white SMFC (South Melbourne Football Club) monogram and white with a red vee.

Find out more about the Sydney Swans Football Club by visiting their Web site at www.sydneyswans.com.au.

West Coast Eagles

In 1987, the West Coast Eagles debuted in the national competition with a bang by defeating the winner of ten premierships, Richmond. Since then, the team has gone from strength to strength.

- **Club colours:** Navy blue guernsey with white and gold vertical blocks and a navy blue and gold eagle logo; navy blue shorts with gold trim; and navy blue socks with a gold band below the knees
- **Founded:** 1986
- **Home ground:** Subiaco Oval
- **Nickname:** The Eagles
- **Premierships:** 1992, 1994 and 2006

The West Coast club was formed in 1986 and played the team's inaugural season the following year. The public company, Indian Pacific Ltd, was given control of the Eagles, whereas the West Australian Football League continued to administer the Western Australian competition.

Formed to foster national competition, the Perth-based Eagles club was successful from the start, defeating Richmond in the team's debut match, finishing the 1987 season in eighth position and making a finals debut the following season.

Coasting along

The West Coast club adopted the nickname Eagles when it entered the League in 1987 because the officials wanted a hard-edged emblem symbolic of the state of Western Australia.

After 1988, the Eagles slipped slightly down the ladder but, under the coaching of Michael Malthouse, in 1991 the team reached the grand final against Hawthorn. The Eagles were trounced in the big match, but bounced back the following year to take the premiership cup out of Victoria for the first time. The Eagles won another flag in 1994 and, in 2006, won their third premiership in defeating Sydney by just 1 point in the grand final.

In the team's short existence, West Coast has been able to boast a number of stars, including:

- **Ben Cousins:** Brilliant midfielder who was appointed West Coast captain in 2001. Won the 2005 Brownlow Medal.
- **Dean Cox:** One of the best ruckmen in modern football. Takes a strong mark and is extremely agile for a player who stands 204 centimetres.
- **Ross Glendinning:** The Eagles' inaugural captain in 1987, Glendinning had won a Brownlow Medal as centre half-back with the Roos in 1983.
- **Glen Jakovich:** Brilliant centre half-back who started with the club in 1991 and won the club's best and fairest awards from 1993 to 1995 and again in 2000.
- **Chris Judd:** Arguably the game's most productive midfielder and a football genius. Won the 2004 Brownlow Medal and captained the Eagles to their 2006 premiership triumph.
- **Dean Kemp:** Courageous half-forward or midfielder who won the 1994 Norm Smith Medal as best on the ground in the grand final.
- **Daniel Kerr:** Prolific ball winner in the midfield, he was runner-up to teammate Ben Cousins in the 2005 Brownlow Medal.
- **Guy McKenna:** Wonderfully reliable half-back who played 267 games with the Eagles from 1988 to 2000 and captained the club from 1999 to 2000.
- **Chris Mainwaring:** Dashing winger who played 201 games with the Eagles from 1987 to 1999. Tragically, he died in 2007.
- **Peter Matera:** A brilliant winger who won the Norm Smith Medal as best on the ground in the 1992 grand final.

✔ **Peter Sumich:** Bulky full-forward who topped the club goal kicking from 1989 to 1994 and again in 1997, with a season's best of 111 goals in 1991.

✔ **John Worsfold:** Tough, fearless defender who captained the club to its 1992 and 1994 flag triumphs. Took over as coach of the Eagles in 2001 and guided the Eagles to the 2006 flag.

The West Coast Eagles entered the national competition in 1987 wearing royal blue guernseys with gold, stylised eagle wings, but later switched to navy blue and added white to the uniform.

You can find out more information on the West Coast Eagles Football Club by visiting www.westcoasteagles.com.au.

Western Bulldogs

The Western Bulldogs began life as the Footscray Imperials. Although the team has never been the strongest of clubs in the national competition, the club can boast some of the game's greatest players.

✔ **Club colours:** Royal blue guernsey with red and white hoops and a white, stylised bulldog logo on the chest; royal blue shorts with red and white trim; and royal blue socks with red and white bands below the knee

✔ **Founded:** 1883

✔ **Home ground:** The Bulldogs have their training and administrative base at the E J Whitten Oval (named after its greatest player) and play their home games at the Telstra Dome.

✔ **Nickname:** The Bulldogs

✔ **Premierships:** (As Footscray) 1954

Footscray, in 1997, decided to abandon its traditional suburban name in favour of that of a broader representation of its area, Melbourne's western suburbs, hence the new name of the Western Bulldogs. Interestingly, the Bulldogs wear a very small FFC (for Footscray Football Club) at the top back of their guernseys in recognition of the club's previous name.

Founded in Melbourne's western suburbs in 1883, at the time of the Prince Imperial (Queen Victoria's third son, Albert), the club was originally called the Footscray Imperials. Shortly after being founded, the club joined the Victorian Football Association; however, the club generally struggled until the stronger clubs broke away to form the Victorian Football League in 1897.

It's a dog's life

Footscray, because of the team's red, white and blue uniforms, was first known as the Tricolours and then the Imperials during the club's early decades. Legend has it that the club changed the nickname in the 1920s after a bulldog wandered onto the ground during a match against Collingwood.

However appealing the dog story is, the more likely reason for the switch in nicknames is that the club's officials wanted a British image and selected the bulldog as a symbol of fighting defiance.

Footscray then won a string of flags and became the dominant team in the Victorian Football Association. Carrying the name the Tricolours because of the team's colours of red, white and blue, the club won the 1924 flag and shortly after played the Victorian Football League's premier club, Essendon, in a charity match. The game against Essendon caused enormous interest, as fans knew the League was considering an expansion of the competition and that Footscray was extremely keen to join the more powerful football body.

Footscray fans were delighted when the team defeated Essendon, and the following year the club was admitted to the Victorian Football League along with Hawthorn and North Melbourne.

By the 1920s, Footscray was known as the Bulldogs, but the new, stronger nickname wasn't much help as the team finished above only Hawthorn in 1925. The team finally made a final in 1938 and then in 1954 the club broke through the mire and made a grand final appearance.

With the ferociously competitive Charlie Sutton as captain and coach, the Bulldogs defeated Melbourne in what has become the team's (so far) only premiership. The Bulldogs' only other grand final appearance was in 1961, when the team went down to Hawthorn. The team was led in the 1961 grand final by Ted Whitten, often rated as one of the greatest footballers the game has ever seen.

Other Footscray stars over the years include:

- ✔ **Simon Beasley:** Colourful full-forward who topped the club goal-kicking record seven times from 1982 to 1989, with a season's best of 105 goals in 1985.
- ✔ **Peter Box:** Talented centreman who won a Brownlow Medal in 1956.

- **Gary Dempsey:** Big-hearted ruckman who won a Brownlow Medal in 1975 before moving to the Kangaroos.

- **Chris Grant:** Brilliant key position player who was club captain from 2001 to 2004.

- **Brad Hardie:** A Western Australian, Hardie won a Brownlow Medal from a back pocket in 1985 in his first year of League football.

- **Doug Hawkins:** A Bulldog favourite, Hawkins played a club record 329 games with the club and was captain from 1990 to 1993.

- **Allan Hopkins:** A brilliant centreman, Hopkins won a Brownlow Medal in 1930.

- **Tony Liberatore:** A great Bulldog favourite, 'Little Libba' was a courageous and tenacious rover who won a Brownlow Medal in 1990.

- **Arthur Olliver:** Champion ruckman who played 272 games with the Bulldogs from 1935 to 1950 and captained the club from 1943 to 1946 and 1948 to 1950.

- **Bernie Quinlan:** Brilliant key forward, from 1969 to 1977, who later won a Brownlow Medal (1981) with Fitzroy.

- **Brian Royal:** Hard-working rover who played 199 games with the Bulldogs from 1983 to 1993.

- **John Schultz:** Big-hearted ruckman who won a Brownlow Medal in 1960.

- **Kelvin Templeton:** Champion key forward who won a Brownlow Medal in 1980 and kicked 118 goals in the 1978 season.

- **Norm Ware:** Powerful ruckman who won a Brownlow Medal in 1941 and captained the club from 1940 to 1942.

- **Scott West:** Brilliant midfielder who is one of the Bulldogs' current stars. To 2007 he had won a club record of seven best and fairest awards.

- **Scott Wynd:** Ruckman who won a Brownlow Medal in 1992 and captained the club from 1994 to 2000.

The Bulldogs have always worn red, white and blue, and the design has changed only slightly over the years. However, for a short period during the 1930s, the Bulldogs wore royal blue guernseys with red and white pinstripes. In 2007, the Bulldogs adopted a white with red and blue bands 'away' guernsey.

Visit the Bulldog's Web site for more news at www.westernbulldogs.com.au.

Chapter 14

The Origin and Structure of the League

*T*he rules of football have been evolving for centuries. The ancient Greeks played a type of football known as *harpaston*, the Romans played a similar sport called *harpastum*, Polynesians played a similar game using a ball made of bamboo fibres and the Inuit of north America played football using a leather ball packed with moss. In 16th-century England, King Henry VIII banned *footeball* (as did many of his predecessors) because the game interfered with military training and work.

None of these cultures, however, played the game in as bloody a manner as the Aztecs of Central America, who substituted a ball with the severed head of a tribal enemy. When heads were hard to come by, the Aztecs occasionally sacrificed the losing captain, whose head became the ball for the next game. Naturally, few volunteered for football leadership.

The unique spin Australians have put on the game comes from many varied influences, so, to understand how Aussie Rules is organised, you need to understand how these components have come together over time. Today, organising a game and keeping up with the rules are such major undertakings that they require an entourage of leaders in the Australian Football League (AFL). In this chapter, I present the specific influences on the development of this unique code of football and discuss its current-day structure and operation.

Creating the Code

Although Australian football can hardly be described as ancient, the sport can be traced back to a number of codes from around the world, and even reportedly includes elements taken from a type of football played by Australia's Aborigines.

Outback origins

Indigenous Australians played a form of football long before Captain James Cook landed on Australia's shores in 1788. Early settlers in the colony of Victoria noted that the local Aborigines played with a ball made of possum skin and filled with crushed charcoal. The ball was kicked around, with players leaping high into the air to take spectacular catches. Unfortunately, little concrete evidence of this football exists, and the debate over whether the Aborigines taught the white settlers the basics of the game continue today. That said, most people agree that these spectacular high-leaping catches had at least a degree of influence on the feature of Australian football called *marking* (catching the ball). (For more information on the skills involved, refer to Chapter 6.)

The Gaelic ingredient

Australian football began to evolve as an organised sport soon after the gold rush of the 1850s, when thousands of Irish immigrants were attracted to the Victorian mining towns of Bendigo and Ballarat. Many of these newcomers started playing the game of football known in the Emerald Isle as Gaelic football.

Combination special with an Irish flavour

The Australian and Gaelic codes are so similar that Australia and Ireland now play international Test matches using a set of what were called *compromise rules* and are now known as *International Rules*.

These Test matches — played with a round ball and a combination of rules from both codes — were initiated in 1984 and are now major sports events on the football calendar on both sides of the world.

Black magic

Many Aboriginal footballers have left their mark on the elite AFL competition. One of the first of these champions was Richmond's Vic Thorp, a star full-back in the era immediately following World War I.

Geelong ruckman Graham 'Polly' Farmer was one of the dominant Australian football stars of the 1960s and is still regarded as one of the game's greatest players. Brothers Phil and Jim Krakouer, who played for North Melbourne (now called the Kangaroos) in the 1970s, are famous for their uncanny skills: Football fans still talk of the brothers' apparent football telepathy, which became known — without a hint of racism — as 'black magic'.

Current Aboriginal football heroes include Adelaide's Andrew McLeod, Sydney's Michael O'Loughlin and Adam Goodes, West Coast's David Wirrpanda and Port Adelaide's Peter and Shaun Burgoyne and Danyle Pearce.

Until early in the 20th century, Gaelic and Australian football were played with an oval-shaped ball on a field with both goal and behind posts. The Irish later switched to a round ball and eliminated the behind posts, but if you watch a game of Gaelic football, the similarity between the two codes soon becomes obvious.

The English element

Although Aborigines, Irish migrants and others played games of football, there were no formal rules. No-one did anything about formalising the game until an advertisement appeared in the *Port Phillip Gazette* on Christmas Day, 1845. It alerted Melbourne sports fans that a 'grand match of the old English game of football' was to be played on an oval adjacent to the Old White Hart Inn in Bourke Street. The event also included games of quoits and skittles and the climbing of greasy poles. The football played on the day was a variation of what we now know as rugby, but with virtually no holds barred.

International interest

Australian football spread rapidly around the world in the 1870s and became popular in New Zealand, South Africa and even Scotland, where a short-lived competition flourished in the Glasgow docks area.

By 1893, 43 Australian football clubs existed in New Zealand, and the Kiwis even competed at the 1908 National Carnival, winning two of four matches and finishing ahead of South Australia,

New South Wales and Queensland. The Kiwis wore black guernseys adorned with a large silver fern leaf motif on the chest.

From these grand beginnings, the game took a nosedive with the advent of World War I and has only recovered the pre-war level of interest overseas in the last decade. For more information on what's happening with the game internationally, refer to Chapter 8.

Indeed, no-one thought of drawing up rules until 1858, when a 23-year-old squatter's son, Thomas Wentworth Wills, returned from a famous rugby school in England and wrote a letter to *Bell's Magazine* suggesting the codification of football as played in the colony of Victoria. Wills set up a meeting with his cousin, Henry C A Harrison (editor of Melbourne's *Morning Herald*), and two friends, J B Thompson and W J Hammersly, to draw up rules for a 'game of our own'. He then argued in a now-famous letter to *Bell's Magazine*:

> *Now that cricket has been put aside for some months to come and cricketers have assumed somewhat of the chrysalis nature (for a time only 'tis true) but at length will burst forth in all their varied hues, rather than allow this style of torpor to creep over them and stifle their now supple limbs, why can they not, I say, form a football club? If a club ever got up, it would be of vast benefit to any cricket club to be trampled upon and would make the turf firm and durable, besides which it would keep those who are inclined to become stout from having their joints encased in useless, super-abundant flesh.*

Wills' letter, published on July 10, 1858, galvanised Melbourne sports fans into action and three weeks later the first recorded match was played. The game was between Scotch College and Melbourne Grammar School and was held on what was then known as Richmond paddock, an area of ground close to the Melbourne Cricket Ground and only metres from what we now know as the Jolimont railway station. The date of this match — July 31, 1858 — is now enshrined as one of the most significant days in Australian football history. The thrilling match lasted over several weekends before Scotch finally won. (See the sidebar 'That first famous match' for more details on this match.)

FOOTY FLASHBACK

That first famous match

Scotch College and Melbourne Grammar School played the first recorded Aussie Rules match in 1858. Both Scotch College (wearing scarlet caps) and Melbourne Grammar (navy blue caps) fielded teams of more than 30 boys, who pushed, shoved and kicked a ball back and forth in an attempt to push the ball over a line at one end of the ground. The match was adjourned to the following Saturday for a result, but the Grammar team failed to show up so the match was resumed on August 21, again with no score. The game again resumed on September 4, with Scotch College this time managing a goal and being declared the winner.

The Melbourne *Morning Herald* wrote of the clash: 'Richmond Park was unusually lively on Saturday. Under the auspices of a fine day and their respective magistrates, the juvenile presbytery (Scotch) and episcopacy (Melbourne Grammar) came out uncommonly strong. Both masters and boys appeared to reach the acme of enjoyment and most jubilant were the cheers that rang out among the gum trees and the she-oaks of the park when Scotch obtained a goal. This event occupied three hours in the accomplishment.'

Encouraged by these developments, Wills, Harrison, Thompson and Hammersley eventually published their rules in 1858 and the genie was out of the bottle. The Melbourne Football Club was formed that year and other clubs mushroomed around Melbourne and then throughout the rest of Victoria, with the Geelong Football Club being formed soon after.

Football matches in the early 1860s were played to a set of rudimentary rules and, as a result, were rough-and-ready affairs. Finally, on May 8, 1866, delegates from the leading clubs met at the Freemason's Hotel on Swanston Street to revise the rules. Significantly, the rules formalised at this meeting included the rule that a player with the ball was forced to dispose of the ball after running 'five or six yards' (about 5 metres), clearly distinguishing the game from rugby.

The game was initially known as Victorian Rules and the code spread quickly to other Australian regions. Before long, objections were raised over the name and, as a result, the term Australian Rules was introduced.

Organising the League

Obviously, having a football club has no point unless you have an opposition to play against. This was evident right from the start of Aussie Rules and football became so popular in the 1870s that, in 1877, the most powerful clubs in Victoria met to form the first major competition under the banner of the Victorian Football Association (VFA). The original clubs were:

- **Albert Park** (later known as South Melbourne and now called Sydney)
- **Carlton**
- **East Melbourne**
- **Essendon**
- **Geelong**
- **Hotham** (later known as North Melbourne and now called the Kangaroos)
- **Melbourne**
- **St Kilda**

The South Australian league, based in Adelaide, was also formed in 1877, and the Western Australian league was founded in 1885. (For more information on these leagues, refer to Chapter 8.)

The composition of the VFA changed considerably over the following 20 years, with clubs coming and going. For example, the now-famous Collingwood club was admitted to the association in 1893, but had to abandon the original name of Britannia in order to have a closer identity with the suburb the club was representing.

The home of football

Buxton's Art Gallery, the birthplace of the Victorian Football League, is today a private home. Found on the first floor of a building built in 1870, the former gallery overlooks the Melbourne Town Hall.

The apartment is reached from a back alley and, until recently, the owners had no idea of the importance their home played in the history of Australian football.

The VFL: In a league of their own

The VFA grew in popularity with each passing season and eventually Melbourne's inner-suburban clubs began to complain about being financial crops for outlying clubs. For example, fans preferred to catch a cable car to Fitzroy or Collingwood rather than to travel across the bay to Williamstown. As a result, representatives of six clubs — Collingwood, Essendon, Fitzroy, Geelong, Melbourne and South Melbourne — held a meeting at Buxton's Art Gallery in Swanston Street on the evening of October 2, 1896, and agreed to form a breakaway competition to be called the Victorian Football League (VFL) — which later became the Australian Football League (AFL).

The six clubs agreed to invite Carlton into the League because of the club's location. St Kilda was also invited to join because of the club's excellent Junction Oval venue. The first VFL matches were played on May 18, 1897, and since then the competition has gone from strength to strength.

The AFL: A larger league

The League has no rules limiting its growth. All it takes to add a club is a vote. Throughout the decades, the League has chosen to add clubs for many different reasons.

FOOTY FLASHBACK

The clever club

The University Football Club, known as the Students, was unusual because each player had to be either a student at the University of Melbourne or the holder of a matriculation or higher certificate.

The club wore black guernseys with a royal blue vee insignia and played home games at the East Melbourne Cricket Ground (now the site of railway yards and private homes). The team played 126 games for 27 wins and 2 draws and managed to defeat every club except for Collingwood.

Famous University players include Albert Hartkopf (who played Test cricket for Australia), Herbert Hurrey and Edward Cordner (father of the Melbourne club's famous Cordner brothers — Don, Denis, Edward and John).

The VFL expanded in 1908 by admitting the Richmond and University clubs, but University — known as the Students — dropped out after the 1914 season due to World War I, and the club never tried to rejoin after the war. Because of the resulting odd number of teams, the League played with a *bye system* (in which one team draws no opponent for a round and automatically advances to the next round) until 1924, when the officials decided to admit a new club to even the competition numbers.

In a surprising move, the League stunned the football world by admitting not just one but three new clubs for the start of the 1925 season. These clubs were:

- **Footscray:** Now called the Western Bulldogs
- **Hawthorn:** Still called Hawthorn
- **North Melbourne:** Now called the Kangaroos

The Victorian Football League became a national organisation in 1982, when the South Melbourne club moved north to become the Sydney Swans. In 1987, the League expanded again, with the inclusion of the newly formed West Coast club of Perth and the Brisbane club.

Due to the presence of these interstate clubs, the league underwent a name change and became the Australian Football League (AFL) in 1990. Subsequent additions to the competition were:

- **1991:** Adelaide
- **1995:** Fremantle
- **1997:** Port Power (Adelaide-based)
- **1997:** Brisbane Lions (the result of a merger between competition founding member Fitzroy and the Brisbane Bears)

The red-tape boys

When the Victorian Football League decided in 1924 to expand the number of clubs in the competition, the league received applications from at least a dozen clubs. One of these was the Public Service Club, and wags at the time suggested the club's players were possibly not quite up to the workload.

The AFL assumed all responsibility for the control and development of Australian football, with the consent of the other states and territories. Aussie Rules is expanding every season and competitions are now held in every Australian state and territory, with organised matches even being played in the United States, Britain, Sweden, Canada, New Zealand and many other countries. Bring on Bangladesh! Develop Dubai! Convert Colombia! For more information on where the game is played, refer to Chapter 8.

People Who Make the Rules

Although early organised games were relatively primitive compared with today's competition, a certain amount of planning did take place, including the formation of a range of rules, a season length and a system of eliminating clubs to end up with the season's premier club.

The Victorian Football League (VFL) originally decided that one delegate from each of the eight clubs would run the competition. As a result, voting became a problem because eight is an even number and the poll may fall four to four, so the delegates decided to appoint a League president and gave him the power to cast a deciding vote. The first president of the VFL was Alex McCracken, a well-known Essendon identity, and the first administrative secretary was E L Wilson.

As the VFL flourished alongside other competitions around Australia, the need for a controlling national body became apparent. As a result, the Australian National Football Council was formed in 1908 and became responsible for the development of game rules, *player clearances* (transfers between clubs) and the general wellbeing of Australian football.

The council's first task was to organise the 1908 National Carnival, a competition between each of the Australian states and New Zealand, subsequently won by Victoria. The Australian National Football Council had a change of name in 1973 and became the Australian Football Council and in 1975 switched again to the National Football League of Australia. It became the National Australian Football Council in 1991.

In the meantime, the VFL was becoming a truly national competition and, after switching to the AFL in 1990, this body assumed all responsibility for the control and development of Australian football, with the consent of the other states and territories.

Smart Alex

The McCracken name crops up again and again in texts about the history of Australian football. And for good reason, as the following shows:

- **Alex McCracken:** Essendon's first club secretary (when he was just a 17-year-old schoolboy attending Scotch College), Essendon president and the first president of the Victorian Football League.

- **Robert McCracken:** Alex's father and Essendon's first president.

- **John McCracken:** Alex's brother and Essendon's first captain.

- **Colyer McCracken:** Alex's brother and Essendon's second captain.

Commission possible

With the VFL growing like Topsy with every season, the 12 club delegates (Footscray, Hawthorn and North Melbourne clubs were admitted in 1925) realised that the competition was becoming so professional that more and more of the organisational work had to be done by the ever-expanding League administration. At the same time, it became apparent that the delegate system was clumsy and didn't always serve the best interests of the game because delegates were representing their respective clubs and, in turn, the clubs' wishes.

The delegates, as the League's board of directors, decided in 1984 to appoint a commission and entrust this new body with the responsibility of running the game from Victoria. The directors retained the power to make decisions on such matters as the admission of new clubs to the competition, the approval of clubs moving out of Victoria and the amendment of any of the laws of the game.

The VFL (now AFL) Commission began operating in 1985, at which time the League's president, Dr Allen Aylett, relinquished his position in favour of Commission chairman, Ross Oakley. Dr Aylett's position was honorary, whereas Ross Oakley, as Commission chairman, acted as CEO.

In 1992, the AFL board of directors adopted a recommendation from the Commission to conduct an independent review of the League's administrative structure. This review is now known as the Crawford Report after David Crawford, a senior partner in the company appointed to conduct the review.

The report was presented on March 1, 1993, and approved just a few months later. The key recommendations included:

- ✔ The appointment of up to eight commissioners
- ✔ The appointment by the Commission of a chairman (currently former Carlton player Mike Fitzpatrick)

  The chairman's duties include chairing Commission meetings, chairing meetings between the Commission and the clubs and acting as a sounding board for the chief executive officer and commissioner (currently Andrew Demetriou)
- ✔ The appointment by the Commission of a chief executive officer (currently Andrew Demetriou)
- ✔ That the Commission holds the power to admit, merge or relocate clubs
- ✔ That all other powers to run the AFL competition be transferred to the Commission and that the AFL board of directors as constituted be abolished

---

The business of football

It takes a rare combination of business acumen and football knowledge to be a commissioner, although, obviously, having played the game is not necessarily a prerequisite. The most important aspect is a love of the game as there is little kudos and plenty of criticism as a commissioner.

AFL Commission chairman Mike Fitzpatrick and chief executive officer Andrew Demetriou are both former AFL footballers:

- ✔ Fitzpatrick played 150 games for Carlton from 1975 to 1976 and 1978 to 1983 and captained the Blues to the 1981 and 1982 premierships. He missed the 1977 season while a Rhodes Scholar at Oxford University, England. He succeeded the late Ron Evans as Commission chairman in 2007.

- ✔ Demetriou played 103 games with North Melbourne (now Kangaroos) from 1981 to 1987 and three with Hawthorn in 1988. He headed the AFL Players' Association before being appointed to the post of AFL General Manager — Football Operations before being appointed CEO in September 2003.

Meet the commish

In 1985, the first commissioners to be appointed were:

- The Hon. Peter Nixon
- Graeme Samuel
- Peter Scanlon
- Dick Seddon

The current AFL commissioners, apart from chairman Mike Fitzpatrick and CEO Andrew Demetriou, are:

- **Justice Linda Dessau:** A justice of the Family Court since 1995 who started the Essendon Women's Network in 1997. She was appointed to the Commission in 2007.
- **Bob Hammond:** A former star South Australian footballer who briefly coached Sydney in 1984. Appointed in 2001.
- **Graeme John:** A former player, coach and president of the Swans, John was appointed in 2000.
- **Bill Kelty:** A well-known trade union identity and a lifelong football fan, Kelty was appointed in 1998.
- **Chris Langford:** A former Hawthorn footballer, Langford played 303 senior games with the Hawks and captained the club in 1994. He was appointed in 1998.
- **Christopher Lynch:** A transport executive who played five games for Geelong from 1972 to 1974, Lynch was appointed in 2007.
- **Sam Mostyn:** A lawyer with a keen interest in football, particularly the Sydney Swans, over the past 20 years, she was appointed to the Commission in 2005.

Colossal changes

When the Victorian Football League organised the first football season in 1897, secretary E L Wilson was an honorary official. Even as recently as the 1950s the League had just three full-time administrative employees — secretary Eric McCutchan, assistant secretary (and later general manager) Jack Hamilton and an office secretary.

The AFL now has more than 100 full-time employees and a substantial office at Telstra Dome at Melbourne's Docklands.

The decision makers

The AFL Commission makes all of the League's major decisions, although the clubs are often consulted about important points. The administration, currently headed by Andrew Demetriou, in turn implements the Commission's policies through a corporate structure, which includes the following:

- ✔ **Appeals board**
- ✔ **Broadcasting and commercial operations**
- ✔ **Development** (covers participation, talent, coaching, umpiring, League and club affiliates, and the game internationally)
- ✔ **Finance and administration**
- ✔ **Football operations** (runs the national competition and associated activities)
- ✔ **Grievance tribunal**
- ✔ **Human resources**
- ✔ **Laws committee** (examines the rules of the game on a year-to-year basis)
- ✔ **Legal and business affairs**
- ✔ **Marketing and communications**
- ✔ **Medical commission**
- ✔ **Membership**
- ✔ **Player payments commission**
- ✔ **Strategy and club support**
- ✔ **Tribunal** (deals with rule infringements such as punching, kicking and — heaven forbid — swearing)

In addition, an *investigating officer* makes sure no-one breaches such rules as exceeding player payments or on-field incidents (such as punching) that aren't seen by umpires or caught on television replays.

Phew! That's enough to keep anyone busy!

Big Business

Although Australian football originated as an amateur sport, a match-payment system crept into the game in the first decade of the 20th century. At one point, the Carlton Football Club was even accused of professionalism. In fact, at the time, no specific rules against payment of players existed, but the practice was considered a breach of the game's etiquette. The payment system was popularly known as shamateurism, but became so popular that in 1911 the League agreed that match payments were a legitimate part of the game.

Although junior football and many senior competitions are played on a strictly amateur basis, with specific rules banning match payments, Australian football at the elite level is today very much a professional game, with even minor leagues making match payments. At the elite AFL level, a player can earn from $60,000 to $700,000 or even more a year.

The League's original makeup of 8 clubs has expanded to 16, and what began as an amateur code has become a highly professional game, with most clubs operating on annual turnovers of $20 million or more. Do the arithmetic and the figure $320 million a year pops up, making the AFL one of the biggest sports operations in the country. And all this to entertain football fans for just six months of the year!

Because the AFL is such big business, the League can charge clubs multi-million dollar licence fees for admission. In 1988, the League decided to buy the debt-riddled Sydney Swans for just $1. I attended the announcement of this decision and, like other reporters, was unable to understand why the League wanted to salvage the club. Yet, just months later, a consortium paid the League $4.7 million for the licence. That's what I call savvy business!

Taking care of the details

Every weekend during the football season, eight AFL matches are played at Australia's far-flung venues. Imagine the scenario of teams flying in every direction, complete with their players, club officials, medicos and equipment. This doesn't just happen by good luck. Making sure everybody is at the right place at the right time takes an enormous amount of organisational skill, which is why the AFL is structured so that every little detail is covered, from the supply of match balls (hey, you can't play the game without this most basic requirement) to umpiring rosters.

For this reason, the AFL operates by using detailed sub-levels, with all sorts of committees and divisions with various organisational duties, and then calls on the individual clubs to carry their own load.

Before each season, the AFL draws up the fixtures (teams, dates and venues) and then the club is responsible for making sure the players arrive at the venue well before a match and are prepared in every way. This includes making sure that the players are wearing the correct uniform, that the players take to the ground at the right time, that the coaches are aware of where their viewing box is and so on.

Taking it from the top

Although the operation of the AFL competition is seen as the League's main responsibility, this is only partly true, because hundreds of other competitions come under the AFL umbrella (refer to Chapter 8). These competitions, professional or amateur, junior or senior, suburban or country, all come under the auspices of the AFL, even though the League does not involve itself directly in the competitions. However, the laws or rules of the game as directed by the AFL must be adhered to by all competitions.

The AFL, as a highly professional body, funds football around Australia and grants are directed to various leagues and organisations, mainly through what is known as *football development*. Competitions aside from these are autonomous, with their own tribunals, umpire-appointment boards, appeal boards, administration divisions and so on. The bigger and higher profile the competition, the bigger the operation. For example, the South Australian National Football League and the West Australian Football League are big organisations in their own right, but still come under the AFL umbrella for game development, rules and so on.

The easiest way to see how the AFL operates is to check out Figure 14-1, which shows a pyramid with the AFL at the base. This pyramid is built on strong foundations, but every brick and every piece of mortar is important. Like the pyramids of ancient Egypt, this structure should stand the test of time . . . perhaps 3,000 years? Who knows!

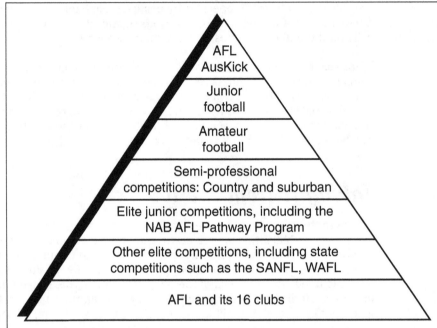

Figure 14-1:
The
structure of
the AFL.

Chapter 15

Roll Out the Honours

In This Chapter

▶ Taking the cup

▶ Choosing the season's fairest and best player

▶ Awarding the best kicker of the season

▶ Picking the best player in the grand final

▶ Matching up the best pre-season player

▶ Deciding the clubs' best and fairest players

The honour boards hanging proudly in each of the 16 AFL clubs are reminders of the glory achieved by the teams and individuals over the past 100 or so years of League competition. The names etched in gold on the honour boards are symbolic of the tradition and heritage passed on from year to year.

Winning a premiership is the ultimate reward in Australian football, to the point that winners of the prestigious Charles Brownlow Medal for the fairest and best player in the competition would gladly swap the medal for a premiership medallion, because team honours come before individual glory.

Although each of the 16 AFL clubs has individual club awards, in this chapter I list the important (and a few not so important) competitions between clubs.

Flagging the Premiers

The AFL competition is played using a system of home and away games, followed by a finals series to decide the premier club of the season. Taking out a premiership is known as *winning the flag* (because a pennant is awarded), *taking the cup* (because a trophy is presented after the grand final) or simply *winning the premiership*. Whichever term is used, the team winning the grand final is the premier club for that season. (To see the list of premiership winners from the Victorian Football League's inception in 1897, check out Appendix A.)

A new premiership trophy is presented each year and held in perpetuity by the winning club. The trophy is a large silver cup with wide handles on both sides. These handles are festooned with ribbons in the colours of the winning club when the cup is presented after each grand final. For example, when Geelong won the premiership in 2007, the trophy was decorated with navy blue and white ribbons.

In the inaugural Victorian Football League season of 1897, finals were played under a round-robin system, with no grand final. The Essendon club won the flag in this first historic series. The same round-robin system was used in 1924, with Essendon again winning the premiership without playing off in a grand final.

Essendon, South Melbourne, Fitzroy and Richmond made up the 'final four' in 1924, and Essendon then defeated Fitzroy and South Melbourne to have the premiership won even before it played its final round-robin match, against Richmond. The Tigers defeated the Dons by 20 points, among allegations that some Essendon players hadn't tried. Fists flew at the club's premiership celebrations and, the next week, Essendon played VFA premier club Footscray (which joined the VFL the following year) in a Dame Nellie Melba charity match at the MCG. Footscray pulled off a shock win among allegations that some Essendon players had been bribed to 'play dead'. Essendon's Tom Fitzpatrick was so angry that he played with Geelong the following season.

All-Australians

Each year a special panel of past players, and experts chooses 22 players, in their playing positions, who the selectors consider would form the best team from among all players and teams of the AFL season. These players then are known collectively as the *All-Australian side* for that year. An All-Australian coach and umpire are also selected. Because no international matches are played (except for the International Rules series against Ireland, which mixes Australian and Gaelic rules — refer to Chapter 14 for more information), this All-Australian selection therefore represents an alternative honour.

The first official All-Australian side was selected in 1953 following a *Carnival series*, in which all states play against each other. All-Australian sides have been selected on an annual basis since 1982. Some players, such as Adelaide's Andrew McLeod, St Kilda's Nick Riewoldt and Robert Harvey, and Sydney's Barry Hall, have all received multiple selections.

In 2007 no less than nine Geelong players were selected for the All-Australian team.

Taking Home the Charlie: The Brownlow

Although a premiership win is the ultimate goal for a club, the Charles Brownlow Medal for the fairest and best player in the competition is the most prestigious award for a player. Winning this medal is referred to as *taking home the Charlie*. The honour was inaugurated in 1924 in memory of former Geelong player and coach and Victorian Football League administrator Charles Brownlow, who died on January 23, 1924.

Ironically, the first Brownlow Medal — as the award is commonly known — was won by a Geelong player, Edward 'Carji' Greeves. Trivia buffs may care to note that the nickname Carji was given to Greeves as a child after a well-known local magician, Carji, the Prince of Bong.

From 1924 to 1930, in every game leading up to the finals, the field umpire awarded a single vote to the fairest and best player on the ground. The League had a one-umpire system at this time, but in 1931 decided that the umpire should award votes on a *3,2,1 basis* for each match (3 points for the lead, 2 for the second and 1 for the third-best player), with the player polling the most overall points being declared the medal winner. Then, in 1976, the League decided there would be two field umpires for each match and both umpires in each match cast votes on a 3,2,1 basis. This approach was too clumsy so, in 1978, the League decided that the two umpires would confer to award one set of 3,2,1 votes for each match. Then, in 1994, a three-umpire system was introduced and it was decided the three umpires for each match would confer for the 3,2,1 votes. The votes are always kept secret until after the last game is played before the grand final. At the end of the home-and-away season, the player polling the most votes is declared the winner of the Brownlow Medal.

From 1924 to 1930, only one player was awarded a medal each year. In the event of a tie, the footballer who had played the fewest games was declared the winner. From 1931 to 1979, a tie was broken by declaring the player with the most '3 votes' the winner (both methods are called the *count-back system*). In 1940, however, South Melbourne's Herb Matthews and Collingwood's Des Fothergill were still even after counting up the '3 votes', so Matthews and Fothergill were declared joint winners. Then, in 2003, there was a three-way tie. Sydney's Adam Goodes, Collingwood's Nathan Buckley and Adelaide's Mark Ricciuto were declared joint winners.

Since 1980, there has been no count-back system and, in the event of a tie, the two or more players polling the highest number of votes are awarded Brownlow Medals. In 1989, the League decided to award retrospective Brownlow Medals to the footballers who had previously been beaten under the count-back system.

As the Charles Brownlow Medal is awarded to the fairest and best player, a footballer who has been suspended during the home-and-away season is ineligible to win the award.

Brownlow Medal night is a glittering affair, with players, club officials, guests and partners (and members of the public) invited to a lavish dinner, with the count of votes televised 'live' around Australia. (To see the list of Charles Brownlow Medal winners, check out Appendix A.)

Every boy who plays Aussie Rules dreams of winning a Brownlow Medal. Not only does it symbolise football brilliance, but its criterion of being awarded to the fairest and best player means it represents all that is good in football — fair play, honest endeavour and biding by the rules of the game. When umpires cast their votes, they keep this criteria in mind, and it's significant that some fine footballers haven't won the medal, possibly because they were not considered the 'fairest' and the 'best'. The AFL has been under pressure for many years to change the criterion to just 'best', thereby dropping the word 'fairest', but it has resisted because the Brownlow Medal is a shining example to young footballers of all they should aspire to in the Australian code.

Father's day

In 1991, Melbourne's Jim Stynes was the favourite to win the Charles Brownlow Medal. On the night of the award, Stynes broke with tradition by not inviting a woman to be his partner for the night, instead inviting his father, Brian, to share any possible glory.

Stynes did indeed win the Brownlow — a remarkable achievement considering that the footballer was recruited from Ireland as a 19-year-old, without ever having seen an Australian football match.

Kicking Up a Storm: The John Coleman

Keeping score of the number of goals kicked by individual players has been part of football from the earliest days of the game. For years newspapers have run special goal-kicking lists, which fans study avidly. Kicking more goals than anyone else in a competition has always been regarded as an honour in any football code, but especially in the AFL. In earlier eras, players known as great goal kickers were called *true-boot artists*. (See Chapter 22 for my list of the top goal kickers.)

From 1981, the AFL has honoured the season's leading goal kicker at the end of the home-and-away rounds (so goals kicked in finals matches aren't included) with a special award called the John Coleman Medal, created in honour of the former Essendon goal-kicking hero. The award was made retrospective to 1955. (To see the list of John Coleman Medal winners, check out Appendix A.) Leading goal kickers from 1897 to 1954 are still honoured, but the AFL acknowledges their award as the Leading Goal Kicker Medal.

Hawthorn's Peter Hudson holds the record in the John Coleman Medal, kicking 146 goals in the home-and-away rounds in 1970. However, also including goals kicked in finals matches, Hudson topped this in 1971, with 150 goals, equalling the full-season record set by South Melbourne's Bob Pratt in 1934. That said, Hudson actually 'broke' the record with a late goal in the 1971 grand final against St Kilda. Hudson had taken a pass from teammate Bob Keddie, but umpire Peter Sheales ruled that the goal be disallowed and that the ball be given back to Keddie, who kicked a legitimate goal.

Coleman kick-starts his career

The Essendon club's John Coleman, after whom the special award for goal kicking is named, started his career in sensational style, kicking 12 goals in his debut match, which was against Hawthorn in the opening round of the 1949 season.

Coleman kicked an amazing 537 goals in 98 games before a serious knee injury prematurely ended his football career. Coleman went on to coach the Essendon team to the 1962 and 1965 premierships. Tragically, Coleman died of a heart attack in 1973, aged just 44.

Voting for the Grandest Player: The Norm Smith

In 1979, the League decided that a medal was to be presented to the best player in each grand final. The medal is called the Norm Smith Medal in honour of the great Melbourne goal kicker and coach who guided the Demons to six premierships.

Smith played 227 games with Melbourne and Fitzroy from 1935 to 1950 and coached a total of 452 games with Fitzroy (55 games), Melbourne (310 games) and South Melbourne (87 games). Smith coached at senior level every year from 1949 to 1972. He died in 1973 at the age of 57. (To see the list of Norm Smith Medal winners, check out Appendix A.)

The Norm Smith Medal is decided by a panel of media experts, who cast votes on a 3,2,1 basis just before the end of each grand final. A new panel is invited to cast votes each year, and to be invited is considered a great honour. I was a panel member in 1987, when Carlton's David Rhys-Jones was the winner.

Incredibly, the first winner of the Norm Smith Medal, Carlton's Wayne Harmes, was actually the nephew of Norm Smith himself. Harmes not only played a brilliant game in the 1979 grand final, but his knock-on to teammate Ken Sheldon for a goal with just minutes to play against Collingwood was vital in the Blues' 5-point win.

Getting a Nip and Tuck: The Michael Tuck

Because the AFL had initiated a 'best on the ground' award for its grand finals, it was decided to do the same for the pre-season competition. Each season, the 16 AFL clubs play competitive matches as a warm-up for the home-and-away season. A trophy is presented to the winning club and, in 1992, the League decided to present a medal to the best player in the grand final of this pre-season competition.

The award was named in honour of Hawthorn champion Michael Tuck, who still holds the distinction of playing the most League games in the history of the competition. Tuck played 426 games with Hawthorn from 1972 to 1991 and was 38 years of age when he retired. Ironically, the first winner of the Michael Tuck Medal was a Hawthorn player, Paul Hudson. (For a list of Michael Tuck Medal winners, see Appendix A.)

Awarding the Best and Fairest

Presenting medals for all competition 'best and fairest' winners is a tradition in Australian football clubs. Most clubs also present medals for the leading goal kicker and for those who play in premierships. Manufacturers probably get metal fatigue churning out the hundreds of medals presented each year.

FOOTY FLASHBACK

Haydn played sweet music

The legendary Haydn Bunton not only won a Brownlow Medal with the Fitzroy club in his first year of League football in 1931, but went on to win another two Brownlow Medals (in 1932 and 1935). Then, in 1938 he crossed to the West Australian Football League to play with the Subiaco club. He then won three Sandover Medals, in 1938 and 1939 and 1941, as the best and fairest in that competition. He therefore is football's most highly decorated player and it's highly unlikely any player will match his extraordinary medal tally.

For example, the South Australian National Football League, based in Adelaide, awards the Magarey Medal each year as its best and fairest award, while the West Australian Football League awards the Sandover Medal. Both these medals, now relatively minor in terms of prestige, once were regarded almost as highly as the Brownlow Medal. Now, with the advent of the AFL's national competition from the early 1980s, these awards have slipped considerably in significance, although still highly esteemed by the residents of Adelaide and Perth respectively.

Saluting the Sandover in the west

The Sandover Medal is presented each year to the best and fairest player in the West Australian Football League (WAFL). This award was inaugurated in 1921, when Perth businessman Alfred Sandover donated a medal to be presented to the competition's most outstanding player. His descendants continue the tradition, with a new medal presented each year. For more information on the WAFL, refer to Chapter 8.

Granting the Magarey down south

The Magarey Medal is presented each year to the best and fairest player in the South Australian National Football League (SANFL). It was inaugurated in 1898 in honour of the SANFL's first chairman, William Magarey. For more information on the SANFL, refer to Chapter 8.

Chapter 16

Grounds for Greatness

In This Chapter

▶ Locating where the action is

▶ Focusing on the fields of old

*T*he earliest games of top-flight Australian football were played on paddocks, complete with rabbit holes and cow dung. Even today, the occasional country ground sports a polka dot arrangement of cow pats. Not so the elite AFL games that are played today at superbly equipped venues, which I discuss in this chapter, along with venues used in the past.

Venues to View the Game

The newest of the venues is the Telstra Dome in Melbourne, which cost a massive $460 million to build. Despite this handsome amount, during the field's debut season, the playing surface came under fire when the turf failed to grow on the shaded side of the ground. This led to players' boots digging up large divets and the ground's management being forced to pay to re-lay new turf. The playing surface at times resembled a patchwork quilt. Kangaroos captain Wayne Carey, however, reminded AFL players of the game's origins on rough-and-ready grounds. The problem was rectified and over recent seasons the playing surface has been magnificent.

Just 20 years ago, Victorian Football League games were mainly played on what were basically glorified suburban grounds, with more mud than grass, and fans standing on terraces. Today, in contrast, standing room is for the most part a distant memory and fans enjoy luxury facilities unheard of a generation ago. Feel like a few slices of sushi or slabs of Hawaiian pizza before the match or at half time? No worries, mate! (That said, the traditional Aussie 'pie and dead horse' — meat pie and tomato sauce — remains the fans' favourite footy food.)

Twelve main AFL venues now exist, although a couple are used only two or three times a season. This section takes you on a tour of the venues, one by one, in alphabetical order.

AAMI Stadium

Although this ground in Adelaide spent most of its life known as Football Park, it attracted sponsorship from an insurance company and in 2002 was renamed AAMI Stadium.

- **Major AFL tenants:** Adelaide and Port Adelaide
- **Crowd capacity:** Slightly less than 60,000
- **Playing surface:** 168 × 133 metres, with goals running from north to south

The home of South Australian football, AAMI Stadium was built at West Lakes, an outer Adelaide suburb, for South Australian National Football League (SANFL) matches. With a superb ground surface and magnificent facilities, the venue was a natural choice as the home of the Adelaide team when the Crows entered the AFL competition in 1991.

Aussie Rules is the only sport played on this ground, and the groundspeople keep it in perfect condition. The bowl-shaped spectator area creates a great atmosphere, especially when the crowd gets behind the home team. In fact, many rivals find it extremely intimidating.

In 1997, when Port Power joined the AFL, the ground became the playing venue for both of South Australia's AFL clubs. (Refer to Chapter 8 for more information on South Australia's teams and Chapter 13 for a listing of all the AFL teams) Originally, AAMI Stadium had an attendance capacity of just under 50,000 (the record attendance for an AFL match at Football Park was 48,522 for a 1993 game between Adelaide and Collingwood). However, in 2002, the building of another grandstand increased the ground's capacity to close to 60,000.

Aurora Stadium

Hawthorn in 2006 entered into an agreement with the Tasmanian government to play four games a season at the Aurora Stadium, Launceston, over the 2007–2011 seasons. This picturesque ground isn't far from the centre of Launceston.

- **Major AFL tenant:** Hawthorn
- **Crowd capacity:** 20,000
- **Playing surface:** 175 × 135 metres, with goals running from north to south

Tasmanian fans have taken to the Hawks as their 'visiting' AFL team (the team flies to Tasmania to play games there). Tasmanians are also proud of the fact that one of Hawthorn's greatest players, Peter Hudson, hailed from the Apple Isle. Hudson played 129 games with the Hawks from 1967 to 1974 and 1977 after being recruited from Tasmanian club New Norfolk. He kicked 150 goals for Hawthorn in 1971 to equal the season's record goal-kicking tally of South Melbourne's Bob Pratt in 1934. This joint record still stands. If you go to a Hawthorn match at Aurora Stadium you'll get the feeling that the Hawks are a home-grown team.

Carrara Oval

Formerly the home ground of the Brisbane Bears, Carrara Oval, on the Gold Coast, returned as an AFL venue in 2007, when it hosted games played by the Kangaroos. The first of these was in round 4, when the Roos hosted the Brisbane Lions. The Roos agreed to play three games a year there from 2007 to 2009.

- ✔ **Major tenant:** The Kangaroos
- ✔ **Crowd capacity:** 14,000
- ✔ **Playing surface:** 160 × 134 metres, with goals running north to south

The Kangaroos defeated the Lions by 24 points in the re-emergence of the Carrara Oval as an AFL venue. Fans noted the ground had changed considerably since the days the Bears played there, with new grandstands and terracing. The AFL in 2006 committed $1 million towards the redevelopment of the ground.

The 'Gabba

Home of the 2001–2003 premiership team, the Brisbane Lions, the 'Gabba (an abbreviation of the suburb in which it is situated — Woolloongabba) is first and foremost a cricket ground and is the home of the Queensland Cricket Association. Test and other first-class cricket matches have been played at the 'Gabba (also known as the Brisbane Cricket Ground) for many decades.

In fact, the ground only became the Brisbane Football Club's playing venue in 1992. Prior to 1992, the Lions played at Carrara Oval.

- ✔ **Major AFL tenant:** Brisbane Lions
- ✔ **Crowd capacity:** Slightly less than 35,000
- ✔ **Playing surface:** 170 × 149 metres, with goals running from east to west

The 'Gabba saw enormous development over the first years of the new millennium: The ground now has spectator facilities and a playing surface that is among the best in the competition. The surface is luxuriant because of the semi-tropical conditions, and the new grandstands, built over several years to 2002, give it a wonderful atmosphere. The ground has a capacity of slightly less than 35,000 and, with the Lions going from strength to strength, crowd records are being set on a regular basis.

Whereas players once had to change in tin sheds at Carrara Oval, the club facilities at the 'Gabba are now world class and the envy of most Victorian-based clubs.

You can find lots more info on the 'Gabba at `www.thegabba.org.au`, including practical stuff like parking and seating, as well as the much more important dates for the Lions' home games!

Manuka Oval

This scenic ground, situated in suburban Canberra, is one of the AFL's newest venues. Located close to Parliament House, it's just ten minutes' drive from Canberra airport.

- ✔ **Major AFL tenant:** None (but the ground is used occasionally by Victorian clubs. Melbourne played Sydney there in 2007.)
- ✔ **Crowd capacity:** Slightly less than 18,000
- ✔ **Playing surface:** Approximately 175 × 152 metres, with goals running east to west

Manuka Oval may not boast the luxury facilities of most AFL venues, but the ground is in a picturesque setting and has a fine grandstand.

Melbourne Cricket Ground (MCG)

One of the world's most famous sports arenas, the MCG (as the ground is more commonly known) hosted the 1956 Olympic Games and has been a superb cricket venue for more than a century. As one of Melbourne's great tourist attractions, you can take daily tours of the famous ground.

- ✔ **Major AFL tenants:** Melbourne, Collingwood, Hawthorn, Kangaroos and Richmond
- ✔ **Crowd capacity:** Slightly more than 98,000
- ✔ **Playing surface:** 159 × 138 metres, with goals running from east to west

Originally an area known as the Police Paddock, the ground was cleared and levelled for cricket in 1854. The venue wasn't used as a football venue until the ground's trustees gave the Melbourne club permission to use the venue for a match against Carlton in 1877.

Following that historic game between Melbourne and Carlton (Melbourne took out the game, by the way), the Melbourne Football Club adopted the MCG as the team's home ground. The first Victorian Football League grand final was played at the venue in 1902, with Collingwood defeating Essendon by 33 points. The MCG is now the traditional venue for the grand final and, in 1970, attracted a record attendance of 121,696 for the grand final between Carlton and Collingwood (Carlton came up trumps).

The MCG wasn't available for League football from 1942 to 1945 because the ground was occupied by American armed forces during World War II and was temporarily renamed Camp Murphy. League matches during the war were played at Toorak Park and Yarraville Oval.

A superb venue with magnificent facilities, including the ultra-modern Great Southern Stand (finished in 1992), the MCG received further improvement for the 2006 Commonwealth Games. The venue currently has a capacity of just over 98,000, following the completion of new stands in 2006.

The Richmond club has shared the MCG with Melbourne since 1965, although the Kangaroos, Collingwood and Hawthorn now play most home games at the famous stadium.

I never tire of going to see matches at the MCG as it's a venue that any city in the world would be proud to call its own. I've seen many fantastic football matches at the 'G', with one of my most vivid memories being the 1996 Sydney–North Melbourne (now Kangaroos) grand final. I'd attended about 30 grand finals at that stage, and always felt like a kid with his nose to the lolly shop window, hoping that one day my team, the Swans, would play in the big match. That dream came true in 1996 but, alas, the Swans went down to the Roos. Fortunately, however, the Swans made it again in 2005 and this time defeated West Coast in the grand final before going down to the Eagles in 2006. Just imagine! Three Swan grand finals in just over a decade! Yet their previous grand final appearance was in 1945 and, even then, the game was played at Princes Park because the MCG was being used by the American military.

The MCG's Web site at www.mcg.org.au is packed with historical and current information. The site even has a page dedicated to Aussie Rules and you can book your tour of the ground online.

Skilled Stadium

Known as Skilled Stadium because of a sponsorship deal with a job-placement company, the ground's original name was Kardinia Park (an Aboriginal word meaning sunrise) and has been the home of the Geelong Football Club since 1944. Until 1940, the Cats played home games at Corio Park, but the ground was taken over by the military during World War II. In the 1941 season, Geelong played at Kardinia Park and then the team went into recess for the 1942 and 1943 seasons as a result of war-related travel restrictions.

- ✔ **Major AFL tenant:** Geelong
- ✔ **Crowd capacity:** Slightly more than 32,000
- ✔ **Playing surface:** 169 × 115 metres, with goals running from north to south

The home ground of the Geelong club has undergone a number of name changes. In the space of just two years to 2002, it was known as (in order) Shell Stadium, Baytec Stadium and, finally, Skilled Stadium, all through sponsorship arrangements.

After the club re-entered the competition in 1944, club officials debated over whether the team should return to the Corio Oval. Finally, after much gnashing of teeth, the head honchos decided the team should stay at Kardinia Park. Despite having an official home ground, the Cats occasionally play home games at Telstra Dome and the MCG.

One of the longest playing arenas in the AFL competition — the ground measures 169 × 115 metres — Skilled Stadium has a capacity of just over 32,000 because of the large amount of seating provided in the old terraces. The ground's record attendance was way back in 1952, when 49,109 fans squeezed into the ground for a match against Carlton.

Melbourne-based football fans think nothing of getting into a car and motoring down to Skilled Stadium to see Geelong home matches. When I was a boy in the 1950s (when the ground was known as Kardinia Park), it was almost an expedition — there was no highway and the drive could take up to two and a half hours. And coming home after the game I was usually miserable, as the Cats were almost invincible on their home turf in that era.

Subiaco

The Subiaco Oval once vied with the Western Australian Cricket Association ground (known as the WACA) as football's premier venue. However, AFL games have not been played at the WACA since the 2000 season.

- ✔ **Major AFL tenants:** West Coast Eagles and Fremantle Dockers
- ✔ **Crowd capacity:** About 38,000
- ✔ **Playing surface:** 171 × 127 metres, with goals running from east to west

The home of the Subiaco Football Club in the West Australian Football League (WAFL), the Subiaco ground has been used as a Victorian Football League and AFL venue since the Perth-based West Coast Eagles joined the competition in 1987. Originally, home games were played at both Subiaco and the Western Australia Cricket Association ground (the WACA) but, in recent times, virtually all AFL games in Perth are played at Subiaco.

When officials decided to use the Subiaco Oval as the sole AFL venue in Perth, it was upgraded. The Perth end of the ground comprised open terraces just a few years ago, but there are now stands all around the ground. With the erection of floodlights, it's also a perfect night venue, especially on warm Perth nights early and late in the season. Because the Perth soil is much sandier than what is used on grounds in the eastern states, muddy conditions are almost unknown. Even after a cloudburst, the ground is almost dry within 15 minutes.

With the Subiaco ground used as the home venue of both the West Coast Eagles and the Fremantle Dockers, which joined the AFL in 1995, most winter weekends see an AFL battle take place at the venue. Recent development of the grandstand and other facilities reduced the ground capacity from just over 50,000 to about 38,000.

Sydney Cricket Ground (SCG)

The Sydney Cricket Ground has been one of the home grounds of the Sydney Swans since the club, as South Melbourne, flew north in 1982. The SCG (as the ground is generally known) has a long and proud tradition as one of the world's finest cricket venues, having hosted Test matches for more than a century. The venue has also been used for rugby league and rugby union Tests and for a time was the venue for rugby league grand finals. The Swans also play several matches a season at the 2000 Olympic stadium, known as Telstra Stadium, at Homebush.

- **Major AFL tenant:** Sydney Swans
- **Crowd capacity:** Slightly more than 35,000
- **Playing surface:** 151 × 136 metres, with goals running from north to south

The Swans' first home game at the SCG was against Melbourne in the opening round of the 1982 season and the team celebrated with a victory.

Because of the Swans' success since making the grand final in 1996, the SCG has become regarded as one of the most difficult away games for most clubs and, at one stage, Swans' fans nicknamed the SCG 'The Fortress'. Regarded as a pocket-sized venue by many fans — 151 × 136 metres — the ground is, in fact, not much smaller than most AFL grounds. Although the SCG usually has a capacity of just over 35,000, in 1997 the Swans managed to attract a record 46,168 fans to the ground for a match against Geelong. However, considerable redevelopment of the ground in recent years has reduced capacity.

The Kangaroos and the Western Bulldogs have also used the SCG as an occasional home venue.

The Sydney Cricket Ground's Web site at www.sydneycricketground.com.au is very user-friendly. Find out what's on and the value of a membership. The site also has interactive maps that show the ground's seating and the view from each — the cyber-approach to try before you buy!

Telstra Dome

Originally known as Colonial Stadium, football's new boutique venue was renamed Telstra Dome at the end of 2002 and is acclaimed as one of the finest sports venues in the world.

- **Major AFL tenants:** Essendon, Carlton, Western Bulldogs and St Kilda
- **Crowd capacity:** 52,660
- **Playing surface:** 159 × 130 metres, with goals running from north to south

Telstra Dome opened to a clash between Essendon and Port Adelaide on the evening of March 9, 2000, and is now an integral part of Melbourne's football culture.

The site, in the Docklands near the heart of the CBD, was chosen by the Victorian government and work started on the venue in October 1997.

Costing $460,000 million, the stadium was designed with fans in mind. For example, the facilities include a retractable roof. Although many games were played with the roof open until early in 2001, the organisers finally decided to play all matches with the cover closed mainly because the shadows interfered with television coverage. The stadium seats 52,660, has six dining rooms with a capacity of 6,500 and even has an underground car park that can accommodate 2,500 vehicles.

The playing area has a natural grass surface built up on several layers of dirt rubble and moisture-retaining material, with a concrete base and a waterproof membrane. Although the venue had a few initial turf and ticketing problems, the stadium is now accepted as being a superb football venue.

Telstra Dome is shared by a number of clubs, with Essendon, Carlton, the Western Bulldogs and St Kilda being the major tenants. However, Telstra Dome isn't reserved for AFL games. For example, the rugby league team, the Melbourne Storm, once used the venue for home matches, and the field plays host to international one-day cricket matches and rugby union internationals. Even superstar singers Barbra Streisand and Robbie Williams have been known to hold court over the Telstra Dome crowd. Soccer club Melbourne Victory also plays home games at Telstra Dome.

My initiation to Melbourne's latest football stadium, Colonial Stadium (now called the Telstra Dome), was early in the 2000 season, just one week after the ground had been opened. I watched Sydney defeat St Kilda and marvelled not only at the modern wonders of this ground, with its retractable roof, but also at the debut of Swans forward Ryan Fitzgerald, who kicked five goals. Sadly, however, Fitzgerald's career was ruined by severe knee and shoulder injuries. He also played briefly with Adelaide and later became a well-known radio and television personality.

Telstra Stadium

Football's newest venue is the 2000 Olympic Games venue, Telstra Stadium, which was known as Stadium Australia before being sponsored by a telecommunications company. The Sydney Swans play several 'home' games at Telstra Stadium each season, playing, for example, West Coast, Collingwood and St Kilda there in 2007, with at least that many games planned there until at least 2018.

Naturally, this stadium is one of the world's greats — just ask the billions around the world who watched the 2000 Sydney Olympics. The grandstands all around the ground are superb and every spectator has a clear view, given that there are no pillars.

Although the ground had a capacity near 100,000 for the Olympics, it was reduced to 80,000 shortly after. To specifically meet the demands of Aussie Rules, seats are electronically moved back to create more playing space. This change allows for around 70,000 for an Aussie Rules match, and the Swans would love to put this figure to the test.

- ✔ **Major AFL tenant:** Sydney Swans
- ✔ **Crowd capacity:** About 80,000
- ✔ **Playing surface:** 178 × 142 metres, with goals running east to west

The first match played at Telstra Stadium was one involving the Sydney Swans as the home team and Essendon as the away team midway through the 2002 season. The match was a thriller, with Essendon winning by just 2 points. Sydney ruckman Ricky Mott had a chance to win the game with a shot for goal on the final siren, but missed. The Swans later in the season defeated Carlton and then Richmond in the only two other games played there.

I've seen two preliminary finals at Telstra Stadium. The first was between Sydney and the Brisbane Lions in 2003. The Swans looked a real chance in trailing narrowly at the final change, but eventually went down by 44 points. The Lions then went on to defeat Collingwood in the grand final. Then, in 2006, I saw the Swans defeat Fremantle by 35 points. Unfortunately, the Eagles defeated the Swans by 1 point in the grand final the following week. I therefore have mixed memories of Telstra Stadium.

If you want to find out more about the Telstra Stadium, check out their Web site at www.telstrastadium.com.au. There you can find construction and design facts, as well as information on upcoming events.

TIO Stadium

The AFL is contracted to play one game at the TIO Stadium at the Marrara
Sports Complex in Darwin, each season. This helps promote the competition
in the Northern Territory, where the AFL is enormously popular. The
Western Bulldogs generally host these games in Darwin and, in 2007, played
Fremantle there. The Bulldogs won by 26 points.

- ✔ **Major tenant:** Western Bulldogs

- ✔ **Crowd capacity:** 14,000

- ✔ **Playing surface:** 175 × 135 metres, with goals running north to south

TIO Stadium provides a wonderful atmosphere for football, and fans really
get into the swing of the games. Football in the Northern Territory is played
in summer because the grounds are usually softer through this 'wet season'.
The AFL also plays one pre-season match each year at the TIO Stadium and
these are often played in torrential downpours.

Venerable Venues

Remarkably, Victorian Football League and AFL matches have been played at
no less than 36 venues! At the start of the competition in 1897, all games were
played at suburban venues. This situation lasted until 25 years or so ago, when
the AFL discovered that fans wanted comfort, comfort and more comfort.

The MCG was by far the best stadium in Melbourne and always attracted a
large attendance. The AFL therefore rationalised its ground policy, and the
old suburban grounds, with their antiquated stands, poor facilities and lack
of parking are now but a memory.

FOOTY FLASHBACK

Having a proper gander

In 1952, the Victorian Football League (now the
AFL) decided to spread the football gospel by
playing what the officials termed a 'propaganda
round' of matches.

The round, which was hotly contested, included
matches in the Victorian country towns of
Euroa and Yallourn, in New South Wales at

Albury and the Sydney Cricket Ground, in
Queensland at the Brisbane Exhibition Ground
and in Tasmania at the North Hobart Oval. The
fact that the VFL didn't repeat this exercise
suggests the experiment was not entirely successful. In reality, it was a novelty, although it
did take the game to new areas — even if only
for one day!

For footy fans with a taste for trivia, the following list shows the venues and the dates the grounds have been used:

- **Albert Park (Lake Oval):** Albert Park, 1897 to 1981
- **Albury:** 1952
- **Arden Street (Gasometer Oval):** North Melbourne, 1925 to 1985. (This ground is still used as the training facility for the Kangaroos.)
- **Brisbane Cricket Ground (the 'Gabba):** Woolloongabba, 1981 and then from 1992 to the present
- **Brisbane Exhibition Ground:** 1952
- **Bruce Stadium:** Canberra, 1995
- **Brunswick Street Oval:** Fitzroy, 1897 to 1966
- **Carrara Oval:** Gold Coast, 1987 to 1992
- **Coburg City Oval:** Coburg, 1965
- **Corio Oval:** Geelong, 1897 to 1940
- **East Melbourne Cricket Ground:** East Melbourne, 1897 to 1921
- **Euroa:** 1952
- **Football Park:** Adelaide, 1991 to the present
- **Glenferrie Oval:** Hawthorn, 1925 to 1973
- **Junction Oval:** St Kilda, 1897 to 1964 and 1970 to 1984
- **Kardinia Park (Skilled Stadium):** 1941 and 1944 to the present
- **Manuka Oval:** Canberra, 1998 to the present
- **Melbourne Cricket Ground (MCG):** Jolimont, 1897 to 1941 and 1946 to the present
- **Moorabbin Oval:** Moorabbin, 1965 to 1992
- **Motordrome:** Richmond, 1932
- **North Hobart Oval:** 1952 and 1991 to 1992
- **Princes Park:** Parkville, 1897 to 2005
- **Punt Road Oval:** Richmond, 1908 to 1964
- **Subiaco Oval:** Subiaco, 1987 to the present
- **Sydney Cricket Ground (SCG):** Paddington, 1903 to 1904, 1952 and 1979 to the present
- **Telstra Dome:** Melbourne Docklands, 2000 to the present
- **Telstra Stadium:** Homebush, 2002 to the present
- **Toorak Park:** Prahran, 1942

- **Victoria Park:** Collingwood, 1897 to 1999
- **Waverley Park:** Waverley, 1970 to 1999
- **Western Australia Cricket Association (WACA):** Perth, 1987 to the present
- **Whitten (Western Oval):** Footscray, 1925 to 1997
- **Windy Hill:** Essendon, 1922 to 1991
- **Yallourn:** 1952
- **Yarraville Oval:** Yarraville, 1942
- **York Park:** Launceston, 2000 to the present

Thanks for the memories

Princes Park, officially known as the Carlton Recreation Reserve, was Carlton's home ground from 1897 to the last AFL match there in 2005. The first match at the ground was against Collingwood on June 22, 1897. That day was a public holiday celebrating the Queen's Birthday, but Collingwood ruined the celebrations (for Blues fans, anyway) by beating Carlton by 4 points.

The ground was in continuous use for more than a century. Over the years, the ground held many claims to fame. For example, in the 1945 grand final, Carlton defeated South Melbourne (now Sydney) here in front of a record attendance of 62,986. Incredibly, the ground in its final season had a capacity of just over 30,000, with most of the old terraces replaced by grandstands. Although Hawthorn, Footscray (now Western Bulldogs) and Fitzroy (now merged with Brisbane) shared the ground with Carlton at various times, the Blues were Princes Park's sole occupants.

I watched many games at Princes Park as a boy because my cousins barracked for the home team, Carlton. I was at the ground when Carlton kicked 30.30 (210) against Hawthorn in 1969. No team to that stage had kicked 200 points in a match and the crowd was frantic with excitement as the Blues neared that magical figure. That day it rained goals!

The last AFL match at Princes Park was played in 2005. The ground remains as Carlton's headquarters and training venue but the team now plays its home games at either the MCG or Telstra Dome. Australian Rugby League club Melbourne Storm also trains at Princes Park, and the ground is used for the Victorian Football League grand final each season and for junior and other matches. However, its days as a major venue are over.

Part V
The Spectator Sport

Glenn Lumsden

*'And this year's winner of the tipping
comp is, of course, Amy from accounts,
who doesn't care about footy and
gets her pet poodle to pick the teams.'*

In this part . . .

Being an Aussie Rules fan is fun, and the keys for making it more so are within the pages of this part.

In Chapter 17, I explain the finer details of becoming a member of an AFL club, including the costs and options available. Thinking of starting your own tipping competition? Then turn to Chapter 18, where you'll also find information on how to follow a footy form guide (it could get you ahead of the rest). And, if you can't get to an AFL game, check out Chapter 19, which details how you can follow the scene through various media. Happy reading on the sidelines!

Chapter 17

The Fanfare of the AFL

You can join the millions of fans who enjoy watching Aussie Rules on television or listening to it on the radio. But an even better approach is to become a member of an AFL club, join one of the team's cheer squads, attend live games or do all three. In this chapter, I discuss each of these activities.

Joining the Member Ranks

If you want to become a member of an AFL club, you can join more than half a million fans who've signed allegiance to one of the 16 AFL clubs. (For details on each of the clubs in the AFL, refer to Chapter 13.)

Ten years ago the total membership was just 267,387 — this figure has more than doubled in a decade. This sharp rise is partly due to the increasing popularity of the AFL competition, but thanks are also due largely to the enormous amount of television coverage the game receives. Games now are shown 'live' on TV around Australia on Friday nights, Saturday afternoons and nights and on Sunday afternoons. There are even Sunday twilight matches and, with a national competition, the audience has widened enormously. Until South Melbourne moved to become the Sydney Swans in 1982, all games in the Victorian Football League (now Australian Football League) were played in Melbourne or Geelong. Now, however, AFL games are played all over Australia and it seems almost every Australian has his or her team.

What's in it for you?

Becoming a member of an AFL club provides you with a number of benefits, such as:

- ✔ **Substantially reduced entry tickets to games:** Membership saves you many dollars on admittance prices to matches over a season.

- ✔ **The opportunity to obtain finals tickets:** You have a better chance of getting finals tickets if you're a member of a club in the finals. A membership ticket does not guarantee you'll be able to buy a ticket if your club makes the grand final, but it certainly makes it a lot easier, as competing teams have an additional allocation.

  Unfortunately, clubs like Essendon or Collingwood, each with well in excess of 30,000 members, cannot supply all their members with grand final tickets. But your chances are higher than they'd be if you were a non-member.

- ✔ **A fulfilment that comes with being a member of a group:** When you belong to a particular football 'tribe', a sense of camaraderie develops.

- ✔ **The satisfaction of financially contributing to and supporting a club:** The money you pay for a membership goes straight to your club, whereas gate money is divided through a complicated formula involving both competing clubs, the AFL and the venue.

- ✔ **Voting rights:** Club memberships generally, but not always, entitle a holder to vote at club elections.

- ✔ **Seasons tickets:** These tickets enable purchasers to sit in a particular area at 'home' games.

To give you an idea of what you may pay for admission as a member, Table 17-1 shows the costs for 2007.

Membership packages on offer

Every club in the League has a range of membership packages available. In fact you may have to choose among hundreds of these packages. Some involve little more than an autographed team photo and regular club newsletters; others involve interstate travel for matches and tickets to events like the club's ball and 'best and fairest' award night.

Table 17-1   The Price of AFL Tickets for Members, 2007

Member category	No. of games included	Price
Adult	11	$120.00
Adult member of an interstate club	11	$96.00
Adult	16	$207.50
Adult	17	$225.00
Adult	18	$242.50
Family (2 adults, 2 children aged under 15)	11	$240.00
Concession	11	$72.00
Concession	11 home and up to 7 away	$111.00
Junior	11	$16.00
Junior	17	$32.00

Basically, most clubs offer junior and adult memberships, for which several options exist and prices vary. All clubs offer $500 memberships, with benefits such as car parking and the opportunity to meet the players at after-match and other functions.

The clubs also have high-profile, high-cost coterie memberships that can cost up to $10,000 a year. Advantages of these memberships might include tickets for club functions and even player sponsorship, complete with a framed photograph of your favourite player and a personalised autograph — one for you and one to hang in the clubroom.

Just the ticket for collectors

Membership tickets have become hot items for collectors. In the earliest era of VFL football, membership tickets were works of art. They were cloth-bound and often gold-embossed with elaborate designs. Now, however, they are plastic, much like credit cards. Some old membership tickets have been known to sell for up to $500 each. In 2001, the Richmond club had a collection of all its membership tickets — except one from 1912. But after a feature I wrote about this fact in *Inside Football*, a fan came forward with a 1912 ticket to complete the club's collection.

Check out each of the club's Web sites for more information on the packages available. You can find links on the AFL's Web site at www.afl.com.au.

Deciding which club to join

Well, I'd recommend any newcomer join the best club of all: The Sydney Swans! But then, I'm extremely biased. If you're a newcomer to the game, I suggest you talk to your friends and colleagues who follow the AFL. In addition, assess the advantages and disadvantages of each particular club by asking these questions:

- ✔ Does the team play close to your home or work?
- ✔ Do you have favourite players at a particular club?
- ✔ Do you want to support the team that your friends or relatives support?
- ✔ Do you prefer supporting a champion or an underdog?
- ✔ Do the club colours appeal to you?

Yes, believe it or not, the team colours can have a big influence on a decision. A friend of mine follows only black-and-white-clothed teams around the world: Collingwood in the AFL, Newcastle United in the English Premier League and Juventus in Italian soccer, for example.

When radio personality Stan Zemanek moved from Sydney to Melbourne in 2002, he had the problem of working out which AFL club he would join. After hearing advice from colleagues and friends, and considering the pros and cons of each, Zemanek (who died in 2007) elected to become a Carlton supporter.

Cheering with the Squad

Every AFL club has a cheer squad, but these are nothing like their American counterparts: You won't find a band or girls in tight sweaters dancing to set-piece chants. Rather, AFL cheer squads are support groups who work tirelessly to support their club on and off the field.

Cheer squads have been part of the AFL for about 45 years and are now seen as an indispensable part of the game. Essentially, they're clubs within clubs, and you pay a small amount to join, with the price varying between AFL clubs.

Cheer squads assume two responsibilities within a club:

- ✔ To design, create and erect match-day run-through banners.
- ✔ To give the team tremendous vocal and visual support in all matches.

Contributing to your team's entry

Banners are now part of the game, yet they originated as simple coloured streamers placed across the players' race at the grounds, especially for grand finals. The team captain, leading his players onto the ground, ran through these streamers and a handful of fans then collected the broken crepe paper.

The idea developed from this to the current use of massive crepe banners requiring ropes and huge, sturdy poles to keep them upright. These banners now measure up to 6 metres in height by 8 metres across. They have messages on both the front and back, sometimes referring to club sponsors, but usually including a rhyme about the opposition. For example, a sign for the Richmond team, who are also known as the Tigers, might read:

> You'll hear the Tiger roar
> When we score more and more
> Watch out Dockers,
> We'll make sure you have shockers!

Corny, but that's the idea!

As you can imagine, these banners take hours and hours to prepare, and they often feature superb portraits of players who may be playing milestones (for example, 200th club game). They are genuine works of art, yet are destroyed in just a few seconds. So if you have an artistic side and aren't too protective of your work, you can become a valuable asset to such a squad.

In addition to helping with creating the banner, cheer squad members hold the ropes and poles of the banner in place at a match. They also pick up the pieces after the team has run through it and take them back to the clubrooms to prepare for the next game.

Showing your support with a group

Cheer squads tend to sit in a specific part of a ground, which is almost always behind one of the two goals. There they wave colourful club flags and streamers. They add enormous colour to the game and often inspire their team in a tight finish. For example, cheer squad members

✔ **Wave huge flags in club colours:** These flags can be very basic, say just black and white stripes for Collingwood, lightning flashes for Port Adelaide (The Power), feature checks in team colours for any club, or player names and/or numbers. For example, the Sydney Swans cheer squad waves a banner that reads 'Hey Jude' in honour of midfielder Jude Bolton.

✔ **Band together by dressing up:** Most cheer squad members wear special club jackets, caps and scarves. However, some have extremely individual outfits. For example, one Collingwood cheer squad member wears a gold suit and matching gold streamer wig.

✔ **Wiggle huge floggers after each club goal:** *Floggers* are long (more than a metre) paper streamers in club colours attached to a long (about a metre) pole. These items are huge and generally are a signal for other supporters to get behind their team.

✔ **Help create and operate special effects:** For example, whenever Richmond scores a goal in a home match, the cheer squad uses a 'roar meter' to determine the volume of noise from the Richmond fans. Consequently, the cheer squad tries to outdo the fans with their own screams.

To join the cheer squad, which can number in the hundreds, depending on the club, all you need to do is contact your favourite club and ask for details. Alternatively, if you live some distance from your club and can't get to cheer squad meetings, you might be able to bond with fellow fans through a supporter group. Just check your club's Web site for details.

Molly, by golly

One of football's most famous former cheer squad members is pop guru Ian 'Molly' Meldrum, who, after over 35 years, is still an ardent St Kilda supporter. Meldrum was a member of the Saints' cheer squad when the club won its only premiership, in 1966, and he still rates it as one of the highlights of his life.

Sitting Happily on the Sidelines

So, you just want to be a fan, not a member of a club and just go to the occasional game. Well, you're in for a pleasant surprise, because the cost of attending an AFL match is incredibly low in comparison with what you'd pay for top-class action in other codes around the world.

As a guide, an admittance ticket for an English Premier League match would set you back a minimum of £30 (about A$82), but usually much more and sometimes as much as £60 (about A$145). In the United States, a ticket for a National Football League match would set you back around US$60 (about A$70).

To see what a bargain you're getting, Table 17-2 shows the AFL prices for the 2007 season. Wow, you must be thinking — how cheap is that! Of course, you pay more for reserved seating, but AFL action still must be one of the least expensive entertainments around.

Table 17-2	AFL Prices for the 2007 Season
Member category	*Price*
Adult	$18.50
Concession	$11.00
Family (two adults and two children under 15 years)	$37.00
Junior (under 15 years)	$2.50
Child (under 4 years)	free

A penny for your sports

Aussie Rules has always been inexpensive. In the VFL's first year of competition, in 1897, the admission price was sixpence (around 5 cents). And football fans could still see a match for less than a dollar right up until 1971, when admission cost 70 cents. Then, in 1972, admission jumped to $1.

Chapter 18

Running a Tipping Competition

*O*ne of the best ways to follow the AFL is through a football tipping competition, in which participants 'tip' which teams are going to win, with points scored on the basis of the results of the weekly matches. A traditional way to follow the game, you'll find tipping competitions in the office, at school or in your neighbourhood, and national competitions through newspapers and via the Internet.

In this chapter, I provide information on how you can set up your own tipping competition or get involved in a professional one. I also detail how you can determine a winning team from resources such as a footy form guide.

Diving into the Tipping Pool

The best place to start a tipping competition is right at the start of the season, which is late March. (For more information on the Aussie Rules season, refer to Chapter 2.) You can run a competition from midway through the footy year, but it doesn't have the same appeal as trying to tip as many match winners as possible over an entire season (March to September).

To start, you need tipsters, and you can have as few as half a dozen or as many as 100 participants. Gather your friends or work colleagues while ye may — the more the merrier. The next step is to decide how much should be wagered on each of the 22 rounds. Most small tipping competitions involve $2 a week, which would set you back a total of $44, unless of course you win! This amount is little more than pocket money for most people, but it provides a lot of fun and, possibly, considerable excitement at the end of the season.

Creating a Tipping Chart

After you have enough tipsters, you need to draw up a chart in order to keep track of their bets and scores each week. To draw up your chart, put the names of your tipsters in a column down the left-hand side and list the 22 rounds in a row at the top, as shown in the example chart in Figure 18-1.

Spreadsheets such as Microsoft Excel are an easy way to create and track tipping competitions. Basically, you just need to enter the relevant data — each tipster's score and the progressive tally — in the spreadsheet's cells.

NAME	ROUND 1	ROUND 2	ROUND 3	ROUND 4	ROUND 5	ROUND 6	ROUND 7	ROUND 8	ROUND 9	ROUND 10	ROUND 11	ROUND 12	ROUND 13	ROUND 14	ROUND 15	ROUND 16	ROUND 17	ROUND 18	ROUND 19	ROUND 20	ROUND 21	ROUND 22
BILL	4/4	3/7	5/12	6/18																		
FRED	5/5	2/7	5/12	5/17																		
JANE	4/4	4/8	5/13	4/17																		
BOB	5/5	3/8	6/14	5/19																		
LIZ	3/3	5/10	5/15	4/13																		
KATH	5/5	5/10	5/15	6/21																		
JOHN	6/6	4/10	4/14	5/19																		
JACK	4/4	4/8	6/14	6/20																		
SUE	3/3	4/7	5/12	6/18																		
DAVE	5/5	5/10	4/14	5/19																		
FRANK	5/5	4/8	5/13	6/19																		
PETER	5/5	5/10	5/15	6/21																		
KAREN	4/4	4/8	5/13	4/17																		

Figure 18-1: A sample tipping chart in progress.

Casting votes

In almost every tipping competition, some poor soul has the task of keeping the chart up to date and collecting the money and tips weekly. However, this is usually a painless task because most tipsters know that their tips must be in by the end of each week.

The best way to ensure that your tipsters get their tips in is to write out the draw for each weekend — the matches to be played — and distribute this list to those involved. Your tipsters can then indicate on the list which teams they predict to win, and return it to you. Alternatively, you could give each person in the pool his or her own *fixture card* (a sheet with the season's games, or fixtures, printed on it) and mark off the tips from week to week.

Keeping tabs

At the end of each round, you need to calculate each tipster's score on your chart. Monday is usually the best day to do this because everybody in the competition wants to know how they did after the weekend matches.

Share scoring duty if you can, particularly if you have a large group of people involved. Many larger offices have a roster system, similar to the monitor system used in schools.

Basically, 1 point is allocated for each winning team correctly picked for each match. With each of the 16 teams playing every weekend, the top score possible each week is 8.

After you've calculated the scores for each of the tipsters involved, you need to write them on your chart, along with the tipsters' progressive tally through the competition. You can do this by drawing a diagonal line through each of the cells in your chart, and putting the score for the round above the line and their progressive total below, as shown in Figure 18-1.

As you can see from the entries in Figure 18-1, in round 1 each tipster's score is a ratio. For example, Bill received 4 points for picking four winning teams, so his progressive total is 4, because that's all he has correct to this point in the competition. In round 2, you can see that Bill picked three winning teams and consequently his progressive total is 7 — the total of his scores in rounds 1 and 2.

Watch the excitement mount as the final round approaches!

Allocating prizes

Most tipping competitions involve no more than a dollar or two each week for each tipster. As an example, say you want to run a $2-a-week competition and have 20 tipsters. This means the 'pot' each week is $40, and over the 22 rounds of an AFL season this amounts to a not inconsiderable $880 grand prize, should you decide to have only one winner.

Sometimes, those who slip behind are less inclined to continue, so most tipping competitions also involve a weekly prize. This additional competition usually takes the form of nominating a match of the round and asking the tipsters not only to nominate the winning team, but also the winning margin.

The weekly winner is whoever tips the winning team and the correct (or nearest) winning margin. Most competitions award half the weekly collect for this prize, so, in the example of a $2-a-week competition with 20 tipsters the prize would be $20.

Taking this approach means that with the weekly prizes amounting to $440 over the season, there is another $440 left in the pot. Given that most tipping competitions allocate first, second and third prizes, following this example means that the season's winner collects $250, the runner-up $125 and the third place-getter $65. Of course, the bigger the pool, the bigger the prizes — so get cracking!

Joining an Organised Competition

Several newspapers, betting agencies and Internet services run their own tipping competitions, and the prizes can be considerable. In 2007, for example, the prizes awarded were:

- ✔ **Yahoo! Tipping:** $6,000
- ✔ **Sportspick:** $10,000
- ✔ **Tatts TipStar:** $225,000

The approach is the same as that for running your own competition: You select the teams you think will win the round and you receive feedback on your progress and how you're doing compared with the other people involved.

Watch for details in your favourite newspaper at the start of a season.

The winner takes it all

In the professional tipping competitions, the winners generally outperform the experts, as, for example, one amateur tipster who, in 2002, tipped far better than any media expert in Australia. Football fan Trevor Button, of Berwick in Victoria, tipped 131 winning teams from the 176 matches over 22 rounds. Although newspapers in 2007 didn't give an overall 'amateur' winner, many stories have circulated over the past few years of children outperforming the experts and, in one classic example, of a pet cat resting a paw on the name of the 'predicted' winner, with considerable success. Yet the best media tipster in 2002 was Melbourne *Age* football writer Linda Pearce, with 123 winners. Next best was the Melbourne *Herald Sun* scribe Geoff Poulter with 121 winners. However, Poulter points out that his newspaper didn't count draws and, if they had, as is the case in most competitions, he would have had 123 winners because there were two drawn matches in 2002.

You'll find a number of Web sites offering tipping competitions on the Internet by typing the words **AFL tipping competition** into a search engine. Most sites just require your details and a visit from you once a week to submit your bets — it's as simple as that. Popular tipping sites, which are free, include OzTips.com (www.oztips.com) and AussieTipster.com (www.aussietipster.com).

Becoming a Football Expert

So, you really want to prove to everyone that you know the AFL well, and you're going to take it very seriously indeed. Well, get yourself the very best statistical information and study the football form.

It's in the book

Several books can help you assess football form, including Stephen Rodgers' wonderful *Every Game Ever Played*, which gives the quarter-by-quarter scores of every VFL/AFL game ever played, and the AFL's yearly publication, the *AFL Record Guide*, which supplies player form and other statistical information.

The *Encyclopedia of AFL Footballers*, a book I wrote with fellow football journalist Russell Holmesby, details the careers of every footballer to have played at least one VFL/AFL game since 1897. Naturally, every current player is listed and you can look up all players for all teams each week to assess capabilities and comparisons. For more information on these books and others that can help you gauge player and team form, see Appendix C.

Newspaper guides

Every daily newspaper around Australia carries football news and many, including the daily newspapers in most capital cities, run comprehensive football form guides. Also, the weekly magazine *Inside Football* runs several pages of football form, including recent results, record margins and so on. Oh, and by the way, you can read my weekly column, 'Mainline', in *Inside Football*! See Chapter 19 for more information on football media.

Information at your fingertips

You can now buy software that provides you with information on the AFL, including match results of every AFL/VFL game played, player statistics, player form and team form against other clubs, and statistics from specific venues. Then you can log on to a Web site and download weekly updates.

Several Web sites detail statistical information on games, teams and players, such as AFL Tables (stats.rleague.com/afl/afl_index.html) and the Swinburne University's School of Mathematical Sciences site (www.swin.edu.au/sport/afl.html).

For software, check out the ProFooty Tipping Software Web site (www.profooty.com.au) and the Footy Tipping Software Web site (www.footy.com.au).

Assessing the footy form guide

Just as you'd analyse a horseracing guide if you were having a bet on a horse race, you can do the same with the AFL. Footy form guides provide you with a wealth of information — such as player status and past performance — that can assist you in deciding who you think will win a particular match in a round.

Footy form guides come out weekly and can be found in a number of publications and Web sites, including:

- ✔ The magazine *Inside Football*
- ✔ Tatts TipStar Web site: www.tipstar.com.au

Inside Football's guide is probably the most comprehensive, but all major daily newspapers carry some facts and figures, as well as written previews by experts. Figure 18-2 shows how *Inside Football* presented its form guide for the Collingwood–Adelaide clash at Telstra Dome in round 22, 2007.

What does this form guide for the Collingwood Magpies–Adelaide Crows clash of 2007 tell you? First, that Collingwood has a win:loss ratio advantage. The records also indicate that the two teams have had an equal share of the match points in four clashes at Telstra Dome (two wins apiece). Adelaide had won four of the past five clashes, but Collingwood had won the previous clash, in round 6, 2007. On this form, you'd probably want to tip Adelaide, but only narrowly. The traits and history of each team indicate that it would be a very close game. So how did this match pan out? Well, you would have been correct in tipping a close game because the final margin was just 19 points, in Adelaide's favour, after leading all the way. However, you can have all the information in the world, yet not be able to pick the winner.

FOOTY FLASHBACK

When the Lions roared

Fitzroy (the Lions, now merged with Brisbane as the Brisbane Lions) pulled off one of the greatest shock results in Aussie Rules history when it defeated Geelong in 1963. Fitzroy had won only one game in 1962 and was on the bottom of the ladder without a win when it played top side Geelong at the Lions' old Brunswick Street Oval in round 10 of the 1963 season. Fitzroy went into the match without captain-coach Kevin Murray, who was on interstate duty for Victoria in Adelaide, but defeated Geelong by 36 points. It was Fitzroy's only win of the season and Geelong went on to win the premiership that year.

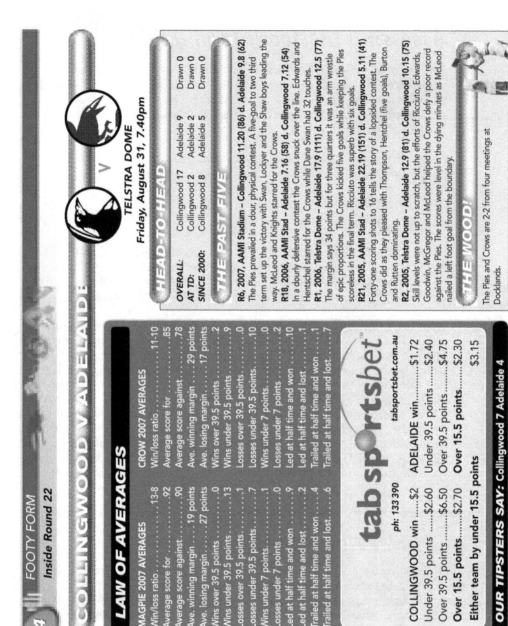

Figure 18-2: A footy form guide from *Inside Football*.

Chapter 19

The Football Media

*W*hen the Victorian Football League (VFL) was formed in 1897, the media coverage was very limited in comparison with what the game receives today. At that time, newspapers like the *Age*, *Sydney Herald* and the now defunct *Australasian* gave fans extensive coverage, but nowhere near the almost blanket coverage of the modern era. The increase in coverage of the game has more to do with the development of the electronic media — radio, television and the Internet — than with anything else.

As these electronic forms of coverage developed, so did interest in the game and, consequently, newspapers started devoting more and more space to Aussie Rules. In the very earliest era of League football, newspapers provided comprehensive match reports and notes about recruits and injuries. Now, however, a League footballer only has to sneeze and it's reported. In this chapter, I look at just how comprehensive the coverage of the AFL scene is in the 21st century and point you to the best media resources you can find to feed your cravings for more info on Aussie Rules.

The Newspaper and Magazine World

Want to read about football? Almost any aspect of the game? Well, any number of publications are available to feed your hunger for footy news.

The Main man on Mondays

I admit to a certain amount of bias when I discuss the *Australian* because I was its chief football writer for ten years and still write the occasional match review for the newspaper I love and respect.

Its Monday review, covering all matches played over the previous weekend, is superb.

Apart from the reports on all matches each weekend, you find superb summaries and analyses, tremendous action photographs, scores and other details on matches in competitions around Australia. A fan can study and enjoy the Monday coverage for hours.

Read all about it — in B&W

You'd have to be living at the Back of Bourke not to get newspaper reports on Aussie Rules and, even then, you'd likely get some coverage. Because every major Australian newspaper reports on Aussie Rules, you can easily follow the game throughout the year, regardless of where you live.

In Melbourne, for example, two daily newspapers, the *Age* and the *Herald Sun*, pride themselves on their coverage of Aussie Rules. They're just as competitive as any of the clubs, and run column after column of previews, reviews, training notes, commentary, features and so on. Newspapers in the capital cities of other states also have extensive coverage, but the Melbourne newspapers usually cover the competition in far greater detail than elsewhere because the competition originally was based in Melbourne and Geelong.

And, if that's not enough for football fans in Victoria, the *Geelong Advertiser* serves the Geelong club (known as the Cats) in particular, and the *Australian* provides excellent national football coverage. On Sundays you can also pick up the *Sunday Herald Sun* and the *Sunday Age*.

In Perth, the *West Australian* and the *Sunday Times* provide great coverage of the AFL; Adelaide has the *Advertiser* and the *Sunday Mail* and Brisbane has the *Courier-Mail* and *Sunday Mail*. The detailed coverage extends to every capital and major country city boasting a daily newspaper.

When you're following the AFL through newspaper reports, keep in mind that every paper has some bias towards the hometown team(s). For example, the *Advertiser* in Adelaide concentrates on that city's two AFL clubs, Adelaide and Port Adelaide. Ditto for the *West Australian* in Perth, with most coverage focusing on hometown teams Fremantle and West Coast.

The magazine world

If newspapers can't adequately feed your footy habit, pick up one of the sport magazines on the market. First, check out the weekly *Inside Football*, for which I've been a columnist and contributor for more than 25 years. When you read my 'Mainline' column, you get a behind-the-scenes glimpse of current events and issues in Aussie Rules! I analyse current football issues and always speak my mind. I also answer reader queries. For example, if you write to me and ask about a certain issue I'll give you my view — even though you may not like it!

Also, the *Football Record* is a wonderful official AFL publication worth picking up. Founded in 1912, primarily to give spectators the player numbers, this glossy magazine has developed over recent years into a truly magnificent publication and is a must to purchase on match days. The numbers are still there, along with all the goal-kicking details, results and other statistics, plus heaps of bright and breezy features and great colour photographs. Some devotees read it from cover to cover on match days and then take it home to read all over again.

Several fanzines — magazines written and produced by the fans of a particular club, sometimes even without club approval — have been produced over recent years. They can be zany and often cover weird and wonderful aspects of the game. Determining which ones will continue into the new season, however, is impossible to tell from year to year. In this respect we lag a long way behind our English soccer counterparts, who produce some very funny fanzines.

Television and Radio Programs

Nothing beats going to the football, but, if you can't get there, the next best thing is to watch a game on television or listen to one on the radio. Fortunately, the AFL is blessed with outstanding electronic coverage of the mighty Australian code of football, with matches being telecast and/or broadcast all over Australia and beyond.

Switching on to the telly

You can now tune into a number of television shows associated with football, from Channel Nine's enormously popular *The Footy Show*, featuring former Geelong champion John 'Sam' Newman and former Melbourne champion forward Garry Lyon, to a wide range of programs on Foxtel. If it's footy you want, you can go square-eyed watching the games and all the accompanying glitz and glamour.

Don't confuse *The Footy Show* featuring Newman and Lyon with the show of the same name on rugby league from Sydney.

Almost from the time football was first televised in 1957, the Seven Network was involved in covering matches — until a consortium of Nine, Ten and Foxtel won the rights in 2002. Suddenly, it was a new ball game, almost literally. With Nine and Ten providing the free-to-air coverage and Fox Footy being the 'pay' network, every game was telecast. Then, at the end of the 2006 season, Seven, Ten and Foxtel won the rights for the following five seasons, with Nine missing out. Sure, in some areas of Australia — particularly in parts of Queensland and New South Wales — the 'delayed' telecasts may not be as early or as frequent, but football now reaches a far wider television audience than it once did. Although coverage varies from area to area, some games may not be covered free-to-air, but are featured on pay TV.

I like to watch as much football as possible, so I subscribe to Foxtel's coverage. That way I can see the occasional game not covered by Seven or Ten. How do I rate the TV coverage teams? To be honest, there's not much difference between them. I love the smooth commentary of Seven's Dennis Cometti, I am a great fan of Ten's Robert Walls, who I consider to be the best match analyst in the business, and Foxtel has a young team whose enthusiasm shows through.

Tuning into radio rules

Aussie Rules on radio? Many fans have made it a tradition not only to be at the game, but to listen to it on radio through a headset. This listen-while-you-watch approach is a great idea because you pick up much more detail. For example, you hear reports on injuries, game analysis and expert commentary that explains such issues as umpiring decisions and tactical moves.

The first footy broadcasts of the game were made in 1923, and the first commentator was radio station 3AR's Wally 'Jumbo' Sharland. Other stars over the years have included Norman Banks, Jack Gurry, Tony Charlton, Harry Beitzel, Jack Dyer and Don Hyde.

The current stars from Melbourne include 3AW's Rex Hunt, the ABC's Dan Lonergan and Triple M's Brian Taylor. These radio stations network around Australia, but equally popular football broadcasting stations are based in other capital cities, including 5AA in Adelaide and 6PR in Perth.

Determining the type of broadcaster you like is really a matter of what suits your style — or rather your eardrums!

For example, four Melbourne-based networks, 3AW, ABC, SEN and Triple M, offer widely varying styles of broadcast. Rex Hunt and the 3AW team have heaps of fun. Hunt, a hugely popular multimedia personality who starred with Richmond, Geelong and St Kilda in a brilliant playing career, is a barrel of laughs because he has nicknames for just about every player and a superbly colourful expression for almost every situation. On the other hand, Dan Lonergan and his ABC team are far more sedate and serious and cater to an entirely different type of fan. They may not be as much fun as the 3AW team, but their calls are clear and concise. If you want fun out of the ABC, tune into Triple J's special broadcast of the grand final, the 'Festival of the Boot', hosted by Roy Slaven and H G Nelson. The Triple M team provides a very high level of excitement and tends to appeal to younger football fans, and sports station SEN joined the coverage in 2007 with a view to winning a share of the market.

Casting the Net

With the ever-increasing popularity of the World Wide Web — also known as the Internet — football is reaching audiences never before imagined. Sports fans around the world can click on Web sites to get all the latest information and even game broadcasts and tele-action.

You wouldn't believe the number of expatriates in London, Chicago and even Beijing who follow the footy news from home through the Internet. A lot of converts from the United States, Britain and elsewhere who have seen AFL matches on TV are also hungry to learn more over the Web. This international audience means that hundreds, maybe even thousands, of Aussie Rules Web sites are accessible to you. Many represent amateur, suburban or country competition or clubs, and quite a few devote themselves to AFL clubs and the AFL scene.

The best way to find out what sites exist is to use a search engine (which is a Web page that contains a huge catalogue of other Web pages), such as Google or Yahoo. Simply type in **Aussie Rules** as a keyword and see what comes up. If you're looking for a particular aspect of the game, such as umpire signals, add this info to your search and your results will be more specific.

The official Web site for the AFL is www.afl.com.au. This site is marvellously comprehensive, covering all aspects of the game, from its history to each of the clubs — basically everything you need to know that is happening with Aussie Rules at the AFL level. The news articles are updated several times a day, even during the off-season, so you know you're getting the latest information. You can also find statistics, columns, player information and links to sites for each of the 16 AFL clubs.

Here are some other especially informative sites to visit:

- ✔ **Fairfax Digital** (www.realfooty.com.au): A top site for getting up-to-date information on the game, as you'd expect from a major media outlet!

- ✔ **The Australian Institute of Sport** (www.ais.org.au): This site has a wide range of information for Aussie Rules players and fans, including information on coaches and current programs. Use the search window to find the information you're looking for.

The beauty of the Web

In 2000, I was in Germany at the time of the AFL's national draft. I was keen to know which players my team, the Sydney Swans, had drafted, so I clicked onto the AFL's Web site at www.afl.com.au and — bingo! — I had everything I wanted to know in five minutes.

Incredibly, a couple of days later I boarded a plane heading back for Australia and bumped, almost literally, into fellow passenger Ron Barassi, a Swan director and playing and coaching legend. Ron had been driving around Italy and was astounded that I had all the draft information. The Internet made me look a lot smarter than I really am! Wherever you travel, stay connected with your favourite team online and you can feel on top of your game as if you were right at home.

Part VI
The Part of Tens

Glenn Lumsden

*'As Gus "Elephant" McKay comes
in to kick his historic 1,000th career
goal ... hang on, some joker in the crowd
has released yet ANOTHER animal ...'*

In this part . . .

1 have followed the Aussie Rules scene for more years than I care to remember and, over these decades, I've seen many champion football individuals and teams. This part of the book is my favourite because I nominate who I believe to be the best players, teams, goal kickers, games and marksmen. I've also tossed in a list of fantastic facts to keep the trivia buffs going.

Chapter 20

Ten Great Players

*W*ho are the ten greatest players in Victorian Football League and AFL history? Ask the same question of 100 football fans and the results are bound to be wildly different.

I, however, am in the superb position of being the author of this book and can please myself as to who I choose to be the ten greatest heroes of Australian football. With all due modesty, I've been covering the VFL/AFL scene for about 40 years and, in that time, I've seen hundreds of games and thousands of footballers. I've written a couple of dozen books on Aussie Rules, from histories to how to play the game. However, I also admit, I'm forced to omit a number of legendary players for technical reasons (for example, I had to overlook champion South Australian player Barrie Robran — an official AFL legend — as he never played at VFL or AFL level). For lists of winners of AFL medals down the years, just turn to Appendix A, and refer to Chapter 15 for information on the medals themselves.

With a heavy heart (and many crossed fingers and toes that I don't incur the wrath of too many fans), the following players — listed in alphabetical order — have earned ten out of ten in my book.

Determined Demon — Ron Barassi

No-one, including me, believes Ron Barassi was one of the game's most skilled players, but he certainly made one of the greatest impacts on the game when he revolutionised the ruck-rover role and took determination to a new level. (For information on the various positions, refer to Chapter 5.)

The son of Melbourne footballer Ron Barassi Snr, who was killed in World War II, Barassi played 204 games with the Melbourne Demons from 1953 to 1964 and played in six premiership sides (including two as captain). Barassi crossed to Carlton as captain and coach in 1965 and guided the Blues to the 1968 and 1970 premiership flags as a non-playing coach. Barassi later coached North Melbourne to premierships in 1975 and 1977 before returning to the Demons as coach from 1981 to 1985 and then guiding the Sydney Swans from 1993 to 1995.

- **Years in the VFL/AFL:** 1953 to 1995 (as player and coach)
- **Teams:** Melbourne, Carlton, North Melbourne and the Sydney Swans

The Maroons' Maestro — Haydn Bunton

Every Victorian Football League club chased Haydn Bunton's signature when the brilliant player was starring in the country team Albury. Bunton finally signed with the Fitzroy Maroons (now merged with Brisbane) and won the Brownlow Medal in his debut season of 1931.

A brilliant rover with uncanny ball skills, Bunton won two more Brownlow Medals in 1932 and 1935. He left Fitzroy at the end of the 1937 season and then won three Sandover Medals as the best and fairest in the West Australian Football League with the Subiaco club. The football champion made a brief comeback to the Victorian Football League in 1942, playing two games with Fitzroy while he was on army service, bringing his total number of games with the Maroons to 119.

- **Years in the VFL:** 1931 to 1942
- **Team:** Fitzroy (now the Brisbane Lions)

King of the Kangaroos — Wayne Carey

The only recent player on my top-ten list, Wayne Carey was the heartbeat of the Kangaroos for a decade and captained the club to the 1996 and 1999 premierships.

A superb mark and an inspirational leader, Carey mixed skill with aggression in the game's most difficult position, centre half-forward. Originally from the country town of Wagga Wagga in New South Wales, Carey played 244 games with the Roos to 2002 and then 28 games with Adelaide from 2003 to 2004 before retiring because of a serious neck injury. During his career with the Roos he was named in the 'All-Australian' side (refer to Chapter 15) seven times, including four as captain. Personal problems saw him leave the Roos just before the start of the 2002 season and, at the end of the season, he indicated he wanted to play with the Adelaide club.

- ✔ **Years in the AFL:** 1989 to 2004
- ✔ **Teams:** Kangaroos and Adelaide

Ace Bomber — John Coleman

John Coleman was an overnight sensation on joining Essendon in 1949. Recruited from the Victorian country club Hastings, Coleman kicked 12 goals in his debut game (against Hawthorn) and went on to kick exactly 100 goals and play in the Bombers' premiership side that season.

Arguably the greatest high mark the game has seen, Coleman's career was cut short when he severely injured a knee in a match against North Melbourne in 1954. Over his career, Coleman kicked 537 goals from just 98 games, played in two Essendon premiership sides and was a non-playing coach of the Bombers, helping the team to premiership victory in the 1962 and 1965 seasons.

- ✔ **Years in the VFL:** 1949 to 1967 (as player and coach)
- ✔ **Team:** Essendon

Polly Good Show — Graham Farmer

Nicknamed Polly, Graham Farmer was arguably the greatest ruckman the game has ever seen. (If you don't know what a ruckman is, refer to Chapter 5.) The star footballer was an expert at directing the ball to teammates and squirting the ball up to 25 metres with pinpoint-perfect handpasses.

Farmer played with East Perth from 1953 to 1961 and won two Sandover Medals before joining the Geelong Cats in 1962. He played 101 games with the Cats to 1967 and played an integral role in the team's 1963 premiership triumph. Farmer returned to Western Australia to play with West Perth in 1968, but returned to Victoria to be a non-playing coach of Geelong from 1973 to 1975.

> ✔ **Years in the VFL:** 1962 to 1975 (as player and coach)
> ✔ **Team:** Geelong

In the Lethal League — Leigh Matthews

Built like a steel barrel, Leigh Matthews was a human battering ram and, in his heyday, combined brilliance with aggression. A ferocious competitor for the Hawthorn club, Matthews consistently won the ball around the ground, but late in his career he swapped his roving role for the full-forward position.

Known as 'Lethal' Leigh, Matthews played 332 games and kicked 915 goals for Hawthorn from 1969 to 1985. He was the non-playing coach of the 1990 Collingwood premiership side before becoming a successful coach of the Brisbane Lions. He played in four Hawks premiership sides and during one memorable match kicked 11 goals.

> ✔ **Years in the AFL:** 1969 to the present (as player and coach)
> ✔ **Teams:** Hawthorn, Collingwood and the Brisbane Lions

Royal Rover — Dick Reynolds

'King Richard', as adoring Essendon fans crowned Dick Reynolds, debuted for the Dons in 1933 and was instantly hailed a champion. A fast and clever rover, Reynolds had great evasive skills and was particularly dangerous near goal.

Reynolds won Brownlow Medals in 1934, 1937 and 1938, and won the Essendon club's best and fairest award seven times. Reynolds played 320 games with Essendon to 1951 and coached the club for an incredible 22 years (including 11 as playing coach), guiding the Bombers to premiership wins in 1942, 1946, 1949 and 1950. The football world mourned Reynolds' death in 2002.

- ✔ **Years in the VFL:** 1933 to 1960 (as player and coach)
- ✔ **Team:** Essendon

Skill by the Tonne — Bob Skilton

When I was a young lad, Skilton was my football idol and I make no apologies for including him in the top-ten list. A superbly gifted footballer who never worked out whether his right or left foot was his natural style, Skilton waltzed through packs and was extremely dangerous near goal.

Skilton won three Brownlow Medals and captained South Melbourne (now the Sydney Swans) from 1961 to 1971. He played 237 games in the red and white from 1956 to 1971 and was captain and coach for the 1965 and 1966 seasons. From 1974 to 1977, Skilton was Melbourne's non-playing coach.

- ✔ **Years in the VFL:** 1956 to 1977 (as player and coach)
- ✔ **Team:** South Melbourne (now the Sydney Swans) and Melbourne

Centre of Activity — Ian Stewart

Recruited from Tasmania to play with St Kilda, Ian Stewart was a football genius and managed time after time to frustrate and conquer rivals. Stewart's foot-passing ability has never been equalled, and the star played the centre position to perfection.

Stewart won Brownlow Medals with the Saints in 1965 and 1966, and added to his Brownlow collection in 1971 as a Richmond player. He played 127 games with St Kilda from 1963 to 1970 and 78 games with the Richmond Tigers from 1971 to 1975. Stewart coached South Melbourne in the 1976 and 1977 seasons and again from 1979 to 1981. In 1978, he coached Carlton for a brief period before resigning due to health problems.

  ✔ **Years in the VFL:** 1963 to 1981 (as player and coach)
  ✔ **Teams:** St Kilda, Richmond

Football's Mr Football — Ted Whitten

Ted Whitten was brilliant in virtually any position, but the champion footballer excelled at either centre half-forward or centre half-back. A magnificent mark with an extremely long kick, Whitten was highly skilled and a ruthless competitor.

Known as 'The Great E J' after his names Edward James, Whitten never won a Brownlow Medal, no doubt as a result of his ferocious playing style. Mr Football, as he was also known, played 321 games with Footscray (now the Western Bulldogs) from 1951 to 1970 and played in the Bulldogs' only premiership side in 1954.

  ✔ **Years in the VFL:** 1951 to 1971 (as player and coach)
  ✔ **Team:** Footscray (now the Western Bulldogs)

And Another Ten I Couldn't Leave Out!

With so many greats of the game, choosing just ten players to put on my list was a struggle, especially as the following football champions were also jostling for a position:

- Kevin Bartlett (Richmond)
- Nathan Buckley (Collingwood)
- Gordon Coventry (Collingwood)
- Jack Dyer (Richmond)
- James Hird (Essendon)
- Peter Hudson (Hawthorn)
- Tony Lockett (St Kilda and Sydney)
- Peter McKenna (Collingwood)
- Bob Pratt (South Melbourne)
- Michael Voss (Brisbane)

Chapter 21

The Top Ten Teams

*E*very club in the history of the Victorian Football League and the AFL has enjoyed days of glory, but a number of teams have shown outstanding levels of performance season after season. The measuring stick for greatness is premiership wins, plus the ability to be consistent, despite problems such as player injuries.

Just as a certain level of agony went into choosing the game's greatest players (refer to Chapter 20), nominating the top ten teams is no easy feat, particularly because a club's level of success can vary greatly from decade to decade. For that reason, the club's golden era is noted after each of the teams, which are listed in chronological order.

Carlton 1906–1908

Carlton failed to win a flag until 1906, but then went on to win the 1907 and 1908 premierships in football's first era of one-club domination. The Blues appointed former Fitzroy player John Worrall as coach in 1902 and the footy expert introduced a regime of professionalism to the team. The Carlton centreline of George Bruce, Rod McGregor and Ted Kennedy is still rated as one of the best player combinations of any era.

Other Carlton stars during this era included:

✔ Norman 'Hackenschmitt' Clark (defender)

✔ George 'Pompey' Elliott (rover)

✔ Jim Flynn (ruckman)

✔ George 'Mallee' Johnson (centre half-back)

Collingwood 1927–1930

The Magpies won a record four consecutive premierships from 1927 to 1930 under the coaching of the legendary Jock McHale. During this era, Collingwood was virtually unstoppable and even managed to finish the 1929 season with just one defeat (by Richmond in a semi-final).

Stars of the Magpies in the team's golden years included:

- Jack Beveridge (centreman)
- Albert Collier (rover)
- Harry Collier (ruckman or defender)
- Gordon Coventry (full-forward)
- Syd Coventry (ruckman)

South Melbourne 1933–1936

South Melbourne only won the 1933 premiership during this era, but the club had arguably the greatest ever combination of players. Sadly, the club was more a team of champions than a champion team, and only bad luck prevented the team from winning all four flags from 1933 to 1936. For example, champion full-forward Bob Pratt was knocked down by a truck and injured on the eve of the 1935 Collingwood grand final against Collingwood. Pratt was forced to miss the big match because of a minor leg injury and South lost a grand final it probably would have won.

In the 1930s, South Melbourne's Bob Pratt was one of the game's greatest full-forwards and Laurie Nash was a magnificent centre half-forward. Other star players included:

- Bill Faul (defender)
- Ron Hillis (full-back)
- Herbie Matthews (forward)
- Len Thomas (centreman)

Melbourne 1939–1941

Melbourne won the three premierships from 1939 to 1941, and many fans believe that only World War II prevented the club from at least equalling Collingwood's record of four consecutive flags from 1927 to 1930. The war depleted the team by no less than four Melbourne 1940 premiership players — Ron Barassi Snr, Harold Ball, Syd Anderson and Keith 'Bluey' Truscott, who were all killed in action.

Coached by Frank 'Checker' Hughes, Melbourne's stars of this era included:

- ✔ Percy Beames (rover)
- ✔ Allan La Fontaine (centreman)
- ✔ Jack Mueller (full-forward)
- ✔ Norm Smith (forward)

Essendon 1946–1951

Essendon played in the grand final every year from 1946 to 1951, winning the 1946, 1949 and 1950 flags. The team was simply desperately unlucky to lose the 1951 flag, mainly as a result of a player suspension.

Coached by triple Brownlow medallist Dick Reynolds, the Bombers had an abundance of talent on every line and, in 1949, recruited the superbly talented John Coleman, who kicked exactly 100 goals in his debut season. However, Coleman was suspended for four matches on the eve of the 1951 finals series for striking (punching) Carlton defender Harry Caspar, no doubt costing Essendon the flag as the team went down to Geelong by just 11 points.

Other Essendon stars of the era included:

- ✔ Bill Brittingham (full-back)
- ✔ Norm McDonald (half-back)
- ✔ Bill Hutchison (rover)

Geelong 1951–1953

During this period, the Cats were virtually impossible to defeat and won the 1951 and 1952 flags before being defeated by Collingwood in the 1953 grand final. In the 1952 and 1953 seasons, the team — coached by former club champion Reg Hickey — managed to go undefeated (with one draw) in 26 games, and bad luck to any team who had to play the Cats at the team's home venue, Kardinia Park (now Skilled Stadium).

Geelong stars of this era included:

- Bob Davis (half-forward)
- Fred Flanagan (centre half-forward)
- George Goninon (full-forward)
- Bernie Smith (back pocket)
- Leo Turner (winger)

Melbourne 1954–1964

Melbourne, under the coaching of the wily Norm Smith, made the finals every year from 1954 to 1964 and every grand final from 1954 to 1960. The team won six premierships during this period — including three consecutive flags from 1955 to 1957 and five flags from seven appearances from 1954 to 1960. During this era, every team in the league went into a game against the Demons with fear in their hearts.

The team's vast number of star footballers included:

- Ron Barassi (ruck-rover)
- John Beckwith (back pocket)
- Denis Cordner (ruckman)
- Bob Johnson (ruckman or forward)
- Noel McMahen (half-back)
- Laurie Mithen (centreman)
- Stuart Spencer (rover)

North Melbourne 1974–1978

Historically, North Melbourne (now the Kangaroos) was an easy team to beat, but the appointment of Ron Barassi as coach in 1973 lifted the club to previously unimagined heights. Thanks also to a massive recruiting drive, North Melbourne made the 1974 grand final (going down to Richmond) before landing the club's first flag in 1975 and then adding to the glory in 1977. North Melbourne played in every grand final from 1974 to 1978 and finished third in 1979 before fading from the game's bright lights.

Stars of this era included:

- Malcolm Blight (full-forward and utility)
- Barry Davis (half-back)
- David Dench (full-back)
- Keith Greig (winger)
- John Rantall (half-back)
- Wayne Schimmelbusch (winger)
- Doug Wade (full-forward)

Hawthorn 1983–1989

Incredibly, Hawthorn made the grand final every year from 1983 to 1989, winning four flags. In addition, the Hawks also made the finals every year from 1982 to 1994, which is a remarkable run in anybody's book. The Hawks' coach at the time was Allan Jeans, except for the 1988 season when, for medical reasons, Alan Joyce took on the coaching duties. The Hawks of this era were tough, ruthless and highly skilled, with a squad of match winners. Leigh Matthews led the team until his retirement in 1985, when Michael Tuck took the reins.

Other Hawthorn stars included:

- Dermott Brereton (centre half-forward)
- Robert DiPierdomenico (winger)
- Jason Dunstall (full-forward)
- Chris Langford (full-back)
- John Platten (rover)

Brisbane Lions 2001–2003

Brisbane was easily the most dominant club over the 2001–2003 seasons, not only winning back-to-back premierships, but setting new standards for skill, toughness and ability to overcome almost every challenge. The Lions started the 2001 season but then stormed home to defeat Essendon comfortably in the grand final. Coached by former Hawthorn champion and 1990 Collingwood premiership coach Leigh Matthews, the Lions proved this victory was no flash in the pan by marching to the 2002 title with a grand final win over Collingwood. Then, in 2003, they made it three flags in a row by defeating Collingwood once again. The Lions almost made it four in a row in 2004, but went down to Port Adelaide in the grand final.

Stars of the Lions' extraordinary 2001–2003 seasons included:

- Michael Voss (midfielder)
- Jason Akermanis (midfielder)
- Simon Black (midfielder)
- Alastair Lynch (full-forward)
- Nigel Lappin (winger)
- Justin Leppitsch (defender)
- Jonathan Brown (forward)

Chapter 22

The Ten Best
True-Boot Artists

In This Chapter

▷ Noting highest scorers

▷ Cheering kicking kings

▷ Acknowledging record breakers

*I*n Australian football, goal kickers are known as true-boot artists and the players who excel at kicking goals have been hailed as heroes since the inception of the Victorian Football League competition in 1897. Working out the game's ten best goal kickers is enormously difficult, because analysing the records is an exacting task (and one that quickly leads to a packet of headache tablets).

Additionally, a number of footballers are without doubt great true-boot artists, but the records indicate otherwise. For example, Sydney and Brisbane's Warwick Capper might have been a great goal kicker, but he didn't set many records. As a result, this chapter kicks off with the top ten kickers in terms of goals scored, and follows with the footballers who I regard as the game's greatest goal kickers, regardless of the players' goal tally.

The Ten Most Prolific Goal Scorers

Crowd numbers, umpires' names, player ages . . . every aspect of Australian football is dutifully recorded for future reference, and the players who kick the goals are no exception, as the following top-ten list (in order of number of goals kicked) shows:

- ✔ **Tony Lockett (St Kilda, Sydney):** 1,360 goals from 281 matches (1983–1999 and 2002)
- ✔ **Gordon Coventry (Collingwood):** 1,299 goals from 306 matches (1920–1937)
- ✔ **Jason Dunstall (Hawthorn):** 1,254 goals from 269 matches (1985–1998)
- ✔ **Doug Wade (Geelong, Kangaroos):** 1,057 goals from 267 matches (1961–1975)
- ✔ **Gary Ablett (Hawthorn, Geelong):** 1,030 goals from 248 matches (1982 and 1984–1996)
- ✔ **Jack Titus (Richmond):** 970 goals from 294 matches (1926–1943)
- ✔ **Leigh Matthews (Hawthorn):** 915 goals from 332 matches (1969–1985)
- ✔ **Peter McKenna (Collingwood, Carlton):** 874 goals from 191 matches (1965–1977)
- ✔ **Bernie Quinlan (Footscray, Fitzroy):** 817 goals from 366 matches (1969–1986)
- ✔ **Kevin Bartlett (Richmond):** 778 goals from 403 matches (1965–1983)

The Ten Greatest Goal Kickers

Over the years, the game has produced many talented goal kickers, but the following ten players (listed alphabetically) stand out from the pack as the greatest of the true-boot artists the game has ever seen. In most cases, injury is the only reason that the players didn't make the records as the best in the game.

Gary Ablett

A legendary player for Geelong, Gary Ablett started his career with Hawthorn in 1982, before drifting into the country to play with the Myrtleford club in 1983. Ablett joined Geelong in 1984 and played with the Cats until 1996, kicking 1,030 goals in his 248 League games, even though the champion player started his career playing as a winger or half-forward. A phenomenal mark, Ablett had tremendous pace off the mark. His best individual match tally was 14, which the star achieved three times — against Richmond in 1989, against Essendon in 1993 and against Sydney in 1994. Ablett's best season total was 129 goals in 1994.

  ✔ **Goal tally:** 1,030 goals from 248 games
  ✔ **Best goal tally from a single game:** 14 (against Richmond in 1989, against Essendon in 1993 and Sydney in 1994)

John Coleman

Essendon's John Coleman was a goal-kicking freak! The star player booted 12 goals in his debut game, which was against Hawthorn in the opening round of the 1949 season. Arguably the greatest high mark the game has seen, Coleman was virtually unstoppable and was deadly accurate within 50 metres. A clever ground player, Coleman kicked 537 goals in 98 matches, a tally that was cut short by a knee injury in 1954.

  ✔ **Goal tally:** 537 goals from 98 games
  ✔ **Best goal tally from a single game:** 14 (against Fitzroy in 1954)

Gordon Coventry

A Collingwood champion, Gordon Coventry kicked 1,299 goals in 306 games from 1920 to 1937 and held the League's goal-kicking record until Sydney's Tony Lockett surpassed the tally in a match against the Magpies in 1999. Coventry, whose brother Syd was also a Collingwood champion, had incredible strength and was virtually impossible to knock off-balance. The star player kicked 7 goals or more in 63 of the 306 matches he played.

  ✔ **Goal tally:** 1,299 goals from 306 games
  ✔ **Best goal tally from a single game:** 17 (against Fitzroy in 1930)

Jason Dunstall

Recruited by Hawthorn from Queensland club Coorparoo, Jason Dunstall failed to be an immediate success on the field. After starting in a forward pocket, the brilliant athlete only became highly successful when he gravitated to the full-forward position and kicked 1,254 goals in 269 matches (making an average of 4.66 goals per match). Dunstall may well have matched the record goal tally of Sydney's Tony Lockett had he been able to fully recover from a fractured skull and, in 1996, a severe knee injury.

✔ **Goal tally:** 1,254 goals from 269 games

✔ **Best goal tally from a single game:** 17 (against Richmond in 1992)

Peter Hudson

Known as 'Peter the Great' by Hawthorn fans, Hudson played an unusual full-forward role in that Hawks coach John Kennedy instructed the team to keep the forward line open so that the Tasmanian star was left alone with an opponent. Hudson played the role to perfection and invariably won the individual duels. Despite his career being interrupted by a severe knee injury, Hudson kicked 727 goals from 129 games (making a superb average of 5.64 goals per match). In 1971, Hudson equalled the League record of 150 goals in a season, set by South Melbourne's Bob Pratt.

✔ **Goal tally:** 727 goals from 129 games

✔ **Best goal tally from a single game:** 16 (against Melbourne in 1969)

Dick Lee

Football's earliest goal-kicking ace was Collingwood's Dick Lee, who terrorised rival defences from 1906 to 1922 and, in an era of low scoring, kicked 7 goals or more in 12 matches. Lee totalled 707 goals from 230 games (making an average of 3.07 goals per match — an incredible ratio for the era). Lee topped the League goal kicking in ten seasons, despite being hampered for much of his career by a severe shin injury, which a doctor had to dress with caustic soda before each game.

✔ **Goal tally:** 707 goals from 230 games

✔ **Best goal tally from a single game:** 11 (against University in 1914)

Tony Lockett

A big, burly full-forward who was never afraid to use his massive frame, Tony Lockett played for St Kilda and Sydney and holds the record for the most goals kicked in League football — 1,360 from 281 matches (making an average of 4.84 goals per match). Surprisingly quick for such a big man, Lockett had astonishingly strong hands and was an excellent team player. The star kicker moved to Sydney in 1995 and was a Swan hero until his retirement in 1999. Lockett made an unsuccessful comeback in 2002, but retired again mid-season after just 3 games for 3 goals.

✔ **Goal tally:** 1,360 goals from 281 games

✔ **Best goal tally from a single game:** 16 (against Fitzroy in 1995)

Peter McKenna

A junior goal-kicking prodigy with West Heidelberg YCW (Young Christian Workers), Peter McKenna played for Collingwood and then Carlton, and kicked 874 goals from 191 games from 1965 to 1977. A magnificently fast lead, McKenna rarely missed a shot for goal with his exquisitely timed drop punts (refer to Chapter 6). McKenna *topped the ton* (which means he kicked over 100 goals in a season) in consecutive years from 1970 to 1972, with a season's best of 143 goals in 1970. The star kicker managed to kick 7 goals or more in a match 45 times. Sadly, however, he suffered a serious kidney injury in 1974, and played the following season in Tasmania before playing briefly with Carlton in 1977 and scoring 36 goals from 11 games.

✔ **Goal tally:** 874 goals from 191 games

✔ **Best goal tally from a single game:** 16 (against South Melbourne in 1969)

Bob Pratt

South Melbourne's Bob Pratt failed to be as prolific as other goal kickers, mainly because he abandoned Victorian Football League competition to play in the Victorian Football Association with the Coburg club. Pratt, recruited from the Mitcham club, kicked 681 goals from 158 games with South Melbourne from 1930 to 1939 and 1946. A superb aerialist, Pratt kicked a record 150 goals in 1934, a feat equalled by Hawthorn's Peter Hudson in 1971.

- **Goal tally:** 681 goals from 158 games
- **Best goal tally from a single game:** 15 (against Essendon in 1934)

Doug Wade

A burly full-forward recruited by Geelong from the Horsham club, Doug Wade was a particularly strong mark and a phenomenally long and accurate shot for goal, mainly through the use of the torpedo punt (refer to Chapter 6). Wade kicked 834 goals from 208 games with the Cats from 1961 to 1972 and then kicked 223 goals from 59 games with North Melbourne from 1973 to 1975. The star player kicked 7 goals or more in a match 40 times, twice kicked more than 100 goals in a season with 127 goals for Geelong in 1969 and 103 for the Kangaroos in 1974.

- **Goal tally:** 1,057 goals from 267 games
- **Best goal tally from a single game:** 13 (against South Melbourne in 1967)

FOOTY FLASHBACK

Fanning the record flames

Melbourne's Fred Fanning holds the record for the most goals in an individual match, scoring 18 against St Kilda at the Junction Oval in the final round of the 1947 season.

Sydney's Tony Lockett may have equalled or even broken Fanning's record in a match against Fitzroy at the Western Oval in 1995 if he hadn't misunderstood a message from coach Ron Barassi. The champion player kicked 16 goals that day but spent 15 minutes on the bench in the belief Barassi had ordered him off the field for a misdemeanour. Rather, Barassi had ordered the club runner to tell Lockett to 'cool it'. Lockett's mistake may have cost him the record!

Chapter 23

Ten Men Earn Top Marks

*N*ominating the game's ten best marking players is extremely subjective because so many great marks have been witnessed and recorded in the history of the game. Besides, how many great marks were taken without a camera or video to record the event?

After looking at thousands of photographs and hours of film footage of football games, I still feel hard pressed to choose just ten great marking players. In the end, my choices are based partly on watching football matches for half a century and partly on that great intangible — football folklore. But, generally speaking, great marking players demonstrate great acrobatic ability, combined with strength and a leap to make Superman envious.

So, with a deep breath, the following are my top ten marking players, in alphabetical order.

Trevor Barker

Although barely 182 centimetres, St Kilda's Trevor Barker played the role of a much taller man and, at full-back, was often up to 15 centimetres shorter than his opponents. Despite being vertically challenged, Barker had a sensational leap and used uncanny judgement to outwit the opposition. Time after time, tall players led Barker to the ball, with the expectation of overpowering the Saints player with ease. Instead, Barker flew into the air to pluck the ball from the taller player's grasp.

The star player was an aerial acrobat who was famous for flying at a pack from any direction and taking truly spectacular marks. Barker played 230 games with the Saints from 1975 to 1989. He died of cancer in 1996.

John Coleman

One of my earliest football memories is watching an Essendon versus South Melbourne match at Windy Hill. In particular, I remember the fans screaming every time the Essendon player wearing number 10 flew for the ball. Time after time the athletic John Coleman rose above the pack and plucked the ball out of the air with such ridiculous ease that his opponents appeared to be glued to the ground.

Coleman was a marking freak and the game lost a hero when a severe knee injury restricted the champion to just 98 games from 1949 to 1954. Old-time Essendon fans insist Coleman wasn't only the greatest mark the game has seen, but that he was also the greatest footballer. High praise indeed!

Gordon Coventry

Because Gordon Coventry played football in the 1920s and 1930s, I have relied on the evidence of history to place him in this top-ten listing. Contemporary reports suggest the Magpies' goal-kicking machine played a similar type of game to the one Tony Lockett adopted in the modern era. This winning style can be seen in a photograph of Coventry grabbing the ball as three opponents desperately cling to his guernsey and arms in a vain attempt to prevent the star from marking.

Coventry, who played 306 games for Collingwood from 1920 to 1937, was bigger and stronger than most players of his era and was greatly feared because of his powerful hands.

Alex Duncan

Few football fans today have heard of Alex Duncan, but the star player was regarded as a marking genius in the 1920s. Reportedly a superb aerialist, Duncan was rarely beaten in marking duels in his 141 games with Carlton from 1921 to 1924 and 1926 to 1930. A centre half-back, Duncan read the play superbly, taking countless marks over a magnificent career. Legendary football writer Wally 'Jumbo' Sharland rated the champion as one of the best marks the game had ever seen.

Duncan was credited with 33 marks in one game against Collingwood in 1927 and was so dominant in the air that the contest is still known as *Duncan's match*.

Jason Dunstall

Hawthorn's Jason Dunstall falls into the Tony Lockett and Gordon Coventry category: The star player took spectacular marks, and his trademark was using his incredible strength to out-position opponents. Like Lockett and Coventry, Dunstall was so dangerous on the field that the star player often had to contend with a gaggle of opponents, all intent on trying to stop him from grabbing the ball. After all, every player knew that, when Dunstall made contact with the ball, a mark was sure to follow.

Strong when taking a mark overhead, Dunstall — who played 269 games for Hawthorn from 1985 to 1998 — was also an excellent lead and therefore was the perfect marking full-forward.

Royce Hart

I watched the great Royce Hart in action for Richmond many times and have included the champion here not because of his ability to fly like Superman, but more because of his courage in taking extremely difficult pack marks. Hart often jumped sideways into a pack, exposing every rib to the opposition players, to pull down a mark. This move took raw, red-blooded courage, because each time the superb athlete risked receiving heavy knocks from ruthless opponents.

Hart, who played 187 games with Richmond from 1967 to 1977, was a supreme aerialist with hands that appeared to magnetically attract the ball.

Alex Jesaulenko

Any football fan worth his scarf and beanie has seen footage of Carlton's Alex Jesaulenko leaping high over Collingwood's Graeme 'Jerker' Jenkin in the famous 1970 grand final. In the footage, 'Jezza' — as the Blues' player was known — is almost two metres off the ground as he wraps his hand around the ball. Arguably, the move is the most famous mark in football history and was brilliant in the extreme.

Jesaulenko pulled down many other superb marks in his career, which included 256 games with the Blues from 1967 to 1979 and 23 games with St Kilda from 1980 to 1981. Jesaulenko had a huge leap and superb judgement and, despite standing just 183 centimetres, was able to mark over much taller opponents.

Tony Lockett

The St Kilda and Sydney champion goal kicker failed to pull down as many spectacular marks as other players on this list, but Tony Lockett took more than his fair share of spectacular grabs (known as *speccies*). More importantly, however, Lockett had hands as strong as a vice and the ball rarely escaped the champion's clutches. A huge man, Lockett used his body to either crash through packs or to stand his ground, often against two or even three opponents.

Once in position to mark, the opposition found it impossible to knock Lockett away; the player's awesome strength usually pulled the ball out of the reach of grappling rival hands. Lockett played a total of 281 games for the Saints and Swans from 1983 to 1999 and in a 3-game comeback in 2002.

Bob Pratt

The great Bob Pratt, who soared with the birds for South Melbourne, was before my time so, to include the player in this list, I've relied on photographic evidence and first-hand accounts from extremely old men who still marvel at the aerial antics of one of the greatest full-forwards the game has seen. One famous photograph of Pratt shows the champion virtually sitting on the shoulder of Collingwood's Jack Regan as he pulls in a mark; another shows him flying over the top of several Richmond opponents.

Pratt, who played 158 games with the Swans from 1930 to 1939 and 1946, is said to have been able to fly as high as his team's namesakes.

Graham Teasdale

Graham Teasdale is a controversial nomination as a great marking player, and the champion's inclusion has a lot to do with the fact that I saw most of Teasdale's games for South Melbourne after he moved to the Swans from Richmond. Teasdale was a truly spectacular high mark, especially when he played in the ruck in his Brownlow Medal-winning season of 1977. During that season, Teasdale pulled down everything but the seagulls gathering over the Lake Oval.

Teasdale had a tremendous leap for such a big man (193 centimetres) and pulled down 'speccie' after 'speccie' in every game. Unfortunately, injuries took their toll, and Teasdale had several lean seasons following his 1977 Brownlow Medal year. The champion played 6 games with Richmond in 1973, 125 games with South from 1975 to 1981 and 14 games with Collingwood in 1982 and 1983.

Chapter 24

The Best Aussie Rules Games

*B*eing paid to watch and report on Aussie Rules football has been one of the great privileges of my life. Occasionally, I've left the ground with a yawn but, most often, the game has held my complete attention from the first bounce to the final siren. Fans love a game where the result is in doubt until the final seconds and/or there is genuine drama, like a player being injured yet kicking the winning goal.

There are many instances in football history when there have been almost unbelievable heroics and/or fighting comebacks. For example, football fans will long remember the 2002 season for the large number of close games and come-from-behind victories. Fans love these games because they get full value right to when the fat lady sings.

So, after a 35-year career of football writing, I humbly nominate the following best games of football (although I certainly don't profess to being old enough to have seen them all!).

South Melbourne v Collingwood — 1918

Since the Victorian Football League was formed in 1897, a number of grand finals have been extremely tight games right to the finish, but the 1918 grand final between South Melbourne and Collingwood had the most exciting finish of them all.

Play was tight throughout the match and fans were kept guessing as to which side was to land the premiership honours. With just a minute to play, Collingwood held a 1-point lead when South swept the ball to the team's forward line. The 39,262 fans roared themselves hoarse as the Southerners landed the ball in the goal square. Finally, South's Chris Laird stuck out a boot and made contact with the ball, dribbling it through for a goal with just a second left to play. South won by 5 points, and legendary football identity John Worrall, writing in the *Australasian*, stated: 'It was the most remarkable victory ever witnessed in a grand final.' The words still ring true today.

- ✔ **Game highlight:** Breathtakingly exciting final goal
- ✔ **My man of the match:** Chris Laird

St Kilda v North Melbourne — 1933

Played on May 27, 1933, the match between St Kilda and North Melbourne was extraordinary because no less than eight St Kilda players were injured as North tried to crash their way to success at the Junction Oval. St Kilda officials branded North's tactics as 'butchery', although the Shinboners (as North Melbourne was then known) denied the allegations and said St Kilda's injuries didn't result from unduly rough play.

During the game, St Kilda's captain, Clarrie Hindson, broke a leg, Bill Mohr suffered two broken ribs and Roy Bence and Matt Cave were concussed. Despite having just a dozen fully fit players left to play the game, St Kilda still managed to win by 14 points, forcing North's president Arthur Calwell to declare St Kilda 'the better side'.

- ✔ **Game 'highlight':** Excessive 'butchery' by North Melbourne
- ✔ **Number of St Kilda players injured:** Eight

Geelong v Collingwood — 1937

Contemporary reports suggest that the 1937 grand final between Geelong and Collingwood was one of the finest games ever played, with the standard of play exceptionally high. A then record crowd of 88,540 at the Melbourne Cricket Ground saw the Cats play superb football to defeat the Magpies by 32 points, which may sound like a comfortable margin, until you realise that the score was level at the final break.

Geelong's captain and coach, Reg Hickey, gambled by giving himself the onerous task of playing on champion Magpie full-forward Gordon Coventry, and restricted the champion goal kicker to just three goals. Both sides played fast, play-on football, and critics raved about the 'sportsmanship on display'.

✔ **Game highlight:** Scores level at the final break

✔ **My man of the match:** Reg Hickey

Carlton v Essendon — 1947

The 1947 grand final clash between Carlton and Essendon is hard to beat for excitement. A crowd of 85,518 fans roared from the game's start to finish as the scores continued to stay tight throughout — although Essendon's inaccuracy (missing shots for goal) in front of goals (8.11 to Carlton's 8.0 at half time) proved costly.

With just 44 seconds to play, the Dons led by 5 points and looked certain to take the flag — until Carlton's Fred Stafford swooped on the ball. Stafford kicked awkwardly around his body and the ball sailed through for a goal to the Blues. Carlton won by just 1 point and, ironically, the goal was one of Stafford's few kicks for the match.

✔ **Game highlight:** Consistently tight scores throughout the match

✔ **My man of the match:** Fred Stafford

Collingwood v Melbourne — 1958

Melbourne had won three consecutive flags from 1955 to 1957 and, in 1958, was attempting to equal Collingwood's record of four consecutive flags (won from 1927 to 1930). The Magpies were desperate to defend this record and were determined to trounce Melbourne.

The Melbourne Demons appeared to have the better combination of players, but Collingwood planned superbly for the defence of their proud record, using Barry 'Hooker' Harrison to restrict Melbourne champion Ron Barassi. Other Collingwood players used raw aggression to outplay Melbourne, and the tactics helped Collingwood defeat the Demons by 18 points. The record was safe.

✔ **Game highlight:** Collingwood's game plan

✔ **My man of the match:** Barry 'Hooker' Harrison

Carlton v Collingwood — 1970

For a number of reasons, the 1970 grand final is rated as the greatest grand final of them all: The game attracted a record crowd of 121,696 fans; Carlton's Alex Jesaulenko took the mark of the century over Collingwood's Graeme 'Jerker' Jenkin and the Blues overcame a 44-point half-time deficit to defeat the Magpies by 10 points.

The standard of play was extraordinarily high throughout the game, and Carlton's comeback was breathtaking. The Blues' hero was reserve Ted Hopkins, who galvanised Carlton after taking the field after half time. Hopkins kicked four goals to inspire the Blues to a victory not even the staunchest fans were dreaming of at the half-time gun.

> ✔ **Game highlight:** Alex Jesaulenko takes the mark of the century
>
> ✔ **My man of the match:** Ted Hopkins

Carlton v Collingwood — 1979

The 1979 grand final between Carlton and Collingwood wasn't necessarily a football purist's delight, but the final moments of the match had more drama than a season at the Old Vic.

The premiership was up for grabs, with just minutes to play, in drizzling conditions, when Carlton, clinging to a narrow lead, worked the ball to the half-forward line and, to the amazement of the 112,845 fans, Carlton's Wayne Harmes knocked the ball to teammate Ken Sheldon. Magpie fans screamed that the ball had been out of bounds and therefore moaned bitterly as Sheldon raced in to take a goal. Carlton won the match by 5 points and, although most football observers now believe the ball wasn't out of bounds, Magpie fans still argue the point to this day.

> ✔ **Game highlight:** Final goal by Ken Sheldon
>
> ✔ **My man of the match:** Ken Sheldon

Sydney v St Kilda — 1994

Sydney and St Kilda were mediocre teams in 1994 and nobody expected the 1994 season clash at the Sydney Cricket Ground to be one of the most sensational of the modern era. The Swans held sway for most of the match and had built up a seemingly impregnable 38-point lead by the final break.

In the final quarter, St Kilda full-forward Tony Lockett turned the match around to give the Saints a 1-point win. Lockett might have finished the game with 11 goals to be hailed his side's hero, but he was later suspended for eight matches after smashing the nose of Sydney's Peter Caven. Ironically, Lockett joined the Swans the following year and instantly became a Swan hero.

✔ **Game highlight:** Massive comeback by St Kilda in the final quarter

✔ **My man of the match:** Tony Lockett

Sydney v Essendon — 1996

I admit to having a Sydney bias but, even allowing for this, the 1996 preliminary final between the Sydney Swans and the Essendon Bombers was a truly extraordinary match. More than 40,000 fans squeezed into the Sydney Cricket Ground for the Saturday night clash to see which team was to make the grand final and, after the lead had changed hands numerous times throughout the match, the scores were level, with just seconds to play.

As the clock ticked down, Sydney's Tony Lockett marked about 52 metres from goal and as he lined up the goals the final siren blared. Any score would put the Swans into the grand final for the first time since 1945, but — as the crowd knew — Lockett was nursing a severe groin injury. Nevertheless, the star player kicked and the ball sailed long and through for a behind. The crowd erupted with a roar! What a sensational finish!

✔ **Game highlight:** Kick for goal as the siren sounds

✔ **My man of the match:** Tony Lockett

Essendon v Kangaroos — 2001

Many fans have hailed the Essendon–Kangaroos match at the MCG on July 20, 2001, as the greatest football game ever played, but the scores were far too high for my liking because the glut of goals reflects a lack of defensive skills.

The first half of the match was ferocious: At one stage, the Kangaroos held a 69-point lead. Incredibly, Essendon clawed their way back into the match to snatch the lead in the final quarter. The Kangaroos again regained the lead, but Essendon came again to win by 12 points — 27.9 (171) to 25.9 (159). The match was great entertainment and had the greatest match comeback in the history of the game.

✔ **Game highlight:** Essendon's Matthew Lloyd kicking nine goals from just ten kicks

✔ **My man of the match:** Essendon's Jason Johnson, a non-stop worker for his team, with 31 possessions (22 kicks and 9 handpasses)

Sydney v West Coast — 2005

I might be biased here, but I've never seen a more exciting game than the Sydney–West Coast grand final of 2005, with little between the teams from start to finish.

Sydney grabbed a break in the second quarter, but West Coast fought back in the third quarter and then took the lead early in the final quarter. The match was tough, tight and relentless, with the tackling ferocious. The Eagles grabbed an 8-point break and most fans at the MCG thought the Western Australian team would cruise over the top of the Swans. However, Sydney forward Barry Hall bombed a goal from outside the 50-metre arc and the Swans were back in the game. Then, halfway through the final quarter, Swan on-baller Amon Buchanan snapped a goal to restore Sydney's lead. The Swans then held on for an incredible 12 minutes as the Eagles mounted attack after attack.

Finally, with just seconds to play, Eagle ruckman Dean Cox kicked long to his team's goal square and teammate Mark Seaby seemed set to take a mark for a winning goal. Yet Sydney's Leo Barry somehow ran from the side of a huge pack to take a soaring fingertip mark to deny the Eagles. It was a match-saving mark and, just a few second later, the final siren blared. Sydney by 4 points in the most exciting grand final of them all.

West Coast had its revenge in the 2006 grand final and, although its 1-point win was wildly exciting, the match lacked the class and spirit of 2005, as the Eagles at one stage led by almost 30 points and the Swans never headed them.

✔ **Game Highlight:** Leo Barry's magnificent last-seconds mark

✔ **My man of the match:** West Coast's Ben Cousins, who never stopped trying, especially after fellow on-baller Daniel Kerr limped off with a leg injury

Chapter 25

Ten Fantastic Footy Facts

*L*iterally thousands of truly amazing incidents have stunned footy fans and officials alike in the history of Australian football. Some have resulted from sheer chance; others have resulted from bizarre circumstances. Although you've probably seen your share of incredible moments on the grounds, the following are my most amazing footy facts. Eat your heart out, Ripley — these gems truly fall into the believe-it-or-not category!

What a Wally!

When Carlton named Chinese footballer Wally Koo-chew for his first League game in 1908, a club member returned his ticket saying Koo-chew's selection 'dealt a death blow' to the nation's White Australia policy. Koo-chew played just four games for Carlton. His low games tally had nothing to do with racism and, rather, more to do with his lack of outstanding football ability. Other Asian footballers to have played the game at the highest level include current Fremantle star Peter Bell, who was born in Korea, and Collingwood and Melbourne's Danny Seow (1986–1990), who was born in Singapore.

Lousy Shot

Richmond plucked Bill James from country club Kyabram to play in the 1920 grand final. The unknown James managed to kick the winning goal in his only League game and then, after being suitably lauded by the press, returned to his life in the country. Not long after, James was accidentally shot in the foot by a friend while rabbit hunting and never played a game of football again. James therefore is unique in the annals of VFL/AFL records, because no other player has won a premiership medal in his only game. James's accident could have been even more serious if he hadn't been wearing an old pair of football boots when shot.

Champion-Ship

Warwick Armstrong, who was known as 'The Big Ship' because of his massive bulk, played brilliantly for South Melbourne in the 1899 grand final against Fitzroy. Even though the Southerners lost the match, Armstrong was hailed a hero of the game, so fans and officials were amazed when, after playing in just 16 League games, the giant elected to dump footy to pursue his cricket career. In fact, the move turned out to be a personal triumph: Armstrong went on to play in 50 Tests over 20 years, scoring 2,863 runs and taking 87 wickets! When Armstrong played football with South Melbourne, he weighed 84 kilograms but, late in his cricket career, weighed 120 kilograms. In private life, he was a whisky merchant who dabbled in journalism.

Unlucky Break

Carlton's Les Witto was playing his sixth match for the Blues in a game against Geelong at Princes Park in 1926 when his arm was broken in a scuffle. Witto was rushed to hospital, but tragically died after tetanus infected the wound. Carlton organised a testimonial for his widow mother in Broken Hill. In another football tragedy, Carlton's Lyle Downs died following a heart attack after training in 1921. Thousands attended the Carlton star's funeral. Downs played 47 games with Carlton from 1917 to his untimely death. Football deaths are extremely rare in Australian football, yet these two at VFL (now AFL) level occurred just five years apart. There have been none at the elite level since.

Cop That!

The occasional tension between the law and football loyalties has sometimes resulted in peculiar entanglements between the police and the game. At the turn of the 20th century, Melbourne's police commissioner decided to ban members of his force from playing football. Undaunted, police constable Will Proudfoot not only led the police band at the 1903 grand final between Collingwood and Fitzroy, he also played for the Magpies under the alias of Wilson. Proudfoot played a pivotal role in the Magpies' 2-point win over the Maroons. In a previous incident, as a police officer at a Victorian Football Association match at North Melbourne in 1896, he was attacked by fans when he went to the rescue of a beleaguered umpire. Proudfoot was severely beaten and his assailant was jailed for three months.

Going Nuts

Champion Collingwood full-forward Gordon 'Nuts' Coventry missed out on playing in the 1936 grand final against South Melbourne because of a suspension. Coventry had been reported for striking Richmond's Joe Murdoch late in the season, but for years after the incident Coventry was still claiming that he had merely retaliated after the Tiger defender had punched boils on the back of his neck. Even more annoying for Coventry was that he was unable to truly share in the glory after the Magpies trounced the Tigers to take out the premiership! Coventry had to serve an eight-match suspension and retired at the end of the following season.

Swan Dive

On the eve of the 1935 grand final between Collingwood and South Melbourne, champion Swans forward Bob Pratt stepped off a tram and was hit by a truck. Pratt's injuries forced him to miss playing in the big match. Collingwood took full advantage of Pratt's absence and went on to win by 20 points. Ironically, the truck driver was a Swans supporter. The hapless truck driver went to Pratt's home to apologise and presented the South champion with a packet of cigarettes in consolation. Pratt was replaced by Roy Moore, who kicked two goals but obviously was not an adequate replacement for one of the greatest goal kickers the game had seen.

She'll Be Apples

In 1970, Geelong and South Melbourne were locked in battle for match points and a place in the finals at Kardinia Park. As Geelong full-forward Doug Wade took a shot for goal late in the match, a South fan threw an apple, which amazingly hit the ball in mid-flight and threw it off-course. The Swans won the game by just 7 points and made the finals. Wade still swears that the ball was on target for a goal and believes his side would have made the finals, not South, if it had not been for that apple. Throwing anything onto the field in Aussie Rules is extremely rare and this shot was a chance in many millions.

Flood of Tears

Although flooding tactics (teams flocking to one end of the ground) is a modern tactic, Footscray used natural flooding to thwart Fitzroy at the Western Oval in 1953. The ground was covered by a sheet of water when a drain became blocked because of torrential rain. Fitzroy was unable to score until the final minute, when captain Allan Ruthven goaled. The water was half a metre deep where Ruthven gathered the ball and his shot for goal slithered through, just saving the Gorillas (as Fitzroy then was known) the embarrassment of being the only team not to score in a VFL/AFL match.

Dark Horse

Fitzroy's Bill Marchbank, a mounted policeman, was refused permission to play with Fitzroy one weekend in the 1911 season and, instead, was rostered on duty for a match between Essendon and South Melbourne. To add injury to insult, Marchbank was thrown from his horse while on duty during the match, hurt his knee and was unable to play for the rest of the season. Marchbank later wore a special guard over his injured knee. Marchbank retired the following season with just 23 games to his credit (1 with Carlton in 1908 and 22 with Fitzroy from 1910 to 1912).

Part VII
Appendixes

Glenn Lumsden

*'I find an easy way to remember
important dates is to pretend
they're footy statistics.'*

In this part . . .

In this part, I've put together some helpful resources for you. Need to know who won the Brownlow Medal in 1966 for your next trivia game? Just turn to Appendix A. Want to fit in with the crowd at the next game? I've listed the common lingo in Appendix B. And if you want to read more about the game, Appendix C supplies a list of some top books to peruse.

Appendix A

Premiership and Medal Winners

Although I like to pride myself on my football knowledge, I'm no walking, talking encyclopedia. I can't recite who won the premiership in most given years, although I can tell you that my side (South Melbourne, now Sydney) won the flag in 1909, 1918, 1933 and, glory of glories, 2005. I'd waited all my life for a Swans premiership and, following a 72-year drought, they defeated the West Coast Eagles in the 2005 grand final. It was the most thrilling grand final for years as the Swans took the lead with 15 minutes to play and held on to win by just 4 points. (Refer to Chapter 24 for a more detailed description of this match.) Here also are the Charles Brownlow Medal dates and winners, along with those of the John Coleman, Norm Smith and Michael Tuck Medals, and other historical information. (Refer to Chapter 15 for more information on these medals.) So, if you don't have a photographic memory, here are the facts at your fingertips.

Premiership Winners

The following teams are winners of the VFL/AFL grand finals:

1897: Essendon	**1911:** Essendon
1898: Fitzroy	**1912:** Essendon
1899: Fitzroy	**1913:** Fitzroy
1900: Melbourne	**1914:** Carlton
1901: Essendon	**1915:** Carlton
1902: Collingwood	**1916:** Fitzroy
1903: Collingwood	**1917:** Collingwood
1904: Fitzroy	**1918:** South Melbourne
1905: Fitzroy	**1919:** Collingwood
1906: Carlton	**1920:** Richmond
1907: Carlton	**1921:** Richmond
1908: Carlton	**1922:** Fitzroy
1909: South Melbourne	**1923:** Essendon
1910: Collingwood	**1924:** Essendon

1925: Geelong
1926: Melbourne
1927: Collingwood
1928: Collingwood
1929: Collingwood
1930: Collingwood
1931: Geelong
1932: Richmond
1933: South Melbourne
1934: Richmond
1935: Collingwood
1936: Collingwood
1937: Geelong
1938: Carlton
1939: Melbourne
1940: Melbourne
1941: Melbourne
1942: Essendon
1943: Richmond
1944: Fitzroy
1945: Carlton
1946: Essendon
1947: Carlton
1948: Melbourne
1949: Essendon
1950: Essendon
1951: Geelong
1952: Geelong
1953: Collingwood
1954: Footscray
1955: Melbourne
1956: Melbourne
1957: Melbourne
1958: Collingwood
1959: Melbourne
1960: Melbourne
1961: Hawthorn
1962: Essendon
1963: Geelong
1964: Melbourne
1965: Essendon
1966: St Kilda

1967: Richmond
1968: Carlton
1969: Richmond
1970: Carlton
1971: Hawthorn
1972: Carlton
1973: Richmond
1974: Richmond
1975: North Melbourne
1976: Hawthorn
1977: North Melbourne
1978: Hawthorn
1979: Carlton
1980: Richmond
1981: Carlton
1982: Carlton
1983: Hawthorn
1984: Essendon
1985: Essendon
1986: Hawthorn
1987: Carlton
1988: Hawthorn
1989: Hawthorn
1990: Collingwood
1991: Hawthorn
1992: West Coast
1993: Essendon
1994: West Coast
1995: Carlton
1996: North Melbourne
1997: Adelaide
1998: Adelaide
1999: North Melbourne
2000: Essendon
2001: Brisbane
2002: Brisbane
2003: Brisbane
2004: Port Adelaide
2005: Sydney
2006: West Coast
2007: Geelong

Charles Brownlow Medal Winners

The Brownlow Medal is awarded annually to the player nominated by the umpires as the 'fairest and best' player of the AFL season. The following footballers are the winners of this prestigious individual honour, named for former Geelong administrator Charles Brownlow:

1924: Edward Greeves (Geelong)
1925: Colin Watson (St Kilda)
1926: Ivor Warne-Smith (Melbourne)
1927: Syd Coventry (Collingwood)
1928: Ivor Warne-Smith (Melbourne)
1929: Albert Collier (Collingwood)
1930: Stan Judkins (Richmond), Allan Hopkins (Footscray), Harry Collier (Collingwood)
1931: Haydn Bunton (Fitzroy)
1932: Haydn Bunton (Fitzroy)
1933: Wilfred Smallhorn (Fitzroy)
1934: Dick Reynolds (Essendon)
1935: Haydn Bunton (Fitzroy)
1936: Dinny Ryan (Fitzroy)
1937: Dick Reynolds (Essendon)
1938: Dick Reynolds (Essendon)
1939: Marcus Whelan (Collingwood)
1940: Herbie Matthews (South Melbourne), Des Fothergill (Collingwood)
1941: Norman Ware (Footscray)
1942–
1945: Award suspended because of World War II
1946: Don Cordner (Melbourne)
1947: Bert Deacon (Carlton)
1948: Bill Morris (Richmond)
1949: Ron Clegg (South Melbourne), Col Austen (Hawthorn)
1950: Allan Ruthven (Fitzroy)
1951: Bernie Smith (Geelong)
1952: Roy Wright (Richmond), Bill Hutchison (Essendon)
1953: Bill Hutchison (Essendon)

1954: Roy Wright (Richmond)
1955: Fred Goldsmith (South Melbourne)
1956: Peter Box (Footscray)
1957: Brian Gleeson (St Kilda)
1958: Neil Roberts (St Kilda)
1959: Bob Skilton (South Melbourne), Verdun Howell (St Kilda)
1960: John Schultz (Footscray)
1961: John James (Carlton)
1962: Alistair Lord (Geelong)
1963: Bob Skilton (South Melbourne)
1964: Gordon Collis (Carlton)
1965: Ian Stewart (St Kilda), Noel Teasdale (North Melbourne)
1966: Ian Stewart (St Kilda)
1967: Ross Smith (St Kilda)
1968: Bob Skilton (South Melbourne)
1969: Kevin Murray (Fitzroy)
1970: Peter Bedford (South Melbourne)
1971: Ian Stewart (Richmond)
1972: Len Thompson (Collingwood)
1973: Keith Greig (North Melbourne)
1974: Keith Greig (North Mebourne)
1975: Gary Dempsey (Footscray)
1976: Graham Moss (Essendon)
1977: Graham Teasdale (South Melbourne)
1978: Malcolm Blight (North Melbourne)
1979: Peter Moore (Collingwood)
1980: Kelvin Templeton (Footscray)

1981: Barry Round (South Melbourne), Bernie Quinlan (Fitzroy)

1982: Brian Wilson (Melbourne)

1983: Ross Glendinning (North Melbourne)

1984: Peter Moore (Melbourne)

1985: Brad Hardie (Footscray)

1986: Greg Williams (Sydney), Robert DiPierdomenico (Hawthorn)

1987: Tony Lockett (St Kilda), John Platten (Hawthorn)

1988: Gerard Healy (Sydney)

1989: Paul Couch (Geelong)

1990: Tony Liberatore (Footscray)

1991: Jim Stynes (Melbourne)

1992: Scott Wynd (Footscray)

1993: Gavin Wanganeen (Essendon)

1994: Greg Williams (Carlton)

1995: Paul Kelly (Sydney)

1996: James Hird (Essendon), Michael Voss (Brisbane)

1997: Robert Harvey (St Kilda)

1998: Robert Harvey (St Kilda)

1999: Shane Crawford (Hawthorn)

2000: Shane Woewodin (Melbourne)

2001: Jason Akermanis (Brisbane)

2002: Simon Black (Brisbane)

2003: Mark Ricciuto (Adelaide), Nathan Buckley (Collingwood), Adam Goodes (Sydney)

2004: Chris Judd (West Coast)

2005: Ben Cousins (West Coast)

2006: Adam Goodes (Sydney)

2007: Jimmy Bartel (Geelong)

John Coleman Medal Winners

This award is given to the footballers who kicked the most goals in a season, excluding finals matches, at the end of the home-and-away rounds. (See the list following the Coleman Medal Winners for leading goal kickers at the end of the finals but not at the end of the home-and-away season.) From 1897 to 1954 the top goals man was simply referred to as 'the leading goal kicker'. In 1981 this feat was rewarded (and made retrospective to 1955) with the John Coleman Medal, named in honour of the former champion Essendon goal kicker, who kicked 537 goals from 98 games from 1949 to 1954. Coleman died following a heart attack in 1973, aged just 44.

1897: Eddy James (Geelong) 22, Jack Leith (Melbourne) 22

1898: Archie Smith (Collingwood) 31

1899: Eddy James (Geelong) 31

1900: Albert Thurgood (Essendon) 24, Ted Lockwood (Geelong) 24

1901: Fred Hiskins (Essendon) 34

1902: Charlie Baker (St Kilda) 30

1903: Ted Lockwood (Collingwood) 33

1904: Vince Coutie (Melbourne) 39

1905: Charlie Pannam (Collingwood) 38

1906: Mick Grace (Carlton) 45

1907: Dick Lee (Collingwood) 45

1908: Dick Lee (Collingwood) 50

1909: Dick Lee (Collingwood) 55

1910: Dick Lee (Collingwood) 51, Percy Martini (Geelong) 51

1911: Harry Brereton (Melbourne) 46

1912: Harry Brereton (Melbourne) 56
1913: Roy Park (University) 53
1914: Dick Lee (Collingwood) 57
1915: Jim Freake (Fitzroy) 65
1916: Dick Lee (Collingwood) 46
1917: Dick Lee (Collingwood) 50
1918: Ern Cowley (Carlton) 35
1919: Dick Lee (Collingwood) 47
1920: George Bayliss (Richmond) 62
1921: Cliff Rankin (Geelong) 61
1922: Horrie Clover (Carlton) 54
1923: Greg Stockdale (Essendon) 64
1924: Jack Moriarty (Fitzroy) 75
1925: Lloyd Hagger (Geelong) 70
1926: Gordon Coventry (Collingwood) 78
1927: Gordon Coventry (Collingwood) 88
1928: Gordon Coventry (Collingwood) 78
1929: Gordon Coventry (Collingwood) 118
1930: Gordon Coventry (Collingwood) 105
1931: Harry Vallence (Carlton) 72
1932: George Moloney (Geelong) 109
1933: Gordon Coventry (Collingwood) 108
1934: Bob Pratt (South Melbourne) 138
1935: Bob Pratt (South Melbourne) 97
1936: Bill Mohr (St Kilda) 101
1937: Dick Harris (Richmond) 64
1938: Ron Todd (Collingwood) 102
1939: Ron Todd (Collingwood) 98
1940: Jack Titus (Richmond) 92
1941: Sel Murray (North Melbourne) 88
1942: Lindsay White (South Melbourne) 67
1943: Fred Fanning (Melbourne) 62
1944: Fred Fanning (Melbourne) 87

1945: Fred Fanning (Melbourne) 67
1946: Des Fothergill (Collingwood) 63
1947: Fred Fanning (Melbourne) 97
1948: Lindsay White (Geelong) 86
1949: John Coleman (Essendon) 85
1950: John Coleman (Essendon) 112
1951: John Coleman (Essendon) 75
1952: John Coleman (Essendon) 103
1953: John Coleman (Essendon) 96
1954: Jack Collins (Footscray) 73
1955: Noel Rayson (Geelong) 77
1956: Bill Young (St Kilda) 56
1957: Jack Collins (Footscray) 74
1958: Ian Brewer (Collingwood) 67
1959: Ron Evans (Essendon) 69
1960: Ron Evans (Essendon) 67
1961: Tom Carroll (Carlton) 54
1962: Doug Wade (Geelong) 62
1963: John Peck (Hawthorn) 69
1964: John Peck (Hawthorn) 68
1965: John Peck (Hawthorn) 56
1966: Ted Fordham (Essendon) 73
1967: Doug Wade (Geelong) 79
1968: Peter Hudson (Hawthorn) 125
1969: Doug Wade (Geelong) 122
1970: Peter Hudson (Hawthorn) 146
1971: Peter Hudson (Hawthorn) 140
1972: Peter McKenna (Collingwood) 130
1973: Peter McKenna (Collingwood) 84
1974: Doug Wade (North Melbourne) 91
1975: Leigh Matthews (Hawthorn) 67
1976: Larry Donohue (Geelong) 99
1977: Peter Hudson (Hawthorn) 105
1978: Kelvin Templeton (Footscray) 118
1979: Kelvin Templeton (Footscray) 91
1980: Michael Roach (Richmond) 107
1981: Michael Roach (Richmond) 86

1982: Malcolm Blight (North Melbourne) 94

1983: Bernie Quinlan (Fitzroy) 106

1984: Bernie Quinlan (Fitzroy) 102

1985: Simon Beasley (Footscray) 93

1986: Brian Taylor (Collingwood) 100

1987: Tony Lockett (St Kilda) 117

1988: Jason Dunstall (Hawthorn) 124

1989: Jason Dunstall (Hawthorn) 128

1990: John Longmire (North Melbourne) 98

1991: Tony Lockett (St Kilda) 118

1992: Jason Dunstall (Hawthorn) 139

1993: Gary Ablett (Geelong) 124

1994: Gary Ablett (Geelong) 113

1995: Gary Ablett (Geelong) 118

1996: Tony Lockett (Sydney) 114

1997: Tony Modra (Adelaide) 81

1998: Tony Lockett (Sydney) 107

1999: Scott Cummings (West Coast) 88

2000: Matthew Lloyd (Essendon) 94

2001: Matthew Lloyd (Essendon) 96

2002: David Neitz (Melbourne) 75

2003: Matthew Lloyd (Essendon) 89

2004: Fraser Gehrig (St Kilda) 103

2005: Fraser Gehrig (St Kilda) 74

2006: Brendan Fevola (Carlton) 84

2007: Jonathan Brown (Brisbane) 77

Leading goal kickers at the end of the finals but not at the end of the home-and-away season (with finals goals in brackets) were:

1902: Ted Rowell (Collingwood) 33 (5)

1911: Vin Gardiner (Carlton) 47 (3)

1913: Jimmy Freake (Fitzroy) 56 (7)

1915: Dick Lee (Collingwood) 66 (5)

1921: Dick Lee (Collingwood) 64 (4)

1933: Bob Pratt (South Melbourne) 109 (7)

1937: Gordon Coventry (Collingwood) 72 (16)

1941: Norm Smith (Melbourne) 89 (4)

1943: Dick Harris (Richmond) 63 (11)

1946: Bill Brittingham (Essendon) 66 (8)

1951: George Goninon (Geelong) 86 (15)

1993: Tony Modra (Adelaide) 129 (10)

2005: Barry Hall (Sydney) 80 (8)

Norm Smith Medal Winners

This award is named in honour of former Melbourne and Fitzroy player Norm Smith, who also coached these clubs and South Melbourne (now Sydney Swans). Smith coached Melbourne to six premierships and, in 2007, was officially named a Legend of the Game. The following footballers have won the trophy for being the best player in the grand final:

1979: Wayne Harmes (Carlton)
1980: Kevin Bartlett (Richmond)
1981: Bruce Doull (Carlton)
1982: Maurice Rioli (Richmond)
1983: Colin Robertson (Hawthorn)
1984: Bill Duckworth (Essendon)
1985: Simon Madden (Essendon)
1986: Gary Ayres (Hawthorn)
1987: David Rhys-Jones (Carlton)
1988: Gary Ayres (Hawthorn)
1989: Gary Ablett (Geelong)
1990: Tony Shaw (Collingwood)
1991: Paul Dear (Hawthorn)
1992: Peter Matera (West Coast)
1993: Michael Long (Essendon)

1994: Dean Kemp (West Coast)
1995: Greg Williams (Carlton)
1996: Glenn Archer (North Melbourne)
1997: Andrew McLeod (Adelaide)
1998: Andrew McLeod (Adelaide)
1999: Shannon Grant (Kangaroos)
2000: James Hird (Essendon)
2001: Shaun Hart (Brisbane)
2002: Nathan Buckley (Collingwood)
2003: Simon Black (Brisbane)
2004: Byron Pickett (Port Adelaide)
2005: Chris Judd (West Coast)
2006: Andrew Embley (West Coast)
2007: Steve Johnson (Geelong)

Michael Tuck Medal Winners

Inaugurated in 1992, this award is named in honour of former Hawthorn champion Michael Tuck, who holds the record for the most games at VFL/AFL level, 426 from 1972 to 1991. The following players have won the Michael Tuck Medal as best on the ground in pre-season grand finals:

1992: Paul Hudson (Hawthorn)
1993: Gavin Wanganeen (Essendon
1994: Garry O'Donnell (Essendon)
1995: Mick Martyn (North Melbourne)
1996: Nicky Winmar (St Kilda)
1997: Craig Bradley (Carlton)
1998: Wayne Carey (North Melbourne)

1999: Paul Salmon (Hawthorn)
2000: Mark Mercuri (Essendon)
2001: Adam Kingsley (Port Adelaide)
2002: Nick Stevens (Port Adelaide)
2003: Andrew McLeod (Adelaide)
2004: Robert Harvey (St Kilda)
2005: Brendan Fevola (Carlton)
2006: Simon Goodwin (Adelaide)
2007: Nick Stevens (Carlton)

Appendix B

Off-field Footy Language

*H*ere's a collection of some of the more colourful expressions used in the great Australian code of football. I've divided them into two groups, one used by the fans when barracking and the other relating to aspects of the game.

Barracking Terms

Baaaaalll!: A crowd exclamation used whenever one of its players tackles an opposition player. They're claiming 'holding the ball', but this has been abbreviated over the years and the elongated use of the word is a plea for a free kick.

Ball magnet: A term used for players who win so much of the ball that the ball seems to follow them wherever they go. In actuality, such players can simply read the play and know where to run to win possession.

Barney: One of numerous terms for a 'fight' among players, which may also be called a 'barney', a 'rumble', a 'blue' or a 'free-for-all'. It can also be a 'bit of biffo'.

Blockbuster: This is usually a top-of-the-table clash; that is, first versus second. It can also be a clash between traditional rivals, guaranteed to draw a capacity crowd.

Chewy on your boot: The chewy is, of course, chewing gum, and this old-time chant is used to distract an opposition forward when he's taking a set shot for goal.

Debacle: Forlorn fans use this expression when their team has been defeated by a huge margin. I've seen the Sydney Swans in many a debacle, especially through their lean years in the early 1990s.

Dog's eye: Rhyming slang for a meat pie, the best possible meal for a day (or night) at the footy. Usually eaten with 'dead horse', rhyming slang for (tomato) sauce.

Down the guts: Fans use this term to implore their players to kick the ball down the centre of the ground, instead of to the wings or flanks.

Fracas: The AFL hates a fracas because it can lead to a melee. It usually involves half a dozen players or more pushing and shoving each other. From there, it can lead to a *barney*, or a 'bit of biffo'.

Go inboard: A plea by fans to players to kick or handpass the ball from the wing or flank into the central corridor of the ground.

Headhunter: A player who has a habit of hitting rivals in the head. This is a serious offence and, like the headhunters of old in the Pacific, few, if any, are still around.

Maggot: See *White leghorn*.

The Magoos: This has nothing to do with myopic cartoon character Mr Magoo, but is rhyming slang for the 'twos', or the reserves side. A player often is demoted from the senior side to 'the Magoos'.

Man-up: Sometimes screamed by fans to their team when the opposition seems to have men everywhere. The fans are telling their players to take a man each to stop the opposition from running free without an opponent.

Own dung hill: A derogatory term for the home ground. Visiting fans take great delight in their team defeating the opposition 'on their own dung hill'.

Sausage roll: Again, rhyming slang, this time for a goal.

Through the hi-diddle-diddle: Rhyming slang to signify that the ball has gone straight through the 'middle' of the goals.

Up there Cazaly: An expression imploring the ruckman to leap higher for a tap to his rover, but it's rarely used today. Originally coined by South Melbourne's Fred Fleiter during the 1920s to call on teammate Roy Cazaly to tap the ball to rover Mark Tandy. The phrase became a catchcry for Australian troops in World War II, and a song title in the 1970s. The song 'Up There Cazaly' was written and recorded by Mike Brady and Peter Sullivan in 1979.

White leghorn: An extremely unkind nickname for field umpires and a reference to their white uniforms, as well as — so it's been claimed down the ages — to their chicken-thin legs. The use of the word 'maggot' is fully suggestive of the fans' view of an umpire's position in football society.

Win the hard ball, you receiver: A suggestion to an opposition player that he's skirting the packs to avoid the prospect of being hurt. He is regarded as a 'receiver', a player who won't win the ball for himself, but waits for a teammate to win it for him, and then receives it.

Descriptions of Play

Another nail in the coffin: A cliché, but it always follows a goal that puts the result beyond doubt and, of course, refers to the losers being dead and all but buried — another cliché.

Blood rule: Refers to the rule that any player bleeding even slightly is ordered from the ground until the blood has been washed away or completely bandaged over.

Centimetre perfect: A wonderfully apt description of the perfect pass from one player to a teammate, which was created by television commentator Denis Cometti (whom many fans regard as the best in the business).

Claret: Any blood spilt during a match.

Daisy-cutter: Used to describe a very low pass to a teammate. The alternative expression *worm-burner* could be considered the trademark of popular radio commentator Rex Hunt.

Done like a dinner: Nothing to do with a Sunday roast but, rather, refers to a team being completely outplayed.

The easy get: The opposite of the *hard ball* — winning the ball in the open and alone.

Electrifying dash: A term used to describe a player running as fast as he can with the ball.

Filling the hole: An expression used to describe the tactic of a player dropping back into an area (the hole) in front of the full-forward to prevent him getting a clear run at the ball.

Flick pass: A type of handpass that is now illegal, although Footscray (now Western Bulldogs) captain and coach Ted Whitten used it successfully in the early 1960s until it was outlawed. The ball is held on the palm of one hand and flicked off with the other. The fist must now be clenched on contact, although the original flick pass is sometimes attempted even now.

Fresh-air kick: Sometimes also known as an 'airy', this occurs when a player fails to make contact with the ball when trying to kick it.

The hard ball: An expression used to describe the difficulty involved in winning possession, often including a risk of physical harm.

Hospital pass: Used to refer to any terrible pass, by hand or foot — one putting a teammate in great physical danger.

Huddle: A term used to describe a team grouping together for a kick-out after a behind has been scored. The players then break to different parts of the ground to confuse the opposition.

Ironed out: See *Shirtfont*.

Junk time: This term represents the last few minutes of a match when the result is already beyond doubt.

Kicking a bagful: Whenever a player kicks six, seven or more goals in one match, fans may suggest that he has 'kicked a bagful'.

Picked his pocket: Used to describe a passage of play in which a player snatches the ball from an opposition player by stealth or surprise.

Shirtfront: This term has nothing to do with sartorial splendour, but in fact describes one player crashing into another player's shirt front, down the middle. The perfect shirtfront can leave a player unconscious, but brings oohs and aahs from the fans.

Spearhead: A term used to describe the team's full-forward, who is leading the attack.

Speccie: This is a 'spectacular' mark, usually high above a pack.

Stacks on the mill: An expression used to describe a huge pack of players fighting for the ball on the ground.

Standing two men: Usually used in reference to a full-forward having to contend with two opponents. The term is a great mark of respect because it means the full-forward is rated as highly dangerous.

Talls and shorts: Terms to describe the different types of players, size-wise, coined by former Carlton coach David Parkin.

Unanswered: Two or more consecutive goals, without a corresponding goal by the opposition.

Veteran player: Any player seen to be nearing the end of his career. The oldest footballer to play at VFL/AFL level was St Kilda's Vic Cumberland, who was 43 years of age when he played his last League game in 1920. Tragically, he died in a motorbike accident just seven years later.

Worm-burner: See *Daisy-cutter*.

Appendix C
Other Useful Books

. . . .

*A*ustralian football has a rich history and tradition, with the AFL (Australian Football League) competition itself more than 110 years old. Of course, over this period a mountain of facts and figures have accumulated — far too many to include in this book, or even perhaps in any book. So, if you're interested in reading more about the game, a number of books are available today, including biographies of star players and coaches, quiz compilations and individual club histories.

Facts and Stats

AFL 2008 (AFL Publishing, 2008)

An annual AFL publication, this book is crammed with just about every piece of information any fan could need: Club records, player records, fixtures, finals details, grand final line-ups, goal kicking, Brownlow Medal statistics and much more. I have a collection of all these annuals and couldn't do without them. They help me enormously with research for feature articles I write for various publications, especially for the AFL match-day program, the *Football Record*. Watch out for the updates over future seasons. I believe this book is a must for all football fans.

Every Game Ever Played by Stephen Rodgers (Viking O'Neill, 1994)

No football fan should be without this regularly updated book, written by football historian Stephen Rodgers. It not only gives the quarter-by-quarter scores for every game played since the first VFL/AFL season of 1897 until 1993, but also lists the top goal kickers of every season, plus ground notes and other snippets of interest. I highly recommend this invaluable title. Hey, Stephen, it's about time we had a new edition.

The Encyclopedia of AFL Footballers by Russell Holmesby and Jim Main (BAS Publishing, 2007)

I know this sounds like a plug for one of my own books but, if you want to know about every footballer who has played the game at the highest level since the AFL was formed as the VFL in 1897, this is it. This book runs to 882 pages and is crammed with all sorts of interesting information, including clubs, games, goals and birth dates. The 2007 edition, for the first time, carries the guernsey numbers worn by most players throughout football history. Numbers were worn in several matches in the first decade of the 20th century, but were not adopted by all clubs until the start of the 1912 VFL season. They're now part of football history and young fans love wearing their favourite club's guernsey, with a particular hero's number on the back. When I was a boy following South Melbourne (now the Sydney Swans), I wore number 4 because my favourite player was Billy Williams, who wore this number in 124 games with the Swans from 1945 to 1951.

Collingwood used to hand out guernsey numbers in alphabetical order. The captain wore number 1 and the vice-captain number 2. Other players then followed in alphabetical order, switching as new players joined the team and making it a nightmare for youngsters who wanted their hero's number on the back of their own guernsey. Star Magpie defender Jack Regan was way down the alphabetical order, and wore 11 separate numbers in his 196 games from 1930 to 1941, 1943 and 1946. At least he got to wear number 1 when he was captain in 1941 and 1943. Collingwood changed its system after World War II, but the captain still wore number 1 until Ray Shaw decided to stick with his number 23 after being appointed captain in 1979.

Game Perspectives

100 Years of Australian Football 1896–1996 (Penguin, 1996)

Although this wonderful book was published in 1996, it's an excellent guide to the first century of VFL/AFL competition. It is beautifully illustrated and is a season-by-season account of the competition. The detail is amazing.

The Book of AFL Finals by Graeme Atkinson (Five Mile Press, 2002)

This book has been regarded as a classic for a long time and is updated every few years. The most recent update was in 2002, making it a superb guide for anyone wanting to know about any finals series since 1897. This is a book that has really stood the test of time.

James Hird: Challenging Times by James Hird and Geoff Slattery (Geoff Slattery Publishing and Lothian Books, 2002)

This is one of the best football books I've read and centres around Hird's diary of events over the 2002 season. A brilliant book that gives you a great insight into what it takes to play Aussie Rules at the elite level.

Other Books

The Champions by Ben Collins (Geoff Slattery Publishing, 2006)

This is a marvellous collection of interviews with such greats of the game as Collingwood's Nathan Buckley and former South Melbourne champion Bob Skilton. It gives real insight as to what makes champion players tick. Very revealing and immensely readable.

The Brownlow various authors, edited by Geoff Slattery (Geoff Slattery Publishing, 2003)

This might be a few years out of date, but contains many wonderful recollections of the winners of football's most prestigious individual award (refer to Chapter 15 for more information). For example, it tells of how 1933 winner, Fitzroy's Wilfred 'Chicken' Smallhorn got his unusual nickname — when Wilfred was a baby, his father had apparently told his mother to look after him 'like a little chicken'.

Index

• C •

• *U* •

• *V* •

• *W* •

FOR DUMMIES

Business

1-74031-109-4
$39.95

1-174031-146-5
$39.95

1-74031-004-7
$39.95

0-73140-710-5
$39.95

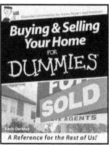

1-74031-166-3
$39.95

1-74031-041-1
$39.95

0-7314-0541-2
$39.95

0-7314-0715-6
$39.95

Reference

Gardening

0-7314-0723-7
$39.95

1-74031-157-1
$39.95

0-7314-0721-0
$39.95

1-74031-007-1
$39.95

FOR DUMMIES®

BESTSELLING BOOK SERIES

2nd Edition
Aussie Rules
For Dummies®

Cheat Sheet

Player positions

Each Aussie Rules team has 22 players; however, only 18 players can take the ground at any one time. These players include:

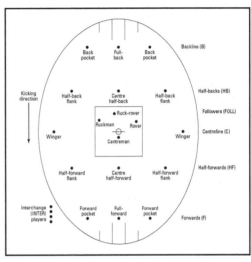

- ✔ **Centre half-forward:** Often the most talented footballer in any team, the centre half-forward is the general who organises teammates within 50–60 metres of goal. The centre half-forward must be an exceptional athlete, capable of running throughout a match, be able to take strong marks and be an accurate kick for goal. This position is said to be the most difficult, and clubs consider they're blessed if they can find a quality centre half-forward. Prototype: Wayne Carey.

- ✔ **Centreman:** As the name suggests, this player acts as the team pivot. The centreman is now commonly known by the generic title of midfielder (each club has several midfielders, even though they might be named on flanks or wings), and his role is to run in an effort to win as many possessions as possible to thrust his side forward. A good midfielder also has defensive skills to be able to shut down the opposition when it has the ball. Prototype: Michael Voss.

- ✔ **Full-back:** As the name implies, this position is the last line of defence — the full-back has the task of restricting the opposition's full-forward. Most full-backs are big and strong, with excellent defensive skills, such as knowing when and how to knock the ball clear instead of trying to mark it. Most modern full-backs are athletic footballers who can turn defence into attack. Prototype: Mal Michael.

- ✔ **Full-forward:** The full-forward plays closer to goal than the centre half-forward and shoulders an enormous responsibility as he is often regarded as the team's main goal scorer. He must be brave and strong, with a sixth sense to allow him to score goals even from half-chances. Prototype: Matthew Lloyd.

- ✔ **Ruckman:** Usually (but not always) the tallest player in the side, the ruckman gets his team moving from stoppages, such as bounce-downs, boundary throw-ins and ball-ups. His main role is to tap or knock the ball to smaller teammates from these stoppages, and his work is called ruck play. According to popular belief, no team can win a premiership without a good ruckman, and some teams have two or three quality 'big men' to provide cover for injuries. A good ruckman can also take marks around the ground. Prototype: Luke Darcy.

For Dummies®*: Bestselling Book Series for Beginners*

2nd Edition
Aussie Rules
For Dummies®

Cheat Sheet

The AFL clubs

Here is a list of the 16 clubs in the AFL, their nicknames and team colours:

- **Adelaide:** Crows; red, navy blue and yellow.
- **Brisbane Lions:** (An amalgamation of the Brisbane Bears and Fitzroy); maroon, royal blue and yellow.
- **Carlton:** Blues; navy blue and white.
- **Collingwood:** Magpies; black and white.
- **Essendon:** Bombers; red and black.
- **Fremantle:** Dockers; green, purple, red and white.
- **Geelong:** Cats; navy blue and white.
- **Hawthorn:** Hawks; brown and gold.
- **Kangaroos:** (Formerly North Melbourne); royal blue and white.
- **Melbourne:** Demons; navy blue and red.
- **Port Adelaide:** The Power; teal, black and white.
- **Richmond:** Tigers; black and yellow.
- **St Kilda:** Saints; red, black and white.
- **Sydney Swans:** (Formerly South Melbourne); red and white.
- **West Coast Eagles:** royal blue, gold and white.
- **Western Bulldogs:** (Formerly Footscray); red, white and blue.

Ten most common umpire signals

Umpires have a range of signals to communicate to the players and each other. These include:

- **Around the neck:** The field umpire puts his right hand across his shoulder.
- **Ball hits a goalpost:** The goal umpire hits the goalpost to signify a 'poster', which is worth one behind, and then waves one flag.
- **Ball-up:** If a field umpire wants to clear player congestion around the ball he crosses his arms in front of his chest.
- **Behind:** The goal umpire raises one finger and then waves one flag.
- **Blood rule:** The field umpire crosses his forearms in front of his face.
- **Goal!!!:** The goal umpire points with a finger on each hand and then waves two flags.
- **Out of bounds on the full:** The boundary umpire raises both arms parallel to the ground.
- **Pushing:** The field umpire announces a free kick by pressing his hands forward in the direction of the push.
- **Travelling for more than 15 metres without bouncing the ball:** The field umpire twirls his wrists over each other.
- **Trip:** The field umpire signifies a free kick for tripping by bending a leg and holding the ankle.

For Dummies®: Bestselling Book Series for Beginners

9 780731 405954